D0641089

THE DOCTRINE AND COVENANTS
A BOOK OF ANSWERS

Sidney B. Sperry

Other volumes in the Sperry Symposium Series
from Deseret Book Company:

Nurturing Faith through the Book of Mormon
The Apostle Paul: His Life and His Testimony
Thy People Shall Be My People
The Heavens Are Open
Doctrines of the Book of Mormon
The Lord of the Gospels
A Witness of Jesus Christ
Doctrines for Exaltation

THE DOCTRINE AND COVENANTS
A BOOK OF ANSWERS

THE 25TH ANNUAL SIDNEY B. SPERRY SYMPOSIUM

Edited by
Leon R. Hartshorn
Dennis A. Wright
Craig J. Ostler

DESERET BOOK COMPANY
SALT LAKE CITY, UTAH

Library of Congress Cataloging-in-Publication Data

Sperry Symposium (25th : 1996 : Brigham Young University)
   The doctrine and covenants, a book of answers : the 25th annual
Sidney B. Sperry Symposium.
      p.   cm
   Includes bibliographical references and index.
   ISBN 1-57345-219-X (HB 6x9)
   1. Doctrine and Covenants—Congresses.   I. Title.
BX8628.S72   1996
289.3'2—dc20   96-42156
                                                                    CIP

Printed in the United States of America

10   9   8   7   6   5   4   3   2   1

CONTENTS

PREFACE

The Doctrine and Covenants is a book of answers. As Elder John A. Widtsoe said: "The first thing to be remembered is that the revelations contained in the Book of Doctrine and Covenants are answers to questions. If that is kept in mind it will help to a better understanding" (*The Message of the Doctrine and Covenants* [Salt Lake City: Bookcraft, 1969], 4–5).

The Saints in the early days of this dispensation asked many questions about specific issues and situations. The answers to their questions came as revelations that they recorded in the Doctrine and Covenants. The Lord encouraged his Saints to develop humility balanced with initiative and independence, and he tutored them as they engaged in the active process of inviting revelation on how best to establish the kingdom of God.

The Prophet Joseph learned early that the Lord responded when asked specific questions. His assignment to translate the Bible initiated many questions; others came from challenges faced by the young Church. Questions from the work of translation preceded such revelations as the visions of glory and the eternal nature of marriage and family. Questions arising from historical events resulted in revelations that defined the nature of priesthood service and the government of the Church. We can more fully appreciate the vitality and vision of the early Saints when we understand the questions that preceded the various revelations.

But the Doctrine and Covenants not only fosters insight into the questions and answers of the past but also gives answers to those who ask their own questions from their own experience.

Those who are searching for answers in the Doctrine and Covenants will find this Sperry Symposium volume a valuable resource in their study. Contributors provide assistance with methods of obtaining answers as well as guidelines in following the Spirit during the process. Some contributors discuss matters of Church government, principles of common consent, the value of trials in our lives, and the importance of marriage and family. Others focus on the answers found in understanding the historical context of the revelations as well as the vision of future events.

This collection encourages a careful study of the Doctrine and Covenants as a book of answers for contemporary questions. The authors have made an earnest effort to provide historical background and doctrinal insight to assist readers in their own pondering of the answers provided in the revelations. It is important to remember that individuals must first ask their own questions and then invite the Lord to assist them in finding answers. As a part of this process, the Doctrine and Covenants is a marvelous book of answers.

We would like to express our appreciation to Patty Smith of Religious Education's Faculty Support Center for her invaluable assistance in organizing and carrying out the symposium and in preparing the manuscript for publication.

CHAPTER ONE

"Read . . . One to Another"

ELAINE L. JACK

How I love the words of the Lord. How I love this gospel, for it brings joy and peace to our lives and lifts us and sustains us as we progress along the path to eternal life.

The Lord commands in the Doctrine and Covenants: "Seek ye out of the best books words of wisdom; seek learning, even by study and also by faith" (D&C 88:118). What does the Lord mean, "seek learning?" What are we to learn?

On most college and university campuses, scholarship is based on masterful texts and perceptive literature that heralds the study of science, art, philosophy, history, languages, and math. We appreciate these works that enlighten and enrich our lives. We are intrigued by the process of discovery and learning exhibited by research and brilliant minds.

We have covenanted to learn truths from the Author of all knowledge, who asks us to "learn that he who doeth the works of righteousness shall receive his reward" (D&C 59:23); "learn to impart one to another as the gospel requires" (D&C 88:123); "learn obedience" (D&C 105:6); "let every man learn his duty" (D&C 107:99); "study and learn and become acquainted with all good books" (D&C 90:15); "learn my will" (D&C 105:1). And this most powerful command of all, "Learn of me" (D&C 19:23).

Elaine L. Jack is general president of the Relief Society of The Church of Jesus Christ of Latter-day Saints.

Our eternal progression is paced by how well, how quickly, and how completely we follow his commandment "Learn of me." With this gentle request, he is calling for us to grasp the dimensions of being a God, to realize "that by him, and through him, and of him, the worlds are and were created" (D&C 76:24). He wants us to learn that we, too, can receive glory and exaltation and be like him "who made the heavens and all the hosts thereof, and by whom all things were made which live, and move, and have a being" (D&C 45:1).

Our efforts to become like God require both spiritual and secular learning. He has said, "Establish . . . a house of learning" (D&C 88:119), and he has promised "the saints shall be filled with his glory, and receive their inheritance and be made equal with him" (D&C 88:107).

Our spiritual knowledge is the base upon which we build all our learning. Elder L. Tom Perry makes this clear: "We are talking about a widening, not a narrowing, window of opportunity to learn if we attend to first things first."[1]

The Lord has given us a curriculum to follow for his course on eternal life. It embraces truth and "knowledge of things as they are, and as they were, and as they are to come" (D&C 93:24). His syllabus makes it clear: "Study my word" (D&C 11:22); "give heed unto my word" (D&C 6:2); "search these commandments" (D&C 1:37); "let your time be devoted to the studying of the scriptures" (D&C 26:1); and this admonition, "I give unto you a commandment, that you rely upon the things which are written . . . by my power you can read them one to another" (D&C 18:3, 35).

Reading the scriptures one to another is what the Sperry Symposium is all about. That the scriptures in the Doctrine and Covenants were directed to leaders and members in this dispensation gives them particular significance. Indeed, we recognize that the Book of Mormon and the Doctrine and Covenants cost "the best blood of the nineteenth century"—that of the Prophet Joseph Smith and his brother Hyrum (D&C 135:6).

All of us share an earnest desire to learn and understand.

But what if we were among the 950 million people in the world who can't begin to understand—because they can't read? In America alone the figure is staggering: one in five are unable to read. Though we don't have specific figures for the Church, we assume that our membership closely parallels the statistics of the broader population. That means that in the United States, twenty percent of the Church membership can't read. How can they follow the Lord's counsel to draw near unto him through his words or seek his spirit through his words—when those words are meaningless symbols on a page?

The issue of literacy is at the heart of spiritual progress. People who can't read often cannot write their names; they can't complete a tithing form, research their family history, or find a scripture reference in a Gospel Doctrine class—let alone read it aloud. Much of the power of the word is lost and with it the opportunity to grow in the gospel.

There is no question that to "give diligent heed to the words of eternal life" (D&C 84:43), we must be able to read them. To "do according to that which [he has] written" (D&C 84:57), we have to comprehend his words before we can act upon them.

What if Joseph Smith had not been able to read? The Prophet recorded in his history: "I was one day reading the Epistle of James, first chapter and fifth verse, which reads: *If any of you lack wisdom, let him ask of God, that giveth to all men liberally, and upbraideth not; and it shall be given him.* Never did any passage of scripture come with more power to the heart of man than this did at this time to mine" (Joseph Smith–History 1:11–12). Joseph Smith opened the door to this dispensation of the fulness of times—in part because he was able to read.

His example is significant for all who seek to gain a testimony, a knowledge "that he lives" (D&C 76:22). Said the Prophet Joseph: "Search the scriptures—search the revelations which we publish, and ask your Heavenly Father, in the name of His Son Jesus Christ, to manifest the truth unto you, and if you do it with an eye single to His glory nothing doubting, He will answer you by the power of His Holy Spirit. You will then know for yourselves and not for another. You will not then be dependent on man for the knowledge of God."[2]

In 1992 President Gordon B. Hinckley announced a churchwide, ongoing, gospel literacy effort: "A great new project is to be undertaken. . . . its consequences will go on and on and be felt in the lives of generations yet to come. . . . It is designed to bring light into the lives of those who can neither read nor write. . . .

". . . Imagine, if you can, the potential of this inspired program. Who dare dream of its consequences?"[3]

President Hinckley is right. Literacy brings light into people's lives: "For the word of the Lord is truth, and whatsoever is truth is light, and whatsoever is light is Spirit, even the Spirit of Jesus Christ" (D&C 84:45).

In all corners of the world, Relief Societies are undertaking literacy programs because learning and education have always been a high priority of our organization. In the early days of settling Zion, the sisters gathered to learn from and to teach one another. Then they took the messages and inspiration home and taught their families. A century later a whole generation of women in the Church were enriched with poetry and prose in a series of lessons, "Out of the Best Books," that focused on great literature. In that course of study we were blessed with a whole new level of learning.

Now in Relief Society we are stressing literacy to help perfect the Saints. This is bold action we are taking, and we are seeing success, one person at a time.

Let me illustrate with a story. A Relief Society president in Blackfoot, Idaho, was the visiting teacher to a young mother of four. Barbara, the visiting teacher, and Kimmie, the young mother, were trying to put up a shelf. Then Barbara was called to the phone. She suggested to Kimmie that she read the instructions and do what came next. When Barbara returned, Kimmie was just sitting there. She hadn't done anything because she could barely read. It affected everything in her life. She was a Primary teacher in her ward—but not a very good one, she would be quick to tell you. After months of playing hangman on the board with the children, she asked to be released. She had bluffed her way through jobs, her GED, her IRS forms and other materials, but she didn't feel right about trying to bluff the Lord. Her visiting teacher, Barbara, offered to tutor her, and Kimmie learned to read.

Says Kimmie, "I am grateful that someone would share time with me to help me change my life. It has made a world of difference to me. I am now reading the scriptures every day and my spiritual strength is growing."[4]

Literacy is a significant issue in the Church. Our current membership as of 1995 worldwide is recorded at 9.3 million. By the year 2000 that number is expected to reach 12 million; by 2020, statistics suggest 35 million; by 2050, approximately 157 million; and by 2080, an estimated 265 million.

The numbers are dramatic, but let's look at them another way. In 1960, 91 percent of the Church lived in the United States and Canada. In 1975 that number was 81 percent. In 1993 only 54 percent of the Church was living in the United States and Canada. By 2020, projections suggest our membership will look something like this: Mexico and Central and South America will account for 71 percent; Asia will contribute 13 percent; Africa, 3 percent; and the United States, Canada and Europe will total 11 percent of the membership of The Church of Jesus Christ of Latter-day Saints.

As I study these projections I recognize what a challenge we face to have all of us reading off the same page. This is a worldwide gospel, and with our growth as a church, we inherit many of the world's problems. One of the most critical is literacy in its many stages. Though we address literacy in more than one hundred languages, literacy hits all of us close to home. Most of us know someone who can't read or hasn't learned to capitalize upon the written word. Many have just learned to cover their inadequacy.

That was apparent to me when my son David, who is a

physician, called to seek some advice on finding a support group for one of his patients. As he talked about the woman's difficulties, he explained that one of her biggest frustrations was that her husband couldn't read. Then he paused and said, "She's related to you." I was stunned. How could any of my relatives not be able to read? And then I look at the numbers: one in five.

The literacy effort instituted just four years ago as described in our *Gospel Literacy Guidelines* is twofold: first, to teach basic gospel literacy skills to those who cannot read or write, and second, to encourage Church members to study the gospel and improve themselves and their families throughout their lives.

The literacy effort doesn't come with a manual and list of specific things to do. The goal is to enhance reading, and if that skill is in place, then the next goal is to work to apply the principles more effectively in our daily lives. When you look at it this way, there are many layers of literacy. The literacy effort has prompted such responses as this one from a fifty-five-year-old man in Washington, "I have hope in the future for me."[5]

In a branch in Seville, Spain, the level of education among the members is extremely low. Most of the women have had few opportunities for schooling. One sister in the ward wrote of the growing emphasis and success of their literacy effort. "Few sisters have gone on to the secondary schools," she says. "Only one has gone on to the university. She is the bishop's wife, and we are all so very proud of her. Some of the women have a difficult time when they are asked to read or write. But since we have become members of the Church our vision has changed . . . we all want to learn."[6] That's the strength of the literacy effort: "We all want to learn."

The literacy effort is focused on developing or participating in a program to suit local literacy needs, but the Church has produced some teaching tools, including the manual, *Ye Shall Have My Words*. The course uses the scriptures as the text. Though many of us used McGuffey readers or "Run, Spot, Run" to learn to read, the Church's manual introduces reading concepts while at the same time teaching precious principles. "Love one another" and "Look unto God," "Beware of pride" and "Repent and be baptized" teach vowels and consonants and the coupling of words and phrases. As members' skills in reading increase, so does their personal understanding of the gospel. The power of the Lord is made known as we read: "Wherefore you can testify that you have heard my voice, and know my words" (D&C 18:36).

In the Dominican Republic, in Guatemala, in Korea and Singapore, in Canada and right here in Utah, Relief Societies are implementing and participating in programs to strengthen literacy. Some are simple; some are far more grand. Lives are changing as levels of reading and comprehension increase. We find women creating reading lists for children, tutoring in schools and juvenile detention centers, offering scripture-study classes for homemaking and great books classes for midweek activities. Hundreds of programs, each suited to the specific needs of the local unit, are being offered in scores of areas. The momentum is building, and the results are impressive. One by one, that light is beginning to shine.

The second stage of the literacy effort stresses reading with our families, encouraging reading in our wards, and enhancing opportunities to learn from the scriptures and the writings of latter-day prophets, using our skills and our spiritual understanding to gain secular knowledge.

"Learn of me" is not an intellectual exercise most effectively accomplished in a quiet carrel or office; it is a dynamic experience that requires action and effort as well as study and thought. It has been a priority in many dispensations. The Nephites and Jaredites produced "many books and many records of every kind" (Helaman 3:15). Nephi, the great prophet leader said, "I was taught somewhat in all the learning of my father" (Nephi 1:1).

No matter our age or circumstance, our reading shapes our understanding of the Savior and his plan. The Lord admonished Emma Smith, "Lay aside the things of this world, and seek for the things of a better" (D&C 25:10).

How different are the words of the Lord compared with the messages scrawled on the side of a building claiming territory for a gang. Where are their mothers? I say to myself when I see this display of blatant disrespect for community and culture. Where are their fathers? And their sense of right and wrong? If they had learned to "study it out in [their] mind" (D&C 9:8), would they have been scrawling incomprehensible commentary on the signs and poles, walls and fences in every neighborhood? I don't think so. Had they learned to read and comprehend and communicate in words, would they be resorting to this display?

Closer to home, we may ask, Are we sending out young missionaries to preach and teach the gospel when they can't read? Or don't read? How can our young converts and our second-generation youth, even third- and fourth-generation, step forward and say, "Here am I, send me" (Abraham 3:27) when those words of Jesus Christ are not in their minds and hearts?

Society, the Church, the ward, the neighborhood, the family—all need the power of the word to give form to this mortal experience, to give meaning to life. Testimonies increase, commitment builds, families draw together, and missionary work surges forward when the word of the Lord, as given in his scriptures and through his prophets, is read, absorbed and honored.

At the BYU Women's Conference last year, Sister Karen Maxwell told of her stake's effort to improve literacy. Two wards in her stake instituted a mentor program in which Relief Society sisters helped encourage the Young Women to reach their goals in scripture reading. The women visited, called, wrote notes and cheered at the progress. One young woman and her Relief Society partner decided to test the thesis it takes just twenty-one days to develop a habit. The Relief Society mentor called the young woman every day for twenty-one days to remind her to stay with it. She did. In another ward, the Young Women make the calls to see if their mentors are keeping up with them in their scripture reading. Says Sister Maxwell, "The relationships developed and the habits thus formed are important elements of the gospel literacy effort." These women have put in practice the Lord's command, "You shall teach one another the doctrine of the kingdom" (D&C 88:77).[7]

Why am I focusing on literacy at the Sperry Symposium, in which analysis of a phrase, a verse, or a pattern may be the rule? All of us can read; some better than others. All of us work to make sense of concepts and teachings and to apply that reasoning to every aspect of our daily lives. All of us take seriously the call to "seek learning." So why address literacy here?

Because literacy is more than being able to read; it is reading regularly, thoughtfully, and prayerfully. The Lord's repeated admonition to study, learn, seek, and ponder are guideposts for us to teach others "line upon line" the principles of the kingdom of God (D&C 98:12). They are guideposts for us to teach ourselves the doctrines of the kingdom and then to branch out to all knowledge, all the Lord has prepared for those that love him (D&C 46:9).

The gospel is a plan whereby we learn to become like God. We have textbooks that are divine and the Holy Spirit as our tutor. The intellect, like testimony, is not worn out when we use it. Engaged, it thrives on the stimulus of learning new and different things, analyzing, processing, storing, and recalling. "Let the solemnities of eternity rest upon your minds" (D&C 43:34) is a reminder to take seriously the opportunity to continue to learn and grow.

Literacy is the foundation of learning. There are layers of literacy that introduce the basics and then stretch us all the way to Joseph Smith's understanding, "Thy mind, O man! if thou wilt lead a soul unto salvation, must stretch as high as the utmost heavens, and search into and contemplate the darkest abyss, and the broad expanse of eternity."[8]

I love the breadth of the messages in the scriptures. In

them we find guidance and focus for secular and spiritual learning.

The Doctrine and Covenants is an inspired resource. What a tool to bridge the Lord's teachings of old with those of this dispensation. And the lessons are the same. Times have always been hard for the righteous: ask Jeremiah or Paul or Jacob of their trials. And yet the Lord says, "Arise and shine forth, that thy light may be a standard for the nations" (D&C 115:5). He also says, "Be thou humble; and the Lord thy God shall lead thee by the hand, and give thee answer to thy prayers" (D&C 112:10).

In section 112 we find guidance appropriate for our discussion of literacy: "Therefore, gird up thy loins for the work. Let thy feet be shod also, for thou art chosen, and thy path lieth among the mountains, and among many nations" (D&C 112:7). Let's apply this to literacy.

It says, "Gird up thy loins," "Let thy feet be shod," or in other words, prepare yourself physically and spiritually "for the work." Why? So that you can be a servant of the Lord, ready to hear his call. And where does he ask you to serve? The familiar reference in Jacob is "the poorest spot in all the land of thy vineyard" (Jacob 5:21). But according to this modern-day admonition, "thy path lieth among the mountains" (D&C 112:7). These are hard places, steep, jagged, rough, and, at times, seemingly insurmountable. They aren't in your own backyard; they lie "among many nations" (D&C 112:7).

This passage from the Doctrine and Covenants takes on special significance when we reach for understanding of its context. What was going on at the time? Section 112 was given on the day that Heber C. Kimball began preaching the gospel in England. It was directed to Thomas Marsh, then president of the Quorum of the Twelve Apostles. Those were not easy times; financial troubles were plaguing the fledgling Church and its leaders. To say "gird up your loins" was to charge them with resolve and new commitment. "You can do this" was the message, and looking back in Church history, their efforts launched the exodus to Zion.

We hope for that same kind of energy in the literacy effort—at every layer. Your own path, no doubt, "lieth among the mountains." It is weaving among ranges of mountains, for there is so much to learn; and when you reach the top of one peak, you see another. Growth, effort, learning. These are the substance of literacy.

Once we have scriptures committed to our mind, they are ours to use, draw upon, work with, compare to, and expand from. Realizing that the scriptures apply beyond our spiritual framework, we begin to use them as the base or standard measure. We don't separate spiritual and secular learning. We recognize that they, too, are ordered. Spiritual understanding boosts and strengthens secular learning. But the reverse is not necessarily true. "Seek ye first the kingdom of God" (3 Nephi 13:33) helps us prioritize. Learning to give priority to learning is a layer of literacy.

We must be prepared if we are to become gods. We are counseled in Doctrine and Covenants 88 to learn about this world, its complexities, its beauty, and its vitality. We are to learn "of things both in heaven and in the earth, and under the earth; things which have been, things which are, things which must shortly come to pass; things which are at home, things which are abroad; the wars and the perplexities of the nations, and the judgments which are on the land; and a knowledge also of countries and of kingdoms" (D&C 88:79).

Our time on earth is spent matching our choices to principles of righteousness and applying our minds to gaining knowledge. President Lorenzo Snow captured this concept in this remarkable couplet:

> As man now is, God once was:
> As God now is, man may be.[9]

Learning.

President Spencer W. Kimball said of the need to learn: "It is obvious that before one can take of the materials in existence and develop them into a world like our own, he must be master of geology, zoology, physiology, psychology, and all the others. It is obvious, also, that no soul can in his short mortal life acquire all this knowledge and master all these sciences, but he can make a beginning and with the foundation of spiritual life and controls and mastery, and with the authorities and powers received through the gospel of Christ, he is in a position to begin this almost limitless study of the secular."[10]

I have always been drawn to Doctrine and Covenants 138, in which President Joseph F. Smith describes the process of receiving revelation through the scriptures: "I sat in my room pondering over the scriptures. . . . I opened the Bible and read the third and fourth chapters of the first epistle of Peter, and . . . I read" (vv. 1, 6). President Smith taught us a valuable lesson in literacy when he described his pondering, letting his mind be filled with the Spirit of the Lord. "As I pondered over these things which are written, the eyes of my understanding were opened, and the Spirit of the Lord rested upon me" (v. 11). The road of eternal progression is a much faster track if you can read.

The Lord has promised: "And to them will I reveal all mysteries, yea, all the hidden mysteries of my kingdom from days of old, and for ages to come, will I make known unto them the good pleasure of my will concerning all things pertaining to my kingdom.

"Yea, even the wonders of eternity shall they know, and things to come will I show them, even the things of many generations.

"And their wisdom shall be great, and their understanding reach to heaven; and before them the wisdom of the wise shall perish, and the understanding of the prudent shall come to naught.

"For by my Spirit will I enlighten them, and by my power will I make known unto them the secrets of my will" (D&C 76:7–10).

May we learn of him, read his word, and share it with the world.

NOTES

1. L. Tom Perry, "Learning to Serve," *Ensign,* August 1996, 15.

2. Joseph Smith, *Teachings of the Prophet Joseph Smith,* sel. Joseph Fielding Smith (Salt Lake City: Deseret Book, 1938), 11.

3. Gordon B. Hinckley, "Ambitious to Do Good," *Ensign,* March 1992, 6.

4. Letter from Kimmie May Jensen to Elaine L. Jack. Used by permission.

5. LaRene Porter Gaunt, "I Have Hope in the Future for Me," *Ensign,* March 1996, 46.

6. "Gospel Literacy International Field Report, Europe: Spain, Seville District," Church Educational System, The Church of Jesus Christ of Latter-day Saints.

7. Karen B. Maxwell, address delivered at Women's Conference, Brigham Young University, Provo, April 1995.

8. Smith, *Teachings of the Prophet Joseph Smith,* 137.

9. Eliza R. Snow Smith, *Biography and Family Record of Lorenzo Snow* (Salt Lake City: Deseret News, 1884), 46.

10. Spencer W. Kimball, *The Teachings of Spencer W. Kimball,* ed. Edward L. Kimball (Salt Lake City: Bookcraft, 1982), 53.

CHAPTER TWO

How to Get Answers to Your Questions from the Doctrine and Covenants

RICHARD O. COWAN

As you search the scriptures, you will probably encounter some questions you cannot answer immediately. Rather than viewing them as obstacles in your study, you might well regard them as opportunities for gaining new understanding.

GENERAL SOURCES OF HELP

There are definite steps to follow in your quest for gospel understanding. Three particular sources of help will be vitally important to your progress:

1.The written scriptures set forth the basic principles of the gospel and are of divine origin. Peter testified that they came into being when "holy men of God spake as they were moved by the Holy Ghost" (2 Peter 1:21). We refer to these scriptures as the standard works because they provide the guidelines by which we can judge the correctness of any concept or idea.

2. Living Church leaders provide valuable insights, particularly into how scriptural principles apply in today's

Richard O. Cowan is professor of Church history and doctrine and chair of the Department of Church History and Doctrine at Brigham Young University.

world. The Lord affirmed that the words of those in authority, spoken "when moved upon by the Holy Ghost shall be scripture, shall be the will of the Lord, shall be the mind of the Lord, shall be the word of the Lord, shall be the voice of the Lord, and the power of God unto salvation" (D&C 68:4).

Elder Brigham Young stressed the importance of living prophets. Referring to the written scriptures, he asserted that "when compared with the living oracles, those books are nothing to me; those books do not convey the word of God direct to us now, as do the words of a Prophet or a man bearing the Holy Priesthood in our day and generation. I would rather have the living oracles than all the writing in the books." The Prophet Joseph Smith then confirmed, "Brother Brigham has told you the word of the Lord, and he has told you the truth."[1]

We should recognize the special stewardship of certain leading General Authorities. President J. Reuben Clark Jr. clarified which Church leaders may add to the standard works: "Only the President of the Church, the Presiding High Priest, is sustained as Prophet, Seer, and Revelator for the Church, and he alone has the right to receive revelations for the Church, either new or amendatory, or to give authoritative interpretations of scriptures that shall be binding on the Church, or change in any way the existing doctrines of the Church." No other person may do any of these things "unless he has special authorization from the President of the Church." President Clark explained that the counselors in the First Presidency and members of the Twelve are also "sustained as prophets, seers, and revelators, which gives them a special spiritual endowment in connection with their teaching."[2]

3. Personal revelation is the only way we can ultimately know the truth. Because the scriptures were written under the guidance of the Holy Ghost and because our inspired leaders speak by that same power, we must have the influence of the Spirit to truly understand them and appreciate the import of their words for us (D&C 18:34–36; 50:21–22).

It is apparent that these channels of help are interrelated—the scriptures were given by personal revelation to living prophets, the teachings of today's prophets are understood within the context of the scriptures and confirmed for us by personal revelation, and we can check our own inspiration against teachings from the scriptures and the living prophets. All three should be employed as we seek our answers.

SOME SPECIFIC SUGGESTIONS

Know the immediate setting of the scripture. Most of the standard works incorporate historical narrative along with inspired teachings. The Doctrine and Covenants, on the other hand, is a collection of revelations with little or no historical material as part of the text. Reading these revelations without background could be like listening to only one end of a telephone conversation. In most cases the needed historical perspective is provided in the section heading.

In section 19 the Lord strongly commanded Martin Harris to repent (vv. 13, 20). Without knowing the historical setting, we are left to wonder what Martin's problem really was. The situation was this: Egbert B. Grandin, who was printing the Book of Mormon at Palmyra, stopped work on the nearly completed project when a group of townspeople vowed that none of them would purchase the book. Anticipating such a crisis, Martin Harris had agreed to pay in advance the publication price of three thousand dollars. He apparently was now reluctant to pay that sum. Understanding this background gives meaning to the admonition that Martin Harris should not covet his property (vv. 25–26) and that he should even give up part of his land if necessary to pay the debt (vv. 34–35). This he did at great sacrifice.

Yet the Lord's revelations often go beyond merely responding to the immediate problem. Note how in section 19, for instance, verses 11 and 12 define "eternal punishment"; verses 16 through 18 shed light on Christ's atoning sacrifice; and verses 29 through 31 define gospel principles we should proclaim.

The composition of section 107 provides quite a different example of the advantage of knowing the historical context. In verse 58 the Lord refers to an earlier revelation. (Note how the next two verses constitute a typical introduction.) A manuscript copy of an earlier revelation, dated November 1831, roughly corresponds to verses 59 through 100 in section 107. This means that the material on the duties of quorum presidencies was made known as early as 1831 rather than 1835, when section 107 was given.

Similarly, verse 93 refers to a "vision showing the order of the Seventy." The precise content of this vision is not known, but it may have been alluded to in a history of the Seventy written by Joseph Young, the first senior president of that quorum. On Sunday, 8 February 1835, the Prophet Joseph Smith invited Brigham and Joseph Young to meet with him privately. After describing a vision "of the state and condition of those men who died in Zion's Camp, in Missouri," the Prophet instructed Brigham Young to have the brethren assemble the following Saturday, when he would "appoint twelve special witnesses, to open the door of the gospel to foreign nations," indicating that Brigham would be one of them.

"He then turned to Elder Joseph Young with quite an earnestness, as though the vision of his mind was extended still further, and addressing him, said: 'Brother Joseph, the Lord has made you President of the Seventies.'"[3] The Quorum of the Twelve Apostles was organized on 14 February 1835, and the Seventy were chosen two weeks later.

See each individual passage in the light of general principles taught throughout the scriptures. God is constant and consistent. He has been described as "the same yesterday, to day, and for ever" (Hebrews 13:8). Hence we need to understand any particular revelation in the broader context of everything else God has spoken.

For example, the command in Doctrine and Covenants

29:7 and 8 that the Saints "be gathered in unto one place" must be applied in the light of the Lord's later declaration that other places would be provided (D&C 101:20–22). Similarly, some individuals have been confused by the provision that the Word of Wisdom should be received "not by commandment or constraint" but rather as a revelation "showing forth the order and will of God" (D&C 89:2). This statement must be understood in the light of the Lord's command given only a few months before that we should "live by every word that proceedeth forth from the mouth of God" (D&C 84:44).

A superficial reading of verse 26 of section 132 seems to suggest that a person married in the temple is guaranteed exaltation no matter what he or she does. This "is the most abused passage in any scripture," asserted President Joseph Fielding Smith. "The Lord has never promised any soul that he may be taken into exaltation without the spirit of repentance. While repentance is not stated in this passage, yet it is, and must be implied."[4] In other words, verse 26 must be interpreted in the light of countless other scriptures that teach that forgiveness of sins comes only after repentance.

Read the scripture carefully. A thoughtful reading of Doctrine and Covenants 132:26 reveals that this verse itself specifies some rather significant requirements that must be met before one can qualify for exaltation. Not only must a couple be married in the temple by proper authority but they also must be "sealed by the Holy Spirit of promise." That means they must have reached the point that they were judged worthy to receive the eternal blessings promised by this sacred ordinance. Obviously this blessing requires a degree of faithfulness far beyond even the high requirements to receive a temple recommend. Those who are to be exalted cannot "shed innocent blood" (D&C 132:27), or, in other words, crucify Christ "unto themselves and put him to an open shame" (D&C 76:35). Furthermore, those who have committed even lesser sins still must be "destroyed in the flesh" and "delivered unto the buffetings of Satan" (D&C 132:26). The exact nature of these sufferings may not be known but concerning their extent the Lord declared: "How sore you know not, how exquisite you know not, yea, how hard to bear you know not" (D&C 19:15).

From a casual reading of Doctrine and Covenants 1:19 we might gain the impression that we should never counsel one another. The next verse clarifies that the Lord is only excluding uninspired counsel because we should always "speak in the name of God" (D&C 1:20). Nephi likewise taught that those who rely on the ideas of men are cursed unless "their precepts shall be given by the power of the Holy Ghost" (2 Nephi 28:31).

A superficial reading of Doctrine and Covenants 42:43 may give the impression that those with sufficient faith do not need to take care of themselves. That, however, is not a conclusion that can logically be drawn from the Lord's instruction that those without faith should be "nourished with all tenderness." Some believe that verse 46 promises that the faithful will never die, but notice what the verse actually says: "And it shall come to pass that those that *die* in me shall not taste of death, for *it [death]* shall be sweet unto them" (emphasis added).

Surrounding verses often provide important clues. Some have concluded that Doctrine and Covenants 76:84 teaches that the telestial kingdom is the same place as "hell." The following verse, however, clarifies that the people going to the telestial kingdom will be "redeemed from the devil" at the last resurrection (D&C 76:85). Some may wonder why followers of such great leaders as Paul, Cephas (Peter), and even Christ inherit only the telestial kingdom (D&C 76:99–100). A careful reading of this passage clarifies that it is speaking of those who merely "say" they are following Christ (v. 100) but are actually vile sinners (v. 103).

A thoughtful study of the scriptures may reveal deeper meanings that casual readers may easily miss. Section 76, verse 58, uses "gods" (a plural noun) whereas verse 59 employs "God's" (a possessive adjective). The first verse emphasizes that as children of our Heavenly Father, we all have the potential of becoming as he is. The second verse stresses that we must depend on and therefore are indebted to Christ, even as he depended on and therefore belongs to the Father.

Verse 43 of section 45 speaks of a gathering to "this place." But where is "this place"? This part of section 45 is a review of the prophecy Christ shared with his disciples on the Mount of Olives (compare the latter part of verse 16 with Matthew 24:1–3). Hence, "this place" refers to the Holy Land, in the Eastern Hemisphere. Knowing this background of section 45 also enables us to understand that "this chapter" in verse 60 refers to Matthew 24, in which the Savior's prophecy to his disciples anciently is recorded.

Many have assumed that the phrase "the glory of God is intelligence" (D&C 93:36) refers only to gaining an education. But "intelligence" can mean either our mental capacity or that part of our being that has existed from the beginning. Reading the context of verse 36 suggests that it is related more to the second of these meanings. Notice how verse 36 equates God's glory with "intelligence, . . . light and truth," and verse 29 indicates that these were attributes of man "in the beginning." The essential message of section 93 is that we had the same qualities that constitute God's glory but we had them only in a small degree, whereas he has them in full. By keeping God's commandments, we can receive truth and light until we have them in full and are glorified (vv. 20, 28). On the other hand, we are cautioned that Satan "taketh away light and truth through disobedience" (v. 39).

Even though section 93 describes a broad process of spiritual growth, seeking learning is an important part in the process. Truth, one of the key attributes of God's glory, is defined as a "knowledge of things as they are, and as they were, and as they are to come" (v. 24). Hence, in an earlier revelation, the Master directed us to "seek learning, even by study and also by faith" (D&C 88:76–80, 118).

Some have used the promise in Doctrine and Covenants

124:59 to support the idea that Joseph Smith's descendants were to succeed him as president of the Church. This passage, however, merely considers the rights of those who invested in the construction of the Nauvoo House and has nothing to do with succession in the presidency. This verse simply affirms that Joseph Smith's heirs were to inherit his stock in the house, according to the pattern commonly followed in the world. Similar inheritances were promised to others (vv. 69, 74–75, 77).

Allusions to other scriptures may have hidden meanings. Labeling today's wicked world as "Babylon" (D&C 1:16) or "Idumea" (D&C 1:36) takes on added meaning when we know that these were ancient kingdoms noted for their hedonistic materialism. Reference in Doctrine and Covenants 117:11 to the abominations of the Nicolaitane band should be understood in the light of John's commending members in the ancient church at Ephesus for hating the deeds of this group (Revelation 2:6).

In Doctrine and Covenants 46 the Lord explained that spiritual gifts include knowing "the differences of administration" and "the diversities of operations" (v. 15–16). These phrases are also found in Paul's list of spiritual gifts (1 Corinthians 12:5–6). Hence, understanding what he meant by these phrases helps us better understand their significance. Sidney B. Sperry explained that the Greek text of Paul's words clarifies their meaning: "Apparently by 'differences of administration' is meant the distinctive varieties of service and ministration by which things are accomplished in the Church." Similarly, Dr. Sperry continued, "diversities of operations" refers to "the workings, results, or effects" of various spiritual gifts. "One who by the gift of the Holy Ghost has the gift of knowing the 'diversities of operation' is one who may correctly discern whether a given service is of God or not."[5] Note that the Lord's revelation in Doctrine and Covenants 46 emphasizes that the gift is to "know," or understand, these things. Priesthood bearers represent the Lord Jesus Christ and so should seek his guidance in their service.

We must clearly understand the actual meaning of words used in the Doctrine and Covenants. In many cases meanings have changed since the days of Joseph Smith. For example, in Doctrine and Covenants 25:7, Emma Smith was told that she would be "ordained" to teach the Church and expound the scriptures. A dictionary published at the time of this revelation indicates that though the principal meaning of *ordain* is "to invest with a ministerial function or sacerdotal [priestly] power," the word also may mean "to set apart for an office; to appoint."[6]

"The term 'ordain' was used generally in the early days of the Church in reference to both ordination and setting apart," explained President Joseph Fielding Smith. "Men holding the Priesthood were said to have been 'ordained' to preside over branches and to perform special work. Sisters also were said to have been 'ordained' when they were called to some special duty or responsibility. In later years we developed a distinction between ordain and setting apart."[7]

The Lord has promised that "the Saints will . . . hardly escape" latter-day tribulations (D&C 63:34). *Hardly* meant "scarcely; barely; almost not," referring to something achieved only "with difficulty; with great labor."[8] The Lord has promised that Zion and her stakes will be places of defense and refuge when the divine wrath will be "poured out without mixture upon the whole earth" (D&C 115:6). Still, the faithful will not be totally shielded from these difficulties, and great effort will be required to maintain the righteous conditions that will spare them (D&C 97:25–26).

Consider insights provided by our living prophets. The foregoing discussion has included examples of how the teachings of our Church leaders significantly clarify the meaning of scriptural passages. Two additional illustrations show how explanations by the Brethren sharpen our understanding of the scriptures. Elder Orson Pratt elucidated the meaning of "Son Ahman," a name used in Doctrine and Covenants 78:20. *Ahman* is the name of the

Father in the pure language of Adam. *Son Ahman* is the name of the Son, and *sons Ahman* is the designation for the remainder of God's children.[9] Nobody is in a better position to explain the meaning of the Lord's revelations than is the Prophet Joseph Smith, through whom they were given. He declared, for example, that "tea and coffee are what the Lord meant when he said 'hot drinks.'"[10]

Nevertheless, Elder Dallin H. Oaks cautioned, "Commentaries are not a substitute for the scriptures any more than a good cookbook is a substitute for food." Elder Oaks pointed out that commentaries may "focus on only one meaning, to the exclusion of others. . . . Sometimes those other, less obvious, meanings can be the ones most valuable and useful to us as we seek to understand our own dispensation and to obtain answers to our personal questions. This is why the companionship of the Holy Ghost is a better guide to scriptural interpretation than even the best commentary."[11]

We must "search" the scriptures. Speaking of the Doctrine and Covenants, the Lord commanded us to "search these commandments" (D&C 1:37). Searching the scriptures involves more than merely reading or even studying them. Reminding us that they were given by his Spirit, the Lord stressed that we must read them by his power to fully comprehend them. If we do that, he promised us that we could "testify that [we] have heard [his] voice, and know [his] words" (D&C 18:36). If we read the scriptures with the same Spirit by which they were given, we will truly understand them, be edified, and, therefore, can rejoice (D&C 50:21–22).

Searching the scriptures also involves pondering their significance and applying them in our daily lives. Nephi declared his intent was to "liken all scriptures unto us" (1 Nephi 19:23). King Benjamin concluded his great discourse with an admonition that certainly applies to our scripture study: "And now, if you believe all these things see that ye do them" (Mosiah 4:10). The Savior similarly warned that hearing his words and failing to live according to them is like building a house on the sand. Lacking a foundation on bedrock, we could fall when storms come (Matthew 7:24–27).

A FINAL CAUTION

Sometimes the best answer to our questions will be "I don't know." Because only the president of the Church, whom we sustain as a prophet, seer, and revelator, has the right to give authoritative interpretations of scripture, we must realize that this certainly is not part of our steward-ship. It is far better to acknowledge our lack of understand-ing than to mislead others by presenting our unfounded opinions as though they were settled doctrine.

Still, there is much we can know. With more complete understanding, we are in a better position to teach the scriptures effectively. "Seek not to declare my word," the Master cautioned Hyrum Smith, "but first seek to obtain my word, and then shall your tongue be loosed; then, if you desire, you shall have my Spirit and my word, yea, the power of God unto the convincing of men" (D&C 11:21).

Let us all become scholars of the scriptures. Great satis-faction comes from understanding God's revelations (2 Nephi 4:15), and even greater joy from sharing them with others (D&C 18:15–16).

NOTES

1. Cited by Ezra Taft Benson, in Conference Report, October 1963, 17.

2. J. Reuben Clark Jr., *Church News,* 31 July 1954, 9, 10.

3. Joseph Young Sr., *History of the Organization of the Seventies* (Salt Lake City: Deseret News, 1878),1–2.

4. Joseph Fielding Smith, *Doctrines of Salvation,* comp. Bruce R. McConkie, 3 vols. (Salt Lake City: Bookcraft, 1954–56), 2:95.

5. Sidney B. Sperry, *Doctrine and Covenants Compendium* (Salt Lake City: Bookcraft, 1960), 196–97.

6. Noah Webster, *American Dictionary of the English Language* (New York: S. Converse, 1828; facsimile reprint, San Francisco: Foundation for American Christian Education, 1980), s.v. "ordain."

7. Joseph Fielding Smith, *Church History and Modern Revelation,* 2

vols. (Salt Lake City: Council of the Twelve Apostles of The Church of Jesus Christ of Latter-day Saints, 1953), 1:126.

8. *Webster's American Dictionary,* s.v. "hardly."

9. Orson Pratt, in *Journal of Discourses,* 26 vols. (London: Latter-day Saints' Book Depot, 1854–86), 2:342.

10. Cited in John A. Widtsoe and Leah D. Widtsoe, *The Word of Wisdom: A Modern Interpretation,* 2d ed. (Salt Lake City: Deseret Book, 1937), 85–86.

11. Dallin H. Oaks, address given at the BYU Studies Academy, 29 January 1993, 7–8.

CHAPTER THREE

DOCTRINAL CONNECTIONS WITH THE JOSEPH SMITH TRANSLATION

ROBERT J. MATTHEWS

The Joseph Smith Translation is a fact of history. It occupied a great amount of the Prophet Joseph Smith's time and energy. But it appears to me that it has generally not been appreciated for what it is and for the influence it has had on Church scripture and doctrine. In reality it has largely been neglected and even ignored by historians and scriptorians. I suppose that because the Joseph Smith Translation is a version of the Bible, historians have not recognized its connections with latter-day revelation, scripture, and history. On the other hand, because the Joseph Smith Translation is not a translation of the Bible in the usual sense of ancient documents and languages, traditional textual enthusiasts have not regarded it as a serious biblical document.

The Joseph Smith Translation of the Bible exerted a substantial influence on the content of the Doctrine and Covenants. The revelations that are now contained in the Doctrine and Covenants—particularly those given during the years 1830 through 1833—have a strong historical, textual, and subject-matter relationship to the Joseph Smith Translation. It has generally been the opinion of those

Robert J. Matthews is former dean of Religious Education at Brigham Young University.

historians who did notice this translation that Joseph Smith corrected the Bible by virtue of the revelations he had previously received and that he was somehow "Mormonizing" the Bible. The truth is, however, that often revelations of doctrinal significance first came to Joseph Smith during his labors with the translation and were thereafter added to the Doctrine and Covenants. This latter view shows the Joseph Smith Translation for what it really is, a preliminary source for many of the theological statements in the Doctrine and Covenants. Such a view adds dignity, grace, and stature to the extensive labors of the Prophet Joseph Smith in making this translation.

THE HISTORICAL SITUATION

Among the obvious facts relating to the Joseph Smith Translation are that the persons, places, and dates associated with it are the same as those pertaining to the Book of Mormon, the Doctrine and Covenants, and various events in early Church history. For example, the persons who worked on the translation include Joseph Smith, Oliver Cowdery, John Whitmer, Sidney Rigdon, and Frederick G. Williams. The places are Harmony, Pennsylvania; Fayette, New York; and Kirtland and Hiram, Ohio. The years when the brethren were working with the Bible in these places were 1830 to 1833. We soon become aware that the work on the translation of the Bible continued on a day-to-day basis, just as it did on the Doctrine and Covenants, as the Prophet sought divine help and received revelation. The kind of revelation we find in the Doctrine and Covenants is also found in the Joseph Smith Translation.

The Doctrine and Covenants contains regulatory and instructional information about the Joseph Smith Translation, giving direction about when to begin, when to pause, who is to be the scribe, and what parts of the Bible to translate next, as well as exhortation to move more rapidly and to make plans for publication. All of these items and more about the Joseph Smith Translation are contained in the revelations in the Doctrine and

Covenants. An examination of the Doctrine and Covenants shows that as some early sections revolve around the translation and printing of the Book of Mormon (parts of sections 3, 5, 8, 9, 10, 17), even so some later sections revolve around the translation and proposed printing of the Joseph Smith Translation (parts of sections 6, 8, 9, 29, 35, 37, 41, 42, 45, 47, 73, 74, 76, 77, 86, 91, 93, 94, 104, and 124). Many verses in the Doctrine and Covenants do not radiate their full meaning and are obscure to a modern reader until he learns that there is a connection to Joseph Smith's translation of the Bible; those passages can then be read in the historical context.

TRANSLATING ANCIENT RECORDS

Following is a brief review of several passages in the Doctrine and Covenants that have a direct relationship to the Joseph Smith Translation. The first three were received close together at Harmony, Pennsylvania, in April 1829. All three refer to Oliver Cowdery, and they are best studied as a unit.

Doctrine and Covenants 6:26–27. The brethren had already commenced the translation of the Book of Mormon. In Doctrine and Covenants 6:26 and 27 the Lord speaks of records containing much of the gospel that have been kept back because of iniquity. Oliver Cowdery is promised that he can assist Joseph Smith to bring this hidden knowledge to light. At first it might seem that this passage is speaking only of the Book of Mormon, but subsequent revelations indicate that other records are also included.

Doctrine and Covenants 8:11. Again, allusion is made in Doctrine and Covenants 8:11 to ancient records that need to be translated and which will reveal sacred knowledge. Like the previous excerpt, if taken alone, this passage may seem to refer to the Book of Mormon only, and it is generally interpreted in that limited scope. Nevertheless, subsequent revelation provides a wider understanding and a larger view of what is meant.

Doctrine and Covenants 9:1–2. A short time before, the Lord had granted Oliver Cowdery the privilege of trying to use the Urim and Thummim to translate the gold plates of the Book of Mormon (D&C 6:25). Because Brother Cowdery had tried but did not succeed in this effort and had returned to writing as the Prophet Joseph translated, the Lord admonished him to remain as the scribe until the translation of the Book of Mormon was finished. The Lord then makes a direct statement about the "other records" he had alluded to in Doctrine and Covenants 6 and 8: "And then [after the Book of Mormon is finished], behold, other records have I, that I will give unto you power that you may assist to translate."

This forthright declaration leaves no doubt that it was the Lord's desire that after the Book of Mormon was translated there were "other records" he wanted the Prophet Joseph and Oliver Cowdery to translate. The footnote in current editions of the Doctrine and Covenants 9:2 states that this passage refers to the Joseph Smith Translation of the Bible and also to the book of Abraham, in both of which Oliver Cowdery assisted the Prophet.

The Book of Mormon came from the press and the bindery the last week of March 1830. The Church was established on 6 April 1830, and the translation of the Bible was begun in June 1830. One event followed another in quick succession. Thus, within just a few weeks after completing the Book of Mormon, these same two brethren were at work in Harmony, making a translation of the Bible. Because hindsight is often clearer than foresight, it should not be difficult for modern readers to see that the Lord in his perfect knowledge had been preparing the Prophet Joseph and Oliver for their work with the Bible by showing them that they would be required to translate other records after the Book of Mormon was finished. Thus we see the direct relationship between passages in the Doctrine and Covenants and the Joseph Smith Translation in the stream of history.

PARALLEL PROCESSES

There is no mention in the Doctrine and Covenants of the exact day on which the Prophet Joseph and Oliver Cowdery began the translation of the Bible, but the manuscript of the Joseph Smith Translation itself begins with the date of June 1830, and it is by this means that the date is established. The manuscript begins in Oliver's hand. Joseph Smith and Oliver Cowdery were living in Harmony, Pennsylvania, at the time. Joseph and Emma were living in a small wooden home not far from Emma's parents. This was the same home in which a little more than a year earlier the Prophet and Oliver had been engaged in the translation of the Book of Mormon. Because of persecutions in May 1829, the Prophet had moved from Harmony and sought seclusion in the Peter Whitmer Sr. home at Fayette, New York, to continue to translate the Book of Mormon. Now in 1830, having commenced the translation of the Bible in the same home in Harmony, with the same scribe, persecution arose; again the Prophet moved from Harmony and sought seclusion in the Peter Whitmer Sr. home in Fayette, this time to continue the translation of the Bible. This latter move was in August 1830, and the Prophet translated the Bible in the Whitmer home in Fayette through the summer and fall of 1830. After Oliver was called on a mission to Missouri (D&C 28:8; 32:1–3), John Whitmer became the scribe. Even a casual reader cannot miss the parallel circumstances between the translation of the Book of Mormon and the Joseph Smith Translation of the Bible.

In the case of the Book of Mormon, the Prophet used an ancient set of plates engraved in an unknown language, which he translated by means of the Urim and Thummim. In the case of the Bible, the Prophet had no ancient text. He used as a base an edition of the King James Version published in 1828 by H. and E. Phinney of Cooperstown, New York. Oliver Cowdery purchased this large, pulpit-sized Bible from the E. B. Grandin Bookstore in Palmyra, New York, on 8 October 1829, for $3.75. By reading the English text, the Prophet, without the aid of the Urim and Thummim, received revelation about the meaning of various passages and also the restoration of lost parts. He dictated these to a scribe. In this manner, a large collection of information was recorded on manuscript pages measuring 8 1/2 by 14 inches, commencing with an independent revelation once given to Moses that Latter-day Saints now know as Moses 1 and continuing with Genesis and eventually the remainder of the Bible.

At Harmony, Joseph Smith received and Oliver Cowdery recorded the vision to Moses. During the summer and early fall of 1830 the translation continued from Genesis 1:1 through approximately Genesis 4. This part of the translation makes up 9 1/4 pages of manuscript written by Oliver Cowdery between June and 21 October 1830. The handwriting then changes to that of John Whitmer on the manuscript dated 21 October, 30 November, and 1 December 1830. This material covers Genesis 5 and was evidently done in the Whitmer home at Fayette, New York, to which Joseph Smith had moved in the last week of August 1830, after Brother Cowdery had departed with others for his mission to the Lamanites in Missouri.

Doctrine and Covenants 29:31–42. Doctrine and Covenants 29 was received by the Prophet Joseph Smith in September 1830 at Fayette, New York. The immediate circumstances that prompted this revelation are not known, yet its content is highly doctrinal, with verses 31 through 42 clarifying the spiritual and temporal aspects of the Creation and also the cause and consequence of the fall of Adam.

It cannot be overlooked that Doctrine and Covenants 29 was received in the same time period during which the Prophet translated Genesis 1, 2, and 3, which also deal with the Creation and the Fall. It is significant that the particular doctrinal emphasis of Doctrine and Covenants 29:31–42 closely parallels the doctrinal emphasis of the Joseph Smith Translation that is not found in the King James Version in Genesis. This circumstance strongly suggests a historical connection between Joseph Smith's translation of Genesis 1–3 (Moses 2–4) and Doctrine and Covenants 29, especially when they were produced within days of each other.

ENOCH AND ZION

The missionaries to the Lamanites, under the direction of Oliver Cowdery, had stopped in the vicinity of Kirtland, Ohio, and baptized a minister named Sidney Rigdon in November 1830. Brother Rigdon was so taken with the concept of the Restoration and the reality of a living prophet that he soon traveled from the Kirtland area to Fayette, New York, to meet the Prophet Joseph. He arrived in Fayette on 5 or 6 December 1830 and within a day or so received the revelation through Joseph Smith now known as Doctrine and Covenants 35, which was received about 7 December.

Doctrine and Covenants 35:20. At the time Brother Rigdon arrived in Fayette, Oliver Cowdery was well on his way to Missouri, and John Whitmer had been called by revelation to preach in Ohio. This left the Prophet Joseph without a full-time scribe. As pointed out in Doctrine and Covenants 35:20, Sidney Rigdon was then called to write for the Prophet, with the promise of the Lord that "the scriptures shall be given, even as they are in mine [the Lord's] own bosom." At this precise juncture, early in December 1830, the manuscript of the Joseph Smith Translation begins showing the penmanship of Sidney Rigdon. We recall that John Whitmer was recording the manuscript as recently as 1 December 1830.

The place at which Brother Rigdon began to write is what we now know as JST Genesis 7:3 (Moses 7:2). This material records valuable information about the patriarch Enoch and his city of Zion, which "dwelt in righteousness; and there was no poor among them" (Moses 7:18). Enoch and his city, we learn from this part of the translation, were all translated and taken to heaven with the promise that in the last days the city would return to the earth and be joined to the New Jerusalem, which the Saints of the latter days would build upon the earth (Moses 7:20–64). None of this detailed information about Enoch—that he had a city or that it had a functioning economic order without any poor—is even hinted at in the King James Version, or in any other version, of the Bible. This information is unique to the Joseph Smith Translation and is of particular importance to the Doctrine and Covenants.

Doctrine and Covenants 37:1–4. Soon after he revealed the Enoch material and during the same month of December 1830, the Lord instructed Joseph Smith to pause in the translation and move the entire Church membership to Ohio. The promise was given a few days later, on 2 January 1831, that the Lord would reveal his "law" to the Church after they arrived in Ohio (D&C 38:32).

Doctrine and Covenants 38:4. The Lord, almost as an aside, refers here to the "Zion of Enoch" being taken into "mine own bosom." Because no Bible has this information but because that very information was revealed to the Prophet Joseph a few days earlier as part of the Joseph Smith Translation, it is evident that this allusion is to information known only through the Joseph Smith Translation.

Doctrine and Covenants 41:7. The revelation in Doctrine and Covenants 41:7, given 4 February 1831, shortly after the Prophet and Sidney Rigdon arrived in Kirtland, indicates that Joseph Smith needs a house to live in where he can "translate." This revelation constitutes divine direction to recommence the translation. The Prophet and Emma were living with others in crowded conditions, which did not provide the serenity and quietness necessary to translate.

Doctrine and Covenants 42:1, 2, 30–55, 59. Five days later, the Lord instructed the Prophet concerning the "law." The law of teaching is stated, as well as other laws and principles pertaining to the kingdom. Of particular significance is the economic order, or law of property and stewardship, that is introduced in section 42. Consecration of property, the role of the bishop, the operation of the storehouse, and building the New Jerusalem are also discussed.

This law regarding material properties would provide for the poor. It cannot be mere coincidence that it came so soon after the great revelation about Enoch, who had a society and a city in which there were no poor. Is it not significant that immediately after receiving the revelation about Enoch while making the translation, the Lord commanded the Prophet to cease translating temporarily, move to Ohio, and there receive the economic law preparatory to building the New Jerusalem in this dispensation? All of these things parallel what was revealed about Enoch, none of which survives in any Bible today.

The next twenty or so sections of the Doctrine and Covenants, after section 42, outline the principles and organizational plan of the consecration of property, which concept had been introduced to the Prophet Joseph while he was translating Genesis.

Doctrine and Covenants 42:56–58. As part of the instruction of the revelation received 9 February 1831 at Kirtland, the Prophet is admonished to "ask" and receive the scriptures, as the Lord has "appointed." The Lord promises that these scriptures would be preserved in safety. He cautions the Prophet not to advertise these new scriptures then but that the time would come when the work would be received "in full," and then they would be taught to all people. Without the background information that Joseph Smith and Sidney Rigdon were translating the Bible almost daily, the real significance of these verses in the Doctrine and Covenants would be lost to our generation. With the knowledge that these brethren were engaged at that very time in the translation of the Bible (Genesis at that date), this passage holds greater meaning and constitutes another admonition for the Prophet to recommence the translation that had been interrupted by the move from Fayette to Kirtland.

Doctrine and Covenants 45:11–12. The revelation recorded in Doctrine and Covenants 45 was received in Kirtland, Ohio, on 7 March 1831. Reference is again made to the great patriarch Enoch and his righteous city who were "separated from the earth" (translated) and "received unto" the Lord. Because neither the King James Version nor any other known Bible has the slightest reference to Enoch having a city or that such a city ever existed on earth or was translated, this passage is a direct reference to the revelation concerning Enoch that was received in December 1830 at Fayette as part of the Joseph Smith Translation.

NEW TESTAMENT TRANSLATION

Doctrine and Covenants 45:60–62. During the course of the revelation recorded in Doctrine and Covenants 45, the Lord reviewed scenes and teachings he had given to the Twelve on the Mount of Olives eighteen hundred years earlier, some of which are recorded in the New Testament. Until this date, 7 March 1831, the Prophet and his scribes had translated only from the early chapters of Genesis. In this revelation the Lord instructed them to begin to translate the New Testament. He gave them the promise that in it (the translation they would make of the New Testament) many important things would be made known to them. Thus we see that the process of translation was a learning and revelatory experience. There can be no mistaking these words: "Wherefore, I give unto you that ye may now translate it [the New Testament], that ye may be prepared for the things to come." The original draft of Joseph Smith's translation of the New Testament shows that the Prophet began translating the book of Matthew the next day, 8 March 1831. The handwriting is Sidney Rigdon's. The first sentence reads: "A translation of the New Testament translated by the power of God." The pages that follow have no chapters or verses and very little punctuation.

Doctrine and Covenants 47:1. On the same day that the translation of the New Testament was started, 8 March 1831, John Whitmer was appointed by revelation to write for the Prophet "in transcribing" all things given from the Lord. One early result of this calling is a manuscript of the New Testament dated 4 April 1831 at Kirtland, which consists of a rewriting of the first draft of the translation of

Matthew, adding chapters, verses, and punctuation, as if for publication. This rewritten document is in the hand of John Whitmer, evidently in fulfillment of his duties.

Doctrine and Covenants 73:3–4. Because of persecution at Kirtland, the Prophet and Sidney Rigdon and their families moved to Hiram, Ohio, on 12 September 1831. The Lord instructed the brethren on 1 December 1831 at Hiram to exert greater efforts in preaching and testifying to the people about the gospel and the Restoration (D&C 71). To fulfill this new assignment, they temporarily laid aside the work of translation for about six weeks. On 10 January 1832, as noted in Doctrine and Covenants 73:3–4, the Lord told the brethren that it was now "expedient to translate again" and to continue with the translation until it was finished.

Doctrine and Covenants 74 headnote. The Prophet recommended the translation of the New Testament sometime between 10 and 25 January 1832. He also received an explanation, by revelation, of 1 Corinthians 7:14. That material does not appear in the Joseph Smith Translation manuscript, however. It is recorded in Doctrine and Covenants 74.

Doctrine and Covenants 76:15–18. While living in the John Johnson home in Hiram, the Prophet and Sidney Rigdon were translating the book of John and came to 5:29, at which point they received the vision of the degrees of glory. Doctrine and Covenants 76:15 through 18 clearly relates this vision to the work of translation to which they had been divinely appointed. The vision was received on 16 February 1832. Most of the New Testament was translated while the Prophet was living in the Johnson home, where he received many other revelations as well.

Doctrine and Covenants 77:1–15. The revelation recorded in Doctrine and Covenants 77, dealing entirely with the book of Revelation, was received in March 1832 at Hiram, Ohio. The Prophet explained the circumstances: "In connection with the translation of the Scriptures, I received

the following explanation of the Revelation of St. John"
(D&C 77, headnote).

FINISHING THE JOSEPH SMITH TRANSLATION

Doctrine and Covenants 86:1–7. After living in Hiram
one year, the Prophet Joseph, Sidney Rigdon, and their
families returned to Kirtland in September 1832. The
Prophet and his family moved into the upper story of the
Whitney store, where one room was designated as the
translating room. Many revelations were received there,
and the work moved forward on the Joseph Smith
Translation. Doctrine and Covenants 86:1 through 7 was
received by revelation on 25 December 1832 while the First
Presidency were reviewing and editing the New Testament
manuscript for publication (D&C 86, headnote).[1] The Old
Testament was at that time unfinished, having been laid
aside in March 1831 in favor of the New Testament as commanded of the Lord in Doctrine and Covenants 45:60–62.

Doctrine and Covenants 90:13. The New Testament
having been translated, the Prophet and Sidney Rigdon
returned to Genesis and translated the remainder of the
Old Testament. It is evident from Doctrine and Covenants
90:13 that they were by this time, 8 March 1833, working
in the books of the prophets. The Lord admonishes them
to continue the work until it is "finished," the translation
even taking precedence over other Church responsibilities.

Doctrine and Covenants 91 headnote. The edition of
the King James Version the Prophet was using contained
the fourteen books commonly called the Old Testament
Apocrypha. The Prophet asked the Lord whether he should
translate that part of the Bible and received word that "it is
not needful that it should be translated" (D&C 91:6).

Doctrine and Covenants 93:53. The revelation received
6 May 1833 at Kirtland, Ohio, now recorded in Doctrine
and Covenants 93, contains doctrinal statements of
remarkable depth. At the end of it the Lord counsels the
brethren to "hasten" to translate the scriptures. This commandment can only have reference to the translation of

the Bible, because the Book of Mormon had been published more than three years earlier and the Egyptian papyrus from which the book of Abraham was obtained would not become available for more than two years.

Doctrine and Covenants 94:10. The revelation recorded in Doctrine and Covenants 94, dated 6 May 1833, instructs the brethren to erect a printing house in Kirtland for "the printing of the translation of my scriptures." Because the translation of the Bible was nearing completion, it follows that a printing shop would soon be the next order of business. We learn from the last page of the manuscript that the translation was finished on 2 July 1833.

Doctrine and Covenants 104:58–59. Doctrine and Covenants 104 was received at Kirtland, Ohio, on 23 April 1834. It deals with several economic problems that were troubling the Church. Because some of the material was of a nature that it needed to be kept from the enemies of the Church at that time, some names, places, and concepts were written in code when this revelation was first published. Because the crises and danger of that time have now passed, the code words are no longer used in the present edition of the Doctrine and Covenants. One important passage was eliminated from the printed revelation and has never been restored. The text is found on page 105 in a manuscript draft in the Church Historical Archives in a collection named the "Kirtland Revelation Book." The passage speaks of the importance of securing copyrights to the publications of Church literature. In addition to the Book of Mormon and the revelations (Doctrine and Covenants), specific mention is made of securing the copyright "of the new translation of the scriptures," which can only mean Joseph Smith's translation of the Bible. The veiled manner in which this instruction has been presented in all printed editions of the Doctrine and Covenants is as follows: "I have commanded you . . . to print my words, the fulness of my scriptures, the revelations, which I have given unto you" (D&C 104:58). Such language prevented the enemies of the Church from knowing the full intent, and because the time is past, there is no real need to restore the entire passage today.

Doctrine and Covenants 124:89. The revelation received at Nauvoo, Illinois, 19 January 1841, and recorded in Doctrine and Covenants 124, specifically commands William Law to use his interest (money) to "publish the new translation of my holy word unto the inhabitants of the earth." Despite Brother Law's high office in the Church at that time, he did not obey the counsel. The passage also indicates the desire of the Lord that the translation be published.

The foregoing are the most prominent references in the Doctrine and Covenants that relate to the Joseph Smith Translation. Not only do many individual verses give regulatory instruction about the daily progress of the translation but whole sections of the Doctrine and Covenants came as a result of the translation.

THE INFLUENCE OF THE JOSEPH SMITH TRANSLATION ON THE DOCTRINE AND COVENANTS

The foregoing evidences are probably sufficient to illustrate that the Joseph Smith Translation has had much influence not only in the text of the Doctrine and Covenants but also in the headnotes and the footnotes. It is also abundantly evident that the Prophet Joseph's work with the Bible has influenced the doctrinal content of the Doctrine and Covenants. Some items, such as the age of accountability and baptism of children, were made known in the Joseph Smith Translation (Genesis 17:1–11) several months earlier than they appear in the Doctrine and Covenants (68:25–27). Many other doctrinal connections also become evident in comparing the text of one with the text of the other. The dates on the manuscript of the Joseph Smith Translation show that in some instances the doctrine in the Joseph Smith Translation was received at the earlier date. The Joseph Smith Translation was often the introductory experience that led to the other revelations and to the established order practiced in the Church.

Is the Joseph Smith Translation a Restoration or Only Inspired Commentary?

Scholars who have devoted a great amount of time and effort in studying the surviving biblical texts and languages sometimes hesitate to view the Joseph Smith Translation as even a partial restoration of what was written originally in the Bible. Because there are no known original documents of the Bible now available, there is no easy comparison.

Nevertheless, no one would say that the Lord could not reveal the original text. We learn from 1 Nephi 13:24 through 40 and from Moses 1:40 and 41 that plain and precious parts would be taken out, lost, held back, and removed from the biblical text—but that these things would be restored. These passages seem to speak not only of a loss of meaning but also of a loss of text (1 Nephi 13:28, 29, 32, 34, 40, and Moses 1:41). The language of these passages seems to mean that actual parts have been taken out of the book of the Jews, which is the Bible.

It is instructive to notice that part of Doctrine and Covenants 45 declares itself to be a repetition of a conversation that Jesus held with the Twelve on the Mount of Olives. Note these words of Jesus to Joseph Smith as recorded in verse 16: "And I will show it plainly as I showed it unto my disciples as I stood before them in the flesh, and spoke unto them, saying: As ye have asked me . . . " The tenor of these words leaves no doubt that Jesus Christ is telling Joseph Smith in the nineteenth century the same things he had told the earlier disciples in the first century—recreating the same scenes from the Mount of Olives, even to the same conversation. It isn't just a similar sermon; it is a reissue of a conversation held nineteen hundred years earlier (D&C 45:15–59).

If the Lord can and did restore one such event, he could and no doubt would do so with other events. Although not every word in the Joseph Smith Translation is necessarily restored text, yet we ought to allow for that kind of revelatory process and hold to the concept that the Joseph Smith

Translation is at the least a restoration of original meaning, doctrinal content, and also of text if necessary.

CONCLUSION

It is evident that the Lord commanded the Prophet Joseph to translate the Bible. It is also evident that the Joseph Smith Translation and the revelations in the Doctrine and Covenants are not merely roots entwined but are in reality the same root, received from the same divine source. The Joseph Smith Translation is neither an orphan nor a stepchild.

The Prophet Joseph's work with the Bible is too important to the restoration of the gospel of Jesus Christ and the revelation of the doctrinal base of this dispensation to be ignored or lightly dismissed. Most of the doctrinal revelations that have guided the Church were received during the years 1830 through 1833, which is the period of time when the Prophet was engaged in translating the Bible. Even Doctrine and Covenants 107 and 132, which are dated later, are based on information revealed in 1831 (D&C 107, headnote; 132, headnote).

It is my experience that when seriously studied in its context, the Joseph Smith Translation of the Bible conveys a wider and deeper appreciation for the history and doctrine of the Doctrine and Covenants.

NOTE

1. Also in Joseph Smith, *The History of The Church of Jesus Christ of Latter-day Saints,* ed. B. H. Roberts, 2d ed. rev., 7 vols. (Salt Lake City: The Church of Jesus Christ of Latter-day Saints, 1932–52), 1:300.

CHAPTER FOUR

WHY DO BAD THINGS HAPPEN TO GOOD PEOPLE?

RANDY L. BOTT

One frequently asked question that, without the benefit of revelation, remains a mystery is, "Why do bad things happen to good people?" Often cast in the form of a bitter challenge, the question may be rephrased into an exclamation: If there were a God who really loved us and was involved with us, he wouldn't let such a tragedy take place![1] The sacred pages of the Doctrine and Covenants can help us to put trials, tribulations, afflictions, and suffering into a more correct, eternal perspective. Additional comments by prophets and apostles of this dispensation are included in the notes.

THE NATURAL CONSEQUENCES OF IMPROPER PRIORITIES

When Joseph Smith wearied the Lord for permission to allow Martin Harris to take the 116 manuscript pages (the book of Lehi) to placate Harris's critics, the Lord warned the Prophet twice about the inadvisability of the proposal. Joseph, apparently not wanting to offend his friend, agreed to ask a third time. At that time the Lord seemed to say, "Joseph, there are lessons of life to learn. You may learn by

Randy L. Bott is assistant professor of Church history and doctrine at Brigham Young University.

precept or you may learn by sad experience, but learn you will."

After the pages were lost, the Lord revealed through the Urim and Thummim a necessary lesson for Joseph Smith and for all of us: "And behold, how oft you have transgressed the commandments and the laws of God, and have gone on in the persuasions of men.

"For, behold, you should not have feared man more than God. Although men set at naught the counsels of God, and despise his words—

"Yet you should have been faithful; and he would have extended his arm and supported you against all the fiery darts of the adversary; and he would have been with you in every time of trouble.

"Behold, thou art Joseph, and thou wast chosen to do the work of the Lord, but because of transgression, if thou art not aware thou wilt fall.

"But remember, God is merciful; therefore, repent of that which thou hast done which is contrary to the commandment which I gave you, and thou art still chosen, and art again called to the work;

"Except thou do this, thou shalt be delivered up and become as other men, and have no more gift" (D&C 3:6–11).

Joseph Smith was not the only one who had to learn to put the Lord at the top of the priority list. David Whitmer received a stern chastisement concerning why he had lost the divine direction and was left to his own devices:

"Behold, I say unto you, David, that you have feared man and have not relied on me for strength as you ought.

"But your mind has been on the things of the earth more than on the things of me, your Maker, and the ministry whereunto you have been called; and you have not given heed unto my Spirit, and to those who were set over you, but have been persuaded by those whom I have not commanded.

"Wherefore, you are left to inquire for yourself at my

hand, and ponder upon the things which you have received" (D&C 30:1–3).

The five mistakes David Whitmer had made are not difficult to translate into today's environment, almost without modification. They were (1) you have feared man (wanted to be socially acceptable); (2) you have not relied on the Lord for strength as you should have (strength received from peers is not nearly as effective as support from God); (3) your mind has been focused on the things of this world rather than on the eternal verities including your present Church calling; (4) you have not listened to the Spirit and those leaders whom the Lord has chosen to guide you; and (5) you have been persuaded by those who seem to know much but have no authority to receive revelations from the Lord for you.

Scattered throughout the Doctrine and Covenants are other warnings, suggesting that the early brethren struggled then as we do now to "Choose ye this day, to serve the Lord God who made you" (Moses 6:33).[2]

FAILURE TO REPENT RESULTS IN SUFFERING

There seems to be an unwritten but painfully evident corollary to the Lord's instructions through Joseph: "There is a law, irrevocably decreed in heaven before the foundations of this world, upon which all blessings are predicated—and when we obtain any blessing from God, it is by obedience to that law upon which it is predicated" (D&C 130:20–21). That corollary is implicit: There is a law, irrevocably decreed in heaven before the foundations of this world, upon which all cursings are predicated—and when we suffer any cursing from God, it is because we have disobeyed the law and received the inescapable consequences of our disobedience.[3] There are many reasons problems come; however, it would be a mistake not to believe that our disobedience is one reason problems come.[4] The Savior sternly warned that persistence in a forbidden path would not be excused: "And surely every man must repent or suffer, for I, God, am endless. . . .

"Therefore I command you to repent—repent, lest I smite you by the rod of my mouth, and by my wrath, and by my anger, and your sufferings be sore—how sore you know not, how exquisite you know not, yea, how hard to bear you know not.

"For behold, I, God, have suffered these things for all, that they might not suffer if they would repent;

"But if they would not repent they must suffer even as I;

"Which suffering caused myself, even God, the greatest of all, to tremble because of pain, and to bleed at every pore, and to suffer both body and spirit—and would that I might not drink the bitter cup, and shrink—

"Nevertheless, glory be to the Father, and I partook and finished my preparations unto the children of men.

"Wherefore, I command you again to repent, lest I humble you with my almighty power; and that you confess your sins, lest you suffer these punishments of which I have spoken, of which in the smallest, yea, even in the least degree you have tasted at the time I withdrew my Spirit" (D&C 19:4, 15–20).

One could hardly accuse the Lord of being unjust for allowing problems to come upon us when we openly defy him or disobey his commandments.[5] In one of the bitterest learning experiences recorded in the Doctrine and Covenants, the Lord revealed through the Prophet the reason for the expulsion of the Saints from Jackson County, Missouri: "I, the Lord, have suffered the affliction to come upon them, wherewith they have been afflicted, in consequence of their transgressions" (D&C 101:2).

A few verses later the Lord listed the "sins" that caused the Saints to "pollute" their inheritance and suffer indescribable deprivations: "There were jarrings, and contentions, and envyings, and strifes, and lustful and covetous desires among them; therefore by these things they polluted their inheritances.

"They were slow to hearken unto the voice of the Lord their God; therefore, the Lord their God is slow to hearken unto their prayers, to answer them in the day of their trouble.

"In the day of their peace they esteemed lightly my counsel; but, in the day of their trouble, of necessity they feel after me.

"Verily I say unto you, notwithstanding their sins, my bowels are filled with compassion towards them. I will not utterly cast them off; and in the day of wrath I will remember mercy" (D&C 101:6–9).

We are left to ponder whether modern Saints are destined to repeat the mistakes of our forbears because of our casual approach to hearkening unto the voice our God.

AFFLICTIONS HELP US LEARN PATIENCE

We need but look at the conditions in the world to know that God has more patience than anyone could possibly believe. Because his stated objective is to help us become like him (Moses 1:39), it would seem apparent that trials, tribulations, and afflictions may come even though we are not breaking any divine laws or really deserve the problems (that is, as a consequence of disobedience). The Lord informed Joseph Smith very early in his ministry: "Be patient in afflictions, for thou shalt have many; but endure them, for, lo, I am with thee, even unto the end of thy days" (D&C 24:8). Hardly a cheery thought, yet it proved to have been stated with godly accuracy.

The warning of tribulations was not reserved exclusively for the Prophet. Newel Knight received a similar injunction with an additional promise. The Lord said: "And again, be patient in tribulation until I come; and, behold, I come quickly, and my reward is with me, and they who have sought me early shall find rest to their souls" (D&C 54:10).

The tribulations will end with the second coming of the Lord. The rewards for enduring tribulations will not be postponed indefinitely. The rest to be found is the "fulness of his glory" (D&C 84:24). Each promise gives the sufferer sufficient hope to endure the trial (Mosiah 23:21–22). Perhaps as a final injunction the Lord again pleads: "Be patient in affliction" (D&C 66:9). Developing patience moves the suffering Saint closer to the eternal goal of personal perfection.[6]

AFFLICTIONS COME FROM VARIOUS SOURCES

We might think that when every external, Satan-controlled factor is marshaled against us, that should suffice (D&C 76:28–29). The Savior consoled the early brethren: "Therefore, fear not, little flock; do good; let earth and hell combine against you, for if ye are built upon my rock, they cannot prevail" (D&C 6:34). In other words, afflictions come from various sources but all of them can move us toward our eternal goal of becoming like God.

Then opposition can be expected from both our visible environment and the invisible dominions of darkness. Isn't that adequate to give us the experiences we need to progress toward becoming celestial people?[7] Thomas B. Marsh was "privileged" to have another source of trouble—his own family. The Lord explained to him: "Behold, you have had many afflictions because of your family; nevertheless, I will bless you and your family, yea, your little ones; and the day cometh that they will believe and know the truth and be one with you in my church" (D&C 31:2).

How could family-generated afflictions possibly turn to his eternal benefit? The Lord continues his instruction to Brother Marsh by explaining: "Be patient in afflictions, revile not against those that revile. Govern your house in meekness, and be steadfast" (D&C 31:9). In other words, be patient with your family. Don't revert to the world's way of solving problems by using force against force. Use meekness and steadfastness in governing your home. As he followed those instructions, the Lord had held out the promise to Thomas Marsh, both in the second and fifth verses of section 31, that "your family shall live." It is not easy to keep serving and governing the house of God when a person's own household is in turmoil. Easy or not, there are lessons to learn that necessitate our complete trust in

God's ability to fulfill the promise that one day our families will be "one with you in my church" (D&C 31:2).[8]

It is a struggle to do everything the Lord reveals, yet the Lord desires a thorough devotion that includes a change of heart. In teaching the early Church members about forgiveness, the Lord said: "My disciples, in days of old, sought occasion against one another and forgave not one another in their hearts; and for this evil they were afflicted and sorely chastened. Wherefore, I say unto you, that ye ought to forgive one another; for he that forgiveth not his brother his trespasses standeth condemned before the Lord; for there remaineth in him the greater sin. I, the Lord, will forgive whom I will forgive, but of you it is required to forgive all men. And ye ought to say in your hearts—let God judge between me and thee, and reward thee according to thy deeds" (D&C 64:8–11).

Not only did the Lord inform his Latter-day Saints about the weaknesses of his former-day disciples but he also warned that they had been "afflicted and sorely chastened" because of their superficial forgiveness, without the requisite attendant change of heart. Apparently, in an attempt to help his Latter-day Saints avoid the same mistake, the Lord warned about the seriousness of withholding forgiveness with our very limited knowledge. In fact, he declared that he would forgive whomever he would, and failure on our part to extend forgiveness to all men would result in the greater sin being levied against us. Perhaps that greater sin is blasphemy, because an unforgiving person would be taking a position preeminent to God (John 10:33).

The Lord also clearly outlined the method of forgiving. Divine justice was not to be escaped by the unrepentant sinner. Judgment was to be left in the hands of God. "Let God judge between me and thee and reward thee according to thy deeds" (D&C 64:11)—as if he were saying, Leave it in my hands. Go on with life. Don't burden yourself by trying to magnify my office. Judgment is mine, and I will repay (see D&C 82:23). The world would have us continually dredge up past wrongs we have suffered. Using worldly philosophies to solve spiritual problems has never worked. The Lord instructs us simply to put the past behind us and surge on to eternal life.[9]

FAILURE TO OBEY THE LORD RESULTS IN AFFLICTIONS

The scriptures are replete with warnings of impending calamities if we fail to follow the Lord's directives.[10] In unfolding to his Saints the definition of modern Zion, the Lord also foretold the calamities that await the wicked: "Nevertheless, Zion shall escape if she observe to do all things whatsoever I have commanded her. But if she observe not to do whatsoever I have commanded her, I will visit her according to all her works, with sore affliction, with pestilence, with plague, with sword, with vengeance, with devouring fire" (D&C 97:25–26).

That conditional protection was reemphasized later when the Lord declared: "Verily, verily, I say unto you, darkness covereth the earth, and gross darkness the minds of the people, and all flesh has become corrupt before my face. Behold, vengeance cometh speedily upon the inhabitants of the earth, a day of wrath, a day of burning, a day of desolation, of weeping, of mourning, and of lamentation; and as a whirlwind it shall come upon all the face of the earth, saith the Lord. And upon my house shall it begin, and from my house shall it go forth, saith the Lord; first among those among you, saith the Lord, who have professed to know my name and have not known me, and have blasphemed against me in the midst of my house, saith the Lord" (D&C 112:23–26).

President Brigham Young clarified the conditions that would determine whether the Latter-day Saints escaped the prophesied calamities: "There is one principle I would like to have the Latter-day Saints perfectly understand—that is, of blessings and cursings. For instance, we read that war, pestilence, plagues, famine, etc., will be visited upon the inhabitants of the earth; but if distress through the judgments of God comes upon this people, it will be because the majority have turned away from the Lord. Let the majority of the people turn away from the Holy Commandments which the Lord has delivered to us, and cease to hold the balance of power in the Church, and we may expect the judgments of God to come upon us; but while six-tenths or three-fourths of this people will keep the commandments of God, the curse and judgments of the Almighty will never come upon them, though we will have trials of various kinds, and the elements to contend with—natural and spiritual elements. While this people will strive to serve God according to the best of their abilities, they will fare better, have more to eat and to wear, have better houses to live in, better associations, and enjoy themselves better than the wicked ever do or ever will do."[11]

The mere reading and pondering of the desolations prophesied upon the heads of the wicked should be sufficient to motivate the Latter-day Saints to be more diligent in following all of the Lord's commandments. It is an interesting study to read the Doctrine and Covenants making a two-column list, one side enumerating the conditions prophesied among the wicked, and the other those promised among the Saints. It takes little discernment to determine in which camp we would prefer to be.

Learning to trust and obey the Lord seems a difficult thing to do in an anthropocentric world. That we must learn obedience is a given. The Lord revealed: "And my people must needs be chastened until they learn obedience, if it must needs be, by the things which they suffer" (D&C 105:6).

TRIBULATIONS SEEM TO BE THE FORERUNNER OF BLESSINGS

Earth life was divinely designed to test us in all areas necessary for future exaltation (Abraham 3:25). Part of that testing is passing through trials and tribulations. The Lord explained: "For verily I say unto you, blessed is he that keepeth my commandments, whether in life or in death; and he that is faithful in tribulation, the reward of the same is greater in the kingdom of heaven. Ye cannot behold with your natural eyes, for the present time, the design of your God concerning those things which shall come hereafter, and the glory which shall follow after much tribulation. For after much tribulation come the blessings. Wherefore the day cometh that ye shall be crowned with much glory; the hour is not yet, but is nigh at hand" (D&C 58:2–4).

The implication of those verses is intriguing: Faithfulness in enduring tribulations results in greater rewards. Greater than what? Greater than if we are not faithful in tribulations. It seems we are destined to pass through trials and tribulations (John 16:33). The important factor is our faithfulness. The Lord said: "For after much tribulation, as I have said unto you in a former commandment, cometh the blessing. Behold, this is the blessing which I have promised after your tribulations, and the tribulations of your brethren—your redemption, and the redemption of your brethren, even their restoration to the land of Zion, to be established, no more to be thrown down" (D&C 103:12–13).

Tribulations seem to be in part the necessary prerequisites to receiving blessings our Heavenly Father desires to bestow on us.[12] If we accept his declaration, our outlook on trials could be brought into alignment with our understanding. Failing to learn this vital principle has resulted in many people becoming embittered against God and (temporarily, at least) losing their faith.

TRIALS PREPARE US FOR SANCTIFICATION

As difficult as it may be for the veiled mind of man to comprehend, a sanctifying effect is associated with trials. Referring in a sobering way to a biblical story of long ago, the Lord continues to enlarge our understanding of trials: "Therefore, they must needs be chastened and tried, even as Abraham, who was commanded to offer up his only son. For all those who will not endure chastening, but deny me, cannot be sanctified" (D&C 101:4–5).

Can the Lord really be intimating that we will all be asked to sacrifice our children as he commanded Abraham?

No, but the principles behind the test of Abraham are very applicable to us. Divorcing ourselves from the actual experience and looking for elements with broader application, we see at least three principles: (1) Abraham was asked to give up something he loved very much; (2) Abraham was asked to do something he really did not want to do; and (3) Abraham was instructed to do something he really did not completely understand.

Every son or daughter of God in that select group who will make up "my jewels" (D&C 101:3) will be required to endure (maybe many more times than once!) the chastening tests of Abraham. Why would a loving Father require such things of his children? President George Q. Cannon gave a convincing explanation: "Here comes the command of God to this man (Abraham) who has been taught so scrupulously about the sinfulness of murder and human sacrifice, to do these very things. Now, why did the Lord ask such things of Abraham? Because, knowing what his future would be and that he would be the father of an innumerable posterity, he was determined to test him. God did not do this for His own sake; for He knew by His foreknowledge what Abraham would do (Abraham 1:22–23); but the purpose was to impress upon Abraham a lesson, and to enable him to attain unto knowledge that he could not obtain in any other way. That is why God tries all of us. It is not for His own knowledge for He knows all things beforehand. He knows all your lives and everything you will do. But He tries us for our own good, that we may know ourselves, for it is most important that a man should know himself. He required Abraham to submit to this trial because He intended to give him glory, exaltation and honor; He intended to make him a king and a priest, to share with Himself the glory, power and dominion which He exercised."[13]

Some of the most difficult tests given to the faithful Saints in the early days of this dispensation surround the events of the Prophet's incarceration during the winter of 1838–39. After many months of suffering beyond imagination, the Prophet complained to the Lord. The Lord's explanation is at once consoling and instructive: "My son, peace be unto thy soul; thine adversity and thine afflictions shall be but for a small moment; and then, if thou endure it well, God shall exalt thee on high; thou shalt triumph over all thy foes" (D&C 121:7–8).

Interestingly, the Lord did not promise Joseph that he would be immediately liberated or that the trials would stop. He just focused the Prophet's attention on the results that were apparently forgotten amidst the suffering. He had previously revealed that there is purpose in trials. He said: "And I give unto you a commandment, that ye shall forsake all evil and cleave unto all good, that ye shall live by every word which proceedeth forth out of the mouth of God. For he will give unto the faithful line upon line, precept upon precept; and I will try you and prove you herewith. And whoso layeth down his life in my cause, for my name's sake, shall find it again, even life eternal. Therefore, be not afraid of your enemies, for I have decreed in my heart, saith the Lord, that I will prove you in all things, whether you will abide in my covenant, even unto death, that you may be found worthy. For if ye will not abide in my covenant ye are not worthy of me" (D&C 98:11–15).

Later, in the revelatory letter written from the Liberty jail, Joseph's perspective was again enlarged. He was not the first nor would he be the last to suffer. Nevertheless, the Lord explained: "Know thou, my son, that all these things shall give thee experience, and shall be for thy good. The Son of Man hath descended below them all. Art thou greater than he? Therefore, hold on thy way, and the priesthood shall remain with thee; for their bounds are set, they cannot pass. Thy days are known, and thy years shall not be numbered less; therefore, fear not what man can do, for God shall be with you forever and ever" (D&C 122:7–9).

There is purpose in suffering that will eventually prove to our eternal benefit.[14] The Savior is aware of all of our suffering, having suffered greater and more than any man has ever suffered. The bounds of our suffering are set, as are the bounds of the persecutors. Said another way, God is in control. Nothing will happen to us that will be to our eternal detriment. We have been allotted a certain time here, and—given our best efforts—our days will not be shortened (D&C 121:25). Even though it may not always be apparent, God's help will be with us in those times of darkest trials.

AFFLICTIONS MAY BE NECESSARY BEFORE BLESSINGS CAN COME

As Latter-day Saints we sometimes become rather self-assured that we are right and the rest of mankind is wrong. In our desire never to be wrong, we may be oblivious to the promptings of the Spirit that are trying to refocus our thinking. If ease is long-lasting, it is easy to become too casual in our remembrance of the Lord.[15] The Lord has a solution for those of us who require such stern correction. Speaking to the Twelve, but with broad application, the Lord said: "And after their temptations, and much tribulation, behold, I the Lord, will feel after them, and if they harden not their hearts, and stiffen not their necks against me, they shall be converted, and I will heal them. Now, I say unto you, and what I say unto you, I say unto all the Twelve: Arise and gird up your loins, take up your cross, follow me, and feed my sheep. Exalt not yourselves; rebel not against my servant Joseph; for verily I say unto you, I am with him, and my hand shall be over him; and the keys which I have given unto him, and also to youward, shall not be taken from him till I come" (D&C 112:13–15).

Meat for a long session of meditation and pondering might be the question: How many of the trials, tribulations, and afflictions that I am experiencing are the result of my stiff neck and unyielding spirit? Could I escape some of those trials if I were more teachable?[16]

TRIALS HELP US LEARN TO LOOK FOR THE GOOD IN ALL THINGS

Many scriptures include the promise that "all these things shall be for thy good." In one grand summary statement, the Lord helps us realize how truly childlike we are in our understanding of him and his marvelous plan for us. He said: "Verily, verily, I say unto you, ye are little children, and ye have not as yet understood how great blessings the Father hath in his own hands and prepared for you; and ye cannot bear all things now; nevertheless, be of good cheer, for I will lead you along. The kingdom is yours and the blessings thereof are yours, and the riches of eternity are yours. And he who receiveth all things with thankfulness shall be made glorious; and the things of this earth shall be added unto him, even an hundred fold, yea, more" (D&C 78:17–19).

Perhaps with all that has been said, we are constrained to say in the end that we do not understand all things. Motivated with an unshakable faith that the Lord is in control, we move forward one step at a time, enduring one trial at a time. Although trials may come in multiples and even though we often fall short of taking full advantage of the test, we are commanded, "Nevertheless, be of good cheer." Our faltering footsteps do not disqualify us from receiving his promised guidance—"for I will lead you along." Mistakes have been and will be made by even the most diligent. The archenemy would have us believe that the promised goal of exaltation has been forfeited by the mistakes we have made. The Lord reassures: "The kingdom is yours and the blessings thereof are yours, and the riches of eternity are yours."

Although it may require almost superhuman effort, we are enjoined to "receive all things with thankfulness." Said another way: Look for the good in everything. Those leaders of the Jews who seemed bent on finding sin in the sinless One found that which was not there (Matthew 12:24; Mark 3:22; Luke 11:15–19). Perhaps the Lord is trying to teach us a vital lesson: You'll find in life exactly what you look for. How disappointing to approach the judgment bar to discover that we really did get just what we looked for. Even before the Church was restored, the Lord promised,

"Verily, verily, I say unto you, even as you desire of me so it shall be unto you" (D&C 6:8; see also 11:8).

It will require an Omnipotent Being to fulfill the promise that follows the injunction made in Doctrine and Covenants 98:1–3: "Verily I say unto you my friends, fear not, let your hearts be comforted; yea, rejoice evermore, and in everything give thanks; waiting patiently on the Lord, for your prayers have entered into the ears of the Lord of Sabaoth, and are recorded with this seal and testament—the Lord hath sworn and decreed that they shall be granted. Therefore, he giveth this promise unto you, with an immutable covenant that they shall be fulfilled; and all things wherewith you have been afflicted shall work together for your good, and to my name's glory, saith the Lord."

TRIALS RESULT IN EXALTATION FOR THE FAITHFUL

The final concept in trying to make sense out of otherwise senseless suffering is perhaps the umbrella encompassing all other concepts. The Lord's desire to provide experiences that will eventually exalt us is paramount: "And all they who suffer persecution for my name, and endure in faith, though they are called to lay down their lives for my sake yet shall they partake of all this glory. Wherefore, fear not even unto death; for in this world your joy is not full, but in me your joy is full. Therefore, care not for the body, neither the life of the body; but care for the soul, and for the life of the soul. And seek the face of the Lord always, that in patience ye may possess your souls, and ye shall have eternal life" (D&C 101:35–38).

When we read the Doctrine and Covenants looking for a specific theme or thread to answer the question, Why suffering? it becomes apparent that the Lord knew and sanctioned the suffering that his Saints would be called upon to endure. Through the Prophet Joseph's successor, Brigham Young, the Lord continued his instruction: "My people must be tried in all things, that they may be prepared to receive the glory that I have for them, even the glory of

Zion; and he that will not bear chastisement is not worthy of my kingdom. Let him that is ignorant learn wisdom by humbling himself and calling upon the Lord his God, that his eyes may be opened that he may see, and his ears opened that he may hear; for my Spirit is sent forth into the world to enlighten the humble and contrite, and to the condemnation of the ungodly" (D&C 136:31–33).

If we would enlarge our understanding of Why suffering? we must be humble enough to be taught from on high.[17] When our understanding becomes one with God's, we will be constrained to admit that "all things have been done in the wisdom of him who knoweth all things" (2 Nephi 2:24). Although incomplete, the points enumerated above serve as a place to begin to understand the "hidden mysteries of my kingdom" (D&C 76:7), which God promised to make known to those who "fear me, and serve me in righteousness and truth unto the end" (D&C 76:5).

NOTES

1. "One cannot look at suffering, regardless of its causes or origins, without feeling pain and compassion. I can understand why someone who lacks an eternal perspective might see the horrifying news footage of starving children and man's inhumanity to man and shake a fist at the heavens and cry, 'If there is a God, how could he allow such things to happen?'" M. Russell Ballard, *Ensign,* May 1995, 23.

2. Examples include D&C 1:19; 3:12–15; 5:21; 6:18–20, 36; 10:6–7; 11:12–14, 19; 12:1–2; 14:2; 15:1; 16:1; 18:3, 18; 19:13.

3. The scriptures clearly tell us that we will be blessed for following God and cursed for rejecting him. Deuteronomy 19, 28, and 30 focus on this principle. A latter-day passage is D&C 24:2–6.

4. "Unfortunately, some of our greatest tribulations are the result of our own foolishness and weakness and occur because of our own carelessness or transgressions. Central to solving these problems is the great need to get back on the right track and, if necessary, engage in each of the steps for full and complete repentance. Through this great principle, many things can be made fully right and all things better. We can go to others for help. To whom can we go? Elder Orson F. Whitney asked and answered this question: 'To whom do we look, in days of grief and disaster, for help and consolation? . . . They are men and women who have suffered, and out of their experience in suffering they bring forth the riches of their sympathy and

condolences as a blessing to those now in need. Could they do this had they not suffered themselves? . . . Is not this God's purpose in causing his children to suffer? He wants them to become more like himself. God has suffered far more than man ever did or ever will, and is therefore the great source of sympathy and consolation' (*Improvement Era,* November 1918, page 7)." James E. Faust, *Ensign,* May 1979, 54.

5. "No one wants adversity. Trials, disappointments, sadness, and heartache come to us from two basically different sources. Those who transgress the laws of God will always have those challenges. . . . If you are suffering the disheartening effects of transgression, please recognize that the only path to permanent relief from sadness is sincere repentance with a broken heart and a contrite spirit. Realize your full dependence upon the Lord and your need to align your life with His teachings. There is really no other way to get lasting healing and peace. Postponing humble repentance will delay or prevent your receiving relief. Admit to yourself your mistakes and seek help now. Your bishop is a friend with keys of authority to help you find peace of mind and contentment. The way will be opened for you to have strength to repent and be forgiven." Richard G. Scott, *Ensign,* November 1995, 16.

6. "Suffering can make saints of people as they learn patience, long-suffering, and self-mastery. The sufferings of our Savior were part of his education. 'Though he were a Son, yet learned he obedience by the things which he suffered;

"'And being made perfect, he became the author of eternal salvation unto all them that obey him' (Hebrews 5:8–9). . . .

"On the other hand, these things can crush us with their mighty impact if we yield to weakness, complaining, and criticism. 'No pain that we suffer, no trial that we experience is wasted. It ministers to our education, to the development of such qualities as patience, faith, fortitude and humility. All that we suffer and all that we endure, especially when we endure it patiently, builds up our characters, purifies our hearts, expands our souls, and makes us more tender and charitable, . . . and it is through sorrow and suffering, toil and tribulation, that we gain the education that we come here to acquire and which will make us more like our Father and Mother in heaven. . . .' (Orson F. Whitney)." Spencer W. Kimball, *Faith Precedes the Miracle* (Salt Lake City: Deseret Book, 1972), 98.

7. "Just when all seems to be going right, challenges often come in multiple doses applied simultaneously. When those trials are not consequences of your disobedience, they are evidence that the Lord feels you are prepared to grow more (see Prov. 3:11–12). He therefore gives you experiences that stimulate growth, understanding, and compassion which polish you for your everlasting benefit. To get you

from where you are to where He wants you to be requires a lot of stretching, and generally entails discomfort." Richard G. Scott, *Ensign,* November 1995, 16–17.

8. "We have learned many things through suffering. We call it suffering; I call it a school of experience. I never did bother my head much about these things; I do not to-day. What are these things for? Why is it that good men should be tried? Why is it, in fact, that we should have a devil? Why did not the Lord kill him long ago? Because he could not do without him. He needed the devil and a great many of those who do his bidding just to keep men straight, that we may learn to place our dependence upon God, and trust in Him, and to observe his laws and keep his commandments. When he destroyed the inhabitants of the antediluvian world, he suffered a descendant of Cain to come through the flood in order that he might be properly represented upon the earth. And Satan keeps busy all the time, and he will until he is bound; and I expect they will then have good times until he is loose again. The time will be when he will be cast into the bottomless pit, and he will not be able to deceive the nations any more until the thousand years have expired. I have never looked at these things in any other light than trials for the purpose of purifying the Saints of God, that they may be, as the Scriptures say, as gold that has been seven times purified by the fire." John Taylor, in *Journal of Discourses,* 26 vols. (London: Latter-day Saints' Book Depot, 1854–86), 23:336.

9. "Brethren, I count not myself to have apprehended: but this one thing I do, forgetting those things which are behind, and reaching forth unto those things which are before, I press toward the mark for the prize of the high calling of God in Christ Jesus." Philippians 3:13–14.

10. Examples include 2 Nephi 5:21; Jacob 2:33; Mosiah 7:28; 9:3; D&C 1:17; 19:15; 45:50; 82:2; 87:5; 109:46; 136:35.

11. Brigham Young, in *Journal of Discourses,* 10:335–36.

12. "To exercise faith is to trust that the Lord knows what He is doing with you and that He can accomplish it for your eternal good even though you cannot understand how He can possibly do it. We are like infants in our understanding of eternal matters and their impact on us here in mortality. Yet at times we act as if we knew it all. When you pass through trials for His purposes, as you trust Him, exercise faith in Him, He will help you. That support will generally come step by step, a portion at a time. While you are passing through each phase, the pain and difficulty that comes from being enlarged will continue. If all matters were immediately resolved at your first petition, you could not grow. Your Father in Heaven and His Beloved Son love you perfectly. They would not require you to experience a

moment more of difficulty than is absolutely needed for your personal benefit or for that of those you love." Richard G. Scott, *Ensign,* November 1995, 17.

13. George Q. Cannon, in Conference Report, April 1899, 66–67.

14. "He led this people in different parts of the United States, and the finger of scorn has been pointed at them. Officers of the Government of the United States have lifted their heel against them, and this people have been driven from town to town, from county to county, and from State to State. The Lord has his design in this. You may ask what his design is. You all know that the Saints must be made pure, to enter into the celestial kingdom. It is recorded that Jesus was made perfect through suffering. If he was made perfect through suffering, why should we imagine for one moment that we can be prepared to enter into the kingdom of rest with him and the Father, without passing through similar ordeals?" Brigham Young, in *Journal of Discourses,* 8:66.

15. "Let any people enjoy peace and quietness, unmolested, undisturbed,—never be persecuted for their religion, and they are very likely to neglect their duty, to become cold and indifferent, and lose their faith." Brigham Young, in *Journal of Discourses,* 7:42.

16. "The plan of happiness is available to all of his children. If the world would embrace and live it, peace, joy, and plenty would abound on the earth. Much of the suffering we know today would be eliminated if people throughout the world would understand and live the gospel." M. Russell Ballard, *Ensign,* May 1995, 23.

17. Elder Richard G. Scott's entire October 1995 general conference talk gives great insight into the purpose and place of suffering in the lives of Latter-day Saints. *Ensign,* November 1995, 16–18.

CHAPTER FIVE

OLIVER COWDERY, SECOND WITNESS OF TRANSLATION AND REVELATION

KEITH W. PERKINS

One important doctrine in the Church is the divine law of witnesses. This law is stated very plainly several times in scripture. "In the mouth of two or three witnesses shall every word be established" (2 Corinthians 13:1; see also Matthew 18:15–16; Deuteronomy 19:15; D&C 6:28). Joseph Fielding Smith taught the importance of this law as it relates to the restoration of the gospel through the Prophet Joseph Smith: "Every time that the heavens were opened and keys had to be restored what happened? We have two witnesses. Joseph Smith was not alone. He was alone in the first vision, alone when Moroni brought the message to him, alone when he received the plates; but after that he was not alone. The Lord called other witnesses."[1]

The divine law of witnesses required Joseph Smith to have a companion who had the same experiences. This law is seen in force in the experiences Joseph Smith and Oliver Cowdery had together in receiving priesthood keys from John the Baptist and Peter, James, and John. In commenting on the experiences Oliver and Joseph shared, President

---

Keith W. Perkins is professor of Church history and doctrine at Brigham Young University.

Joseph Fielding Smith said: "It was Oliver Cowdery and Joseph Smith who received the keys in the Kirtland Temple on the 3rd of April, 1836, when Christ appeared, when Moses appeared, when Elias appeared, when Elijah appeared. And every time when the keys of a dispensation were bestowed it was to Joseph Smith and Oliver Cowdery—not Joseph Smith alone. Why? Just because of what the Savior said: 'If I bear witness of myself, my witness is not true' (John 5:31)."[2]

Two types of witnesses can come to an individual— spiritual and physical. We see the Lord giving both types of witnesses to the truthfulness of the Book of Mormon, for example. The Three Witnesses heard the voice of God and saw the angel, the plates, and other sacred objects. The Eight Witnesses were able to handle the plates of the Book of Mormon.

Doctrine and Covenants 6 through 9 show us another aspect of the importance of witnesses and Oliver's role as a witness. Not only was he to be one of the Three Witnesses to the Book of Mormon but he was a witness of the gift of translation. He became the second witness of the Restoration and the assistant president of the Church, holding all the keys that Joseph Smith held (D&C 124:94–96).

Historical Background

Oliver Cowdery's role as the second witness of the Book of Mormon came about in an interesting way. In the winter of 1829 Oliver Cowdery taught school in the Manchester area of New York and boarded for a time with Joseph Smith's parents. The Smiths told him about events surrounding the coming forth of the Book of Mormon, and Oliver gained a testimony of the truth of the work: "The subject . . . seems working in my very bones, and I cannot, for a moment, get it out of my mind."[3] He resolved he would go with Samuel Smith, a younger brother of the Prophet, to Pennsylvania to spend the spring with Joseph. He stated that he had made it a matter of prayer and firmly believed that it was the will of the Lord that he should go. "If there is a work for me to do in this thing," Oliver stated, "I am determined to attend to it."[4] Oliver was not the only one praying about this work; Joseph Smith was praying for someone to assist him in the work of translation. The Lord told Joseph that assistance would be coming in a few days. Three days later, on 5 April 1829, Oliver arrived.[5] He had decided to assist Joseph in the work because he had gained a testimony of the Book of Mormon when the Lord appeared to him and showed him the gold plates in a vision.[6]

How grateful Joseph must have been to have help again in the important work of translating the Book of Mormon after Martin Harris lost the 116 manuscript pages of the Book of Mormon. This gratitude is expressed in the Prophet's history: "Two days after the arrival of Mr. Cowdery (being the 7th of April) I commenced to translate the Book of Mormon, and he began to write for me, which having continued for some time, I inquired of the Lord through the Urim and Thummim, and obtained the following: [D&C 6]."[7]

THE SECOND WITNESS OF THE GIFT OF TRANSLATION

It is impossible to fully understand sections 6 through 9 of the Doctrine and Covenants unless we understand clearly the importance of the divine law of witnesses. It is not a coincidence that Joseph Smith received four revelations within one month of the arrival of Oliver Cowdery. It shows us something of the nature of Oliver Cowdery. He had a very questioning mind and needed answers. It also demonstrates the importance of witnesses in his kingdom.

In the first revelation given to Oliver Cowdery through Joseph Smith, the Lord begins to lay out the pattern for the law of witnesses. The Lord informed Oliver that he had a gift that was "sacred and cometh from above" (D&C 6:10). He then told Oliver that when he exercised this gift he would "know mysteries which are great and marvelous" (D&C 6:11).

Oliver was promised by the Lord that if he desired, the Lord would grant to him the gift of translation, "even as my servant Joseph" (D&C 6:25). The purpose of this gift was to bring forth records which "contain much of my gospel, which have been kept back because of the wickedness of the people" (D&C 6:26). Oliver was promised the same keys of the gift of translation that Joseph held; he would then be the second witness of this gift. That would allow him to assist in bringing to light "those parts of my scriptures which have been hidden because of iniquity" (D&C 6:27–28).

I believe it is not a coincidence that Doctrine and Covenants 7 was the next revelation given to Joseph Smith and Oliver Cowdery. The Lord had told Oliver in the previous revelation that he would assist in bringing forth, with his newly acquired gift, hidden scriptures held back because of iniquity. Section 7 is an example of a translation of an ancient scriptural record that had been hidden (the parchment of John).

In the next revelation, section 8, the Lord grants Oliver permission to use his gift of translation. Oliver was told that he would receive knowledge of "the engravings of old records, which are ancient" (D&C 8:1). This gift was made possible because of the gift of the Holy Ghost, which is the spirit of revelation. He was warned that his gift, like all other spiritual gifts, could not be exercised without faith, and he must not doubt or he would be unable to do anything (D&C 8:8, 10). Finally, he was told to "translate and receive knowledge from all those ancient records which have been hid up, that are sacred; and according to your faith shall it be done unto you" (D&C 8:11).

Doctrine and Covenants 9 describes Oliver's success and failure in the translation process. Apparently he did begin to translate (D&C 9:5), but he did not continue; therefore the Lord took the privilege away from him (D&C 9:5). Oliver appears to have made two mistakes. First, he did not understand the process of translation and revelation. He mistakenly assumed that all he had to do to translate was simply to ask (D&C 9:7). But such revelation does not come without effort on the part of the recipient as he seeks divine assistance (D&C 9:8). Second, he forgot the Lord's warning about doubt and fear. Peter, the ancient apostle, had commenced to walk to Him on the water of the Sea of Galilee, but fear caused him to sink. In his failure the Lord asked him, "O thou of little faith, wherefore didst thou doubt?" (Matthew 14:31).

Oliver was like Peter. When we think of Peter trying to walk on water, we focus on his failure. Jesus had to rescue him. We must never forget that Peter *did* walk on water (Matthew 14:29). The Savior told him that he failed after he commenced to walk on water because of his doubt and lack of faith (see Matthew 14:31). So it was with Oliver Cowdery. When he gave in to his fears, his efforts at translation faltered. We focus on Oliver's failure to translate when he did translate for a time (D&C 9:5); but, like Peter, he failed to accomplish his desire (D&C 9:1) because he feared (D&C 9:11). Yet Oliver translated enough to qualify him as the second witness of the gift of translation, thus fulfilling the divine law of witnesses (D&C 6:28). Further research on the original manuscript of the Book of Mormon may show that Joseph Smith acted as scribe for Oliver Cowdery when Oliver translated a portion of the Book of Mormon.

Oliver was informed by the Lord that having failed to "continue as you commenced" in the translation of the Book of Mormon, his assignment now reverted to his previous one, that of being a scribe for Joseph Smith, until the translation of the Book of Mormon was finished (D&C 9:5). He was not to be discouraged, though, because there were "other records" that the Lord would "give unto you power that you may assist to translate" (D&C 9:2). The full extent of Oliver's work is not clear, but it was fulfilled in part as Oliver acted as scribe for Joseph Smith for some of the Joseph Smith Translation of the Bible and the book of Abraham. Why did we not get other records? Perhaps because the Latter-day Saints neglected the Book of

Mormon, as the Lord warned us in Doctrine and Covenants 84:54 through 57.

President Joseph Fielding Smith explained that "these records [D&C 9:2] of ancient inhabitants on this American continent were not translated. It is possible that some of them might have been translated had the people received the Book of Mormon with full purpose of heart and had been faithful to its teachings."[8] The Lord had promised Mormon he would try the faith of the people and when they were willing to accept the "lesser part," the Book of Mormon, then He would make known to them the "greater things" (3 Nephi 26:9). President Smith said it is obvious we have not passed the test outlined by Mormon, for we have not received the "greater things" the Lord has in store for us. President Ezra Taft Benson told us: "The Lord has revealed the need to reemphasize the Book of Mormon to get the Church and all the children of Zion out from under condemnation—the scourge and judgment (see D&C 84:54–58)."[9] Oliver Cowdery was a party to this failure, President Smith explained, when he turned away from the Church when his service was desperately needed: "He therefore lost his privilege to translate through his own disobedience, and the people have lost the privilege of receiving the 'greater things' spoken of by the Lord."[10]

From this experience Oliver Cowdery learned a great deal about revelation—what it is, how to receive it, and the active role that we must play in receiving it.

THE SPIRIT OF REVELATION

Doctrine and Covenants 6, 8, and 9 describe, define, and explain the spirit of revelation. We learn from these and other revelations that the life-giving force in the Church is revelation. The Lord states that this is the only "true and living church" (D&C 1:30). It is living because it is guided by continuing revelation through the Holy Ghost.[11]

In these revelations, which Joseph Smith received at the request of Oliver Cowdery, Oliver was told that he had already been receiving revelation. The Lord told him that if he asked and knocked, he would receive (D&C 6:5). Oliver was reminded that he had a gift that was sacred and that if he inquired of the Lord, he would know "mysteries which are great and marvelous" (D&C 6:10–11). He was further told that in the past when he inquired of the Lord he had received answers—that was the reason he had come to Pennsylvania to find Joseph (D&C 6:14).

Revelation comes when the Lord enlightens our mind; that enlightenment is "the Spirit of truth" (D&C 6:15). A number of things are essential if we expect to receive revelation: desire, treasuring up the word of God, faithfulness, and diligence in keeping the commandments of God (D&C 6:20).

The Lord reminded Oliver of the time He had given him a marvelous revelation in the Manchester, New York, area. Oliver had cried unto the Lord to know if the things he had heard about the coming forth of the Book of Mormon were true. In response to this prayer, the Lord spoke peace to his mind. Joseph Fielding McConkie explained the meaning of the word *peace* in this context: "As Oliver grew into his understanding of the spirit of revelation, the first great lesson he had to learn was the unobtrusive, quiet nature of that Spirit. The witness of the Spirit always involves feelings, and chief among those feelings is that of peace. No other word is as consistently used in scriptural descriptions of the presence of angels, the Lord, or his Spirit, than 'peace.' It was also important for Oliver to learn how easily the spirit of revelation can be overlooked or missed if we do not learn to pay attention to it. Oliver was being prompted, directed, and enlightened, without even being conscious of it. These quiet operations of the Spirit provide a marked contrast with the feelings of spiritual ecstasy so often professed in spiritual counterfeits."[12]

Because the Lord didn't answer in a dramatic form of revelation, Oliver, like so many of us, didn't realize the significance of the revelation he had received. We are often like the Lamanites when the Holy Ghost fell upon them and "they knew it not" (3 Nephi 9:20). As President

Spencer W. Kimball taught us: "In our day, as in times past, many people expect that if there be revelation it will come with awe-inspiring, earth-shaking display. For many it is hard to accept as revelation those numerous ones in Moses' time, in Joseph's time, and in our own year—those revelations which come to prophets as deep, unassailable impressions settling down on the prophet's mind and heart as dew from heaven or as the dawn dissipates the darkness of night.

"Expecting the spectacular, one may not be fully alerted to the constant flow of revealed communication. I say, in the deepest of humility, but also by the power and force of a burning testimony in my soul, that from the prophet of the Restoration to the prophet of our own year, the communication line is unbroken, the authority is continuous, and light, brilliant and penetrating continues to shine. The sound of the voice of the Lord is a continuous melody and a thunderous appeal. For nearly a century and a half there has been no interruption."[13]

Revelation comes to us by the Holy Spirit speaking to our mind and heart. By this same type of revelation Moses led the children of Israel out of Egypt and through the Red Sea (D&C 8:1–3).

Elder Marion G. Romney explained the importance of revelation as discussed in Doctrine and Covenants 9:6 through 9: "This is the kind of revelation we can all live by. One need not make serious mistakes in life. Such can be avoided by following this formula. It will guide us in all our activities, if we will become sensitive to it."[14]

REVELATION, LIVING PROPHETS, AND SCRIPTURE

We are not dependent for guidance only upon revelations recorded in the scriptures. Church leaders have emphasized this truth from the beginning of this dispensation. President Wilford Woodruff recalled a meeting he had attended: "Brother Brigham took the stand, and he took the Bible and laid it down; he took the Book of Mormon, and laid it down: and he took the Book of Doctrine and

Covenants, and laid it down before him, and he said, 'There is the written word of God to us, concerning the work of God from the beginning of the world, almost, to our day.' 'And now,' said he 'when compared with the living oracles, those books are nothing to me; those books do not convey the word of God direct to us now, as do the words of a Prophet or a man bearing the Holy Priesthood in our day and generation. I would rather have the living oracles than all the writing in the books.' That was the course he pursued. When he was through, Brother Joseph said to the congregation: 'Brother Brigham has told you the word of the Lord, and he has told you the truth.'"[15]

Brigham Young gave us even more detail of that meeting in Nauvoo: "At this meeting in Joseph's house Hyrum worked hard. He took the bible, the Book of Mormon, and the book of doctrine and covenants, and said he, that is the law which god has given us by which to build up his Church and Kingdom in the last days, and anything more than these is of man, and is not of God. When he sat, Joseph, with his hands still over his face, and nudging me with his elbow, said, 'brother Brigham, now, come, get up.' I got up, and previous to getting up I had become pretty well charged with plenty of powder and ball, and my lungs were not so weak as they are now. I could talk then so as to be heard a mile. I felt like a thousand lions. I took the books, and laid them down one by one, beginning with the bible, and said 'there lies the bible, the book of Mormon, and the book of Doctrine and Covenants, the revelations God has given through Joseph for the salvation of the people in the 19th Century, yet I would not give the ashes of a rye straw for these three books, so far as they are efficacious for the salvation of any man, that lives without the living oracles of God. That was my text, and I think that before we got through the congregation was perfectly satisfied. I showed them that if we did not have the living oracles we were no better than the sectarian Churches of the world. After I got through, Hyrum arose and made a handsome apology, and confessed his wrong which he had committed in his excess of zeal, and asked pardon."[16]

This doctrine was also confirmed by President George Q. Cannon, who said, "We have the Bible, the Book of Mormon and the Book of Doctrine and Covenants; but all these books, without the living oracles and a constant stream of revelation from the Lord, would not lead any people into the Celestial Kingdom."[17]

MOST REVELATION COMES AS CONFIRMATION

The Lord teaches us that most revelation comes as confirmation; that is, we first study the problem out in our mind, and then we counsel with the Lord and ask him if the decision is right. If it is, the confirmation comes by a quiet burning within our bosom—essentially a feeling (see 1 Nephi 17:45). If we have made an incorrect decision, instead of a quiet assurance in our heart, we will have a stupor of thought (D&C 9:8–9).

We often ask how to know when we have received revelation. Joseph Smith described it this way: "A person may profit by noticing the first intimation of the spirit of revelation; for instance, when you feel pure intelligence flowing into you, it may give you sudden strokes of ideas, so that by noticing it, you may find it fulfilled the same day or soon; (i.e.,) those things that were presented unto your minds by the Spirit of God, will come to pass; and thus by learning the Spirit of God and understanding it, you may grow into the principle of revelation, until you become perfect in Christ Jesus."[18]

President Harold B. Lee stated the same principle this way: "When there come to you things that your mind does not know, when you have a sudden thought that comes to your mind, if you will learn to give heed to these things that come from the Lord, you will learn to walk by the spirit of revelation."[19] On another occasion he stated: "When your heart tells you things that your mind does not know, then the Spirit is guiding you."[20]

CONCLUSION

We have seen the role Oliver Cowdery played in the beginning of the Church and his role in the work of translating the Book of Mormon and learning more about the process of revelation. He had been sustained and ordained second elder of the Church on 6 April 1830. After the First Presidency was organized, it became necessary to clarify his ecclesiastical position; therefore, he was ordained as assistant or associate president of the Church on 5 December 1834. President Joseph Fielding Smith explained that the purpose of this office was to hold the keys of the kingdom of heaven and to act as spokesman to the Church the same as Aaron.[21]

Unfortunately Oliver fell from his position as associate president of the Church, and Hyrum Smith was called to that position (D&C 124:94–95). The divine law of witnesses was again fulfilled when the second elder, or associate president, of the Church sealed his testimony with his blood in Carthage Jail, along with the president of the Church (D&C 135:1, 3). Had Oliver remained faithful, perhaps he would have been the one to have had that great honor.[22]

NOTES

1. Joseph Fielding Smith, *Doctrines of Salvation: Sermons and Writings of Joseph Fielding Smith,* comp. Bruce R. McConkie (Salt Lake City: Bookcraft, 1954), 1:210.

2. Ibid., 211.

3. Lucy Mack Smith, *History of Joseph Smith,* ed. Preston Nibley (Salt Lake City: Bookcraft, 1958), 139.

4. Ibid.

5. Ibid., 141.

6. Dean C. Jessee, ed., *The Papers of Joseph Smith* (Salt Lake City: Deseret Book, 1989), 1:10; see also D&C 6:37.

7. Joseph Smith, *History of The Church of Jesus Christ of Latter-day Saints,* ed. B. H. Roberts, 2d ed. rev., 7 vols. (Salt Lake City: The Church of Jesus Christ of Latter-day Saints, 1932–51), 1:32–33.

8. Joseph Fielding Smith, *Church History and Modern Revelation,* 4 vols. (Salt Lake City: The Council of the Twelve Apostles of The Church of Jesus Christ of Latter-day Saints, 1946), 1:48.

9. Ezra Taft Benson, *Ensign,* May 1986, 78.

10. Smith, *Church History and Modern Revelation,* 1:49.

11. See James E. Talmage, *The Articles of Faith* (Salt Lake City: The Church of Jesus Christ of Latter-day Saints, 1949), 304.

12. Joseph Fielding McConkie, "The Principle of Revelation," in Robert L. Millet and Kent P. Jackson, eds., *The Doctrine and Covenants,* Studies in Scripture Series, vol. 1 (Salt Lake City: Randall Book, 1984), 82.

13. Spencer W. Kimball, *Ensign,* May 1977, 78; emphasis added.

14. Marion G. Romney, in Conference Report, April 1964, 125.

15. Wilford Woodruff, in Conference Report, October 1897, 22–23.

16. Remarks of President Brigham Young, at the Semi-Annual Conference, Great Salt Lake City, 8 October 1866, reported by G. D. Watt; typescript in author's possession; spelling modernized.

17. George Q. Cannon, *Gospel Truth,* sel. Jerreld L. Newquist (Salt Lake City: Deseret Book, 1987), 252.

18. Joseph Smith, *Teachings of the Prophet Joseph Smith,* sel. Joseph Fielding Smith (Salt Lake City: Deseret Book, 1976), 151.

19. Harold B. Lee, in Conference Report, Mexico City Area Conference 1972, 49.

20. Harold B. Lee, *The Teachings of Harold B. Lee,* ed. Clyde J. Williams (Salt Lake City: Bookcraft, 1996), 509.

21. Smith, *Doctrines of Salvation,* 1:212.

22. Ibid., 1:221–22.

CHAPTER SIX

THE LAW OF
COMMON CONSENT

MATTHEW O. RICHARDSON

In Latter-day Saint sacrament meetings, time may be allotted for "ward business." Part of the procedure with items of business is an invitation to the congregation to sustain fellow Church members in their callings by raising their right hand. If members are opposed to the proposed action, they can also make it known in the same manner. This practice, formally known as the law of common consent, is not only a noticeable part of our meetings but an essential principle in proper gospel government and personal progression.

Unfortunately, the law of common consent is viewed by many members as nothing more than an accompaniment to a business agenda. Perhaps because of the frequency of the event, application of the law of common consent may become an automated raising of a hand in mechanical approval. Some might say that the law of common consent is too common and therefore feel that it is a commonplace occurrence in the Church that signifies more tradition than actual function. Although common consent is familiar to Church members, it is anything but common. President J. Reuben Clark Jr. taught: "It is clear that the sustaining vote by the people is not, and is not to be regarded as, a mere matter of form, but on the contrary a matter of the last gravity."[1]

Matthew O. Richardson is assistant professor of Church history and doctrine at Brigham Young University.

Perhaps this important gospel principle has become a matter of form to some not because of familiarity with it but because of a lack of familiarity. For example, some members may understand the proper procedure but have never learned, or have forgotten, the purposes of the principle. Others may be acquainted with the purposes and practices of common consent but have failed to see the doctrinal significance as emphasized in the Doctrine and Covenants and throughout Church history. As the Saints learn about the law of common consent, it becomes anything but common. Obviously it requires more than raising a hand on Sundays to become familiar with the law of common consent. To develop a deeper familiarity with this practice, it is helpful to obtain a basic understanding of Christ's government in his kingdom. Next, a historical overview of common consent reveals its historical precedence and underscores its importance and necessity. With this background, it is easier to understand the proper practice or procedure of this principle. Finally, the deep meaning of common consent is found in its intended purposes. When understood correctly, common consent becomes a meaningful rite of worship for the Saints, which ultimately brings them closer to the Savior.

THE GOVERNMENT OF THE CHURCH

To better understand common consent, it is important first to understand the workings of the government of God. Elder Harold B. Lee described the government of the kingdom of God as a theocracy but also "something like a democracy."[2] This description is a simple clarification of a seemingly complex and often misunderstood organization. Elder Lee highlighted two significant pillars in the Lord's government: theocracy and democracy. The first pillar, theocracy, accents Christ's undeniable position as head of the kingdom—the sole proprietor. The second pillar, democracy, emphasizes the people's opportunity to participate in their government. This combination of terms, however, immediately raises questions from traditional political sciences. How can a theocracy also be described as a democracy? On the surface these terms not only seem incompatible but provoke a jealous power struggle. A democracy doesn't seem to fit with a theocracy because of the world's understanding and definition of democracy. But thankfully, when this term is properly understood, the powerful second pillar not only fits but is seen for the essential principle in gospel government and doctrine it is.

The pillar of democracy that Elder Lee described in the Lord's kingdom was something *like* a democracy. In a traditional democracy, power is vested in the people and they hold participatory rights. The role of the people under a conventional theocracy, on the other hand, is being part of the kingdom rather than of its governmental process and procedure. The Lord's kingdom, unlike a conventional theocracy, allows the members to participate in its government. This unique combination in which all power is vested in the Lord (theocracy) with the participation of the people (democracy) has thus been called a theodemocracy,[3] which is a form of government in which the decisions for the kingdom of the Lord are his decisions but his people have been given the opportunity to exercise their presence in that kingdom. Members of the Lord's kingdom exercise their democratic presence through the principle of common consent.

THE HISTORICAL PERSPECTIVE OF COMMON CONSENT

The unique relationship between Christ and his disciples in divine government is found throughout religious history. A glimpse into the past reveals the precedence, patterns, and practice of common consent as it underscores its vitality and importance. This principle was practiced in one form or another during the lifetime of Moses (Exodus 24:3), Joshua (Numbers 27:19–22), Peter (Acts 1:26), and Mosiah (Mosiah 29:25–26). According to Elder Bruce R. McConkie, the law of common consent "has been operative in every dispensation."[4] Thus, this principle is of necessity part of modern Church government. Common consent is another of the many witnesses that The Church of Jesus Christ has been literally restored.

The law of common consent in the modern dispensation was first revealed to Joseph Smith and Oliver Cowdery in Peter Whitmer's home in June 1829. At that time, Joseph and Oliver were instructed to ordain each other to the office of elder and then to ordain others as it was made known unto them. Their ordination was deferred, however, until "such times as it should be practicable to have our brethren, who had been and who should be baptized, assembled together, when we must have their sanction to our thus proceeding to ordain each other, and have them decide by vote whether they were willing to accept us as spiritual teachers or not."[5]

Because priesthood ordination is of obvious doctrinal importance, that historical event also teaches the relative importance of common consent and its necessity to God's kingdom. Elder Orson F. Whitney explained the significance of that event as follows: "What!—exclaims one. After these men had communed with heavenly beings and received from them commandments for their guidance; after receiving divine authority to preach the Gospel, administer its ordinances, and establish once more on earth the long absent Church of Christ! After all this must they go before the people and ask their consent to organize them and preside over them as a religious body? Yes, that was precisely the situation. Notwithstanding all those glorious manifestations, they were not yet fully qualified to hold the high positions unto which they had been divinely called. One element was lacking—the consent of the people. Until that consent was given, there could be no church with these people as its members and those men as its presiding authorities. The Great Ruler of all never did and never will foist upon any of his people, in branch, ward, stake or Church capacity, a presiding officer whom they are not willing to accept and hold."[6]

Further instruction concerning ordinations and the "vote" of brethren was later revealed to Joseph Smith, in early April 1830. Joseph was instructed to organize the Church and kingdom of God. Included in those specific instructions was the "law of common consent," which reemphasized that "no person is to be ordained to any office in this church, where there is a regularly organized branch of the same, without the vote of that church" (D&C 20:65–66).

On 6 April 1830 Joseph Smith, Oliver Cowdery, and members of the Smith and Whitmer families gathered in Peter Whitmer's home in Fayette, New York, to organize the Church of Jesus Christ. It was anticipated that at this gathering Joseph and Oliver would be ordained elders. Before that ordination, however, Joseph and Oliver needed to receive a sanctioning vote from those present. "According to previous commandment [given in June 1829 and recorded in D&C 20:65–66], the Prophet Joseph called upon the brethren present to know if they would accept himself and Oliver Cowdery as their teachers in the things of the kingdom of God; and if they were willing that they should proceed to organize the church according to the commandment of the Lord. To this they consented by unanimous vote."[7] Joseph then proceeded to ordain Oliver an elder, after which Oliver likewise ordained Joseph.

The early emphasis of common consent seems centered upon the selection of ecclesiastical leadership; however, doctrinal and procedural issues were also presented before the people for their "vote." Also during the organizational meeting on 6 April 1830, those at Peter Whitmer's home were to consent to organizing the Church according to the commandments of the Lord. Three months later, in July 1830, Joseph was instructed that "all things shall be done by common consent in the church, by much prayer and faith, for all things you shall receive by faith" (D&C 26:2). This revelation has become a foundation to the government of the Lord's kingdom and defines the order of proper Church procedure.

After the events leading to the establishment of the doctrine of common consent in July 1830 (D&C 26), instructions for its operation, reemphasis of it as a principle, and evidences of its practice can be found throughout the other revelations in the Doctrine and Covenants. Some examples include the role of revelation and common consent, which was revealed in September 1830 (D&C 20:13, 63, 65, 66). Members who were appointed to service to give relief to the poor and needy or to leadership positions within the Church organization were appointed by "the voice of the church" (D&C 38:34–35; 41:9–10; 51:4, 12; 104:64, 71–77, 85; 124:124–44). In February 1831, the "law of the Church" (D&C 42) reemphasized that anyone possessing authority must be "known to the church" (D&C 42:11).[8] One final example found in the Doctrine and Covenants comes from the minutes of the organization of the first high council of the Church on 17 February 1834 in Kirtland, Ohio (D&C 102:9) and neatly sums up the law of common consent as practiced by the Saints over the previous five years. A "voting" took place to acknowledge those called by revelation in their administration "by the voice of the church" (D&C 102:9). Evidences of the law of common consent are found throughout other journals, histories, and records of the restored Church. Although there is ample historical precedent, instruction, and evidence of common consent in early religious history, some of the early Saints, like some modern Saints, still misunderstood exactly how to practice the law properly.

PRACTICE AND PROCEDURE

Many early members of the Church felt that common consent meant they would be involved in making decisions and policies and in determining the course of the Church. In other words, some of them felt that the Church would follow the standard of parliamentary procedure. After all, many of the revelations and instructions concerning common consent described this procedure as the members' opportunity to *consent* or *vote* for all things in the Church (D&C 20:63, 65, 66; 26:2; 28:13; 102:19; 104:21, 72, 85; Official Declarations 1 and 2). These words generally summon the images of electioneering and all the trappings of politics. It was revealed that there is an "order" (D&C 28:13; 43:3–6), which common consent follows. Members' participation according to the order of the Lord's kingdom is clearly described by President J. Reuben Clark Jr., who said: "In the Church the nominating power rests in a group, the General Authorities, but the sustaining or electing power rests in the body of the Church, which under no circumstances nominates officers, the function of the Church body being solely to sustain or to elect. . . .

"The sole function of this constituent assembly today, is, as already stated, to accept or reject the General Authority or other officers proposed to them. This assembly may not propose others to be voted upon.

"Furthermore, the actual procedure for voting is normally by the uplifted hand of those present. No electioneering, no speech-making, no stating of objections, no proposing of candidates, no vocal demonstration of any kind is in order. Anyone seeking to do any of these things would not only be out of order as a matter of procedure, but would be likewise breaking the peace of the State by interrupting and disturbing a public assembly, would be subject to arrest as a disturber of the peace, and if necessary, would have to be so dealt with as a matter of public order. This assembly might be called the 'voting booth' of the Church. This will be clear to all our listeners."[9]

It is clear that the principle of common consent distinctly defines the practice and procedures of participation within Church government. Limited to "the voice of the church" or members of the Church of Jesus Christ (D&C 38:34; 41:9; 51:4; 58:49; 102:9), practice of the law of common consent is a privilege given to every member of the Church in good standing. This privilege of voting is more an act of ratifying leadership callings and decisions rather than actually making those decisions. Such decisions are left to the Lord and his anointed servants. Because politicking is not part of the process of voting within the Church, members signify their approval of a proposed action by raising their right hand. The method of manifesting a vote was a little different in earlier times. For example, Peter and the original apostles "cast lots,"[10] and earlier procedures in the latter-day Church required members to cast their votes by standing rather than by raising their hands. Today, however, it is common practice to raise the right hand in approval or disapproval of proposed actions.

Some members are concerned whether it is appropriate for them to vote when visiting a ward or branch other than their own. Generally, members called to most Church positions are sustained by a vote of those belonging to the organization in which they will serve. For example, a stake president is sustained by his stake members, a bishop is sustained by his ward members, and an elders quorum president is sustained by those in the elders quorum rather than by the entire ward. Thus, the vote of members of a given organization (whether the entire Church, as at general conference, a deacons quorum, or members of a Beehive class) manifest their approval of the Lord's will concerning them and their governance.

CONCLUSION

When we become more familiar with the law of common consent, we understand the uncommon blessing it is in Church government and to our lives. We become more like Christ through common consent because it affords the opportunity to recognize Christ as the sovereign King, make our will like his, sustain our fellow Saints, bind ourselves to him through solemn covenants, and exercise our agency by choosing as he would choose. Elder Packer taught that "there is an obedience that comes from a knowledge of the truth that transcends any external form of control. We are not obedient because we are blind, we are obedient because we can see."[11] As Saints exercise common consent, they are in a better position to see as Christ sees.

The exercise of common consent would never be

considered common by those who can see in its purpose doctrinal necessity as well as the example of the Savior. As Saints become familiar with the law of common consent, they cannot help but become more familiar with Christ. When we exercise our privilege to consent to Christ, "we shall be like him; for we shall see him as he is" (1 John 3:2). The day will come, because of this perspective, that we consent to Christ's will because we have become like him in every way.

NOTES

1. J. Reuben Clark Jr., in Conference Report, April 1940, 73.

2. Harold B. Lee, "The Place of the Living Prophet, Seer, and Revelator," *Charge to Religious Educators*, 2d ed. (Salt Lake City: The Church of Jesus Christ of Latter-day Saints, 1982), 105.

3. Hyrum M. Smith and Janne M. Sjodahl, *Doctrine and Covenants Commentary* (Salt Lake City: Deseret Book, 1965), 131–32.

4. Bruce R. McConkie, *Common Consent* (Salt Lake City: Church of Jesus Christ of Latter-day Saints, n.d.), 4.

5. Joseph Smith, *History of The Church of Jesus Christ of Latter-day Saints,* ed. B. H. Roberts, 2d ed. rev., 7 vols. (Salt Lake City: Deseret Book, 1980), 1:61.

6. Orson F. Whitney, in Conference Report, October 1930, 45.

7. B. H. Roberts, *A Comprehensive History of The Church of Jesus Christ of Latter-day Saints, Century One,* 6 vols. (Provo: Brigham Young University Press, 1965), 1:196.

8. The first revelation concerning proper authority was revealed in September 1830 and is recorded in D&C 28. At the time, Hiram Page professed to receive through a stone revelation concerning the order of Church and thereby deceived many members. Section 28 established the order of revelation for the Church. Later, in February 1831, a Mrs. Hubble went to Kirtland, claiming to receive revelation, and confused many of the newly converted Saints. The Lord again reminded the Saints of the proper order of revelation for the Church (D&C 43). Both incidents of deception were preceded by revelations to the Prophet of the proper procedure and the role of common consent regarding revelation and authority (D&C 26; 42).

9. J. Reuben Clark Jr., in Conference Report, April 1940, 71–72.

10. Elder Bruce R. McConkie described "casting lots" as "sustaining votes." See Bruce R. McConkie, *Doctrinal New Testament Commentary,* 3 vols. (Salt Lake City: Bookcraft, 1971), 2:32.

11. Boyd K. Packer, *Ensign,* April 1983, 66.

CHAPTER SEVEN

THE HIRAM PAGE STONE: A LESSON IN CHURCH GOVERNMENT

DENNIS A. WRIGHT

It began with a curious, small, flat stone that Hiram Page wore on a chain around his neck. He believed that the stone held special powers and used it to seek inspiration. Foolish as the practice may now seem, Hiram lived at a time when many devout Christians believed in the use of such objects as rocks and tree branches to divine hidden truths or to learn the will of God.[1] Folk superstition supported Hiram's claim to have a spiritual gift that enabled him to use his stone for inspiration, causing some to comment on his supposed gifts.[2]

Hiram Page spent his early years learning folk medicine in preparation for a career as a physician. His travels took him to Fayette, New York, where he met the Peter Whitmer Sr. family. In November 1825 he married Peter's daughter Catherine and made his new home with the Whitmers. Through his association with the Whitmer family he met Oliver Cowdery and the Prophet Joseph Smith. Hiram became an avid supporter of the young Prophet and was invited to be one of the Eight Witnesses of the gold plates. For the rest of his life he testified that he had actually seen

Dennis A. Wright is associate professor of Church history and doctrine at Brigham Young University.

the plates from which Joseph Smith translated the Book of Mormon. [3]

Hiram learned of the Urim and Thummim and the part it played in the translation of the Book of Mormon. He knew that Joseph possessed a seerstone and used it in his prophetic calling.[4] Hiram assumed that his own gift of seership, exercised through the stone he wore around his neck, was of divine origin. He continued to use his stone as a source of "inspiration," even after he joined the Church.

Before the September 1830 conference of the Church, Oliver Cowdery and the Whitmers became interested in Hiram's supposed spiritual gift and encouraged him to use his stone to seek information about Zion and the government of the Church.[5] Teachings in the Book of Mormon prompted Oliver, the Whitmer family, and other members to consider the establishment of Zion in the latter days (3 Nephi 16; 21; Ether 13). Their interest in Church government developed from their apparent misunderstanding of the prophet's role. The acceptance of Hiram's revelations by Oliver and the Whitmers fostered considerable discussion among Church members.

Joseph Smith recognized in Hiram Page's revelations a threat to the already revealed principles of Church government.[6] Members of the Church had first accepted those principles in the 6 April 1830 organizational meeting by voting to accept Joseph and Oliver as their "teachers in the things of the Kingdom of God."[7] During that meeting Joseph received a revelation emphasizing the unique role of the prophet as a "seer, a translator, a prophet, an apostle of Jesus Christ, an elder of the church" (D&C 21:1). The revelation counseled those present to "give heed unto all his words and commandments which he shall give unto you as he receiveth them, . . . for his word ye shall receive, as if from mine own mouth" (D&C 21:4–5). In accepting this word, the members received a promise that "the gates of hell shall not prevail against you . . . and the Lord God will disperse the powers of darkness from before you" (D&C 21:6). The revealed government of the new Church placed the prophet at the head as the authorized spokesman in matters of revelation and divine guidance.

At the June 1830 conference Joseph formalized the events of the April meeting by presenting revelations entitled "Articles and Covenants." The members voted unanimously to accept the revelations as the constitution of the Church.[8] That document, now sections 20 and 22 in the Doctrine and Covenants, identifies the unique role of the prophet as the first elder in matters related to revelation and Church government.

Although the members agreed in principle to the revealed doctrine, some misunderstood the unique role of the prophet. Shortly after the conference, Oliver Cowdery and the Whitmers "began to conceive of themselves as independent authorities with the right to correct Joseph and receive revelation."[9] In July Oliver wrote Joseph and commanded him "in the name of God" to change the word *works* in a revelation (D&C 20:37) to *faith,* so that priestcraft might not be part of the Church.[10] Apparently Oliver and the Whitmers felt it their responsibility to question Joseph on certain matters. The Prophet spent considerable effort persuading those involved that the wording should remain as it was first revealed.[11] David Whitmer described a decline of confidence in Joseph's seership when the Prophet announced that he would no longer use the Urim and Thummin or the seerstone in the revelation process. Some felt that without the Urim and Thummin or the seerstone Joseph would experience a diminished power of seership.[12] Oliver and the Whitmers felt justified in acting counter to the revealed order of the Church by challenging the Prophet's role as the only spokesman for the Lord.[13] This feeling contributed to an acceptance of Hiram Page's seership and his revelations regarding Zion and the government of the Church as it showed their belief that the keys of revelation for the Church did not reside solely with the prophet. Support for this view came from others who opposed an authoritarian ministry. In this way, the matter became more than belief in false revelation, for it struck at the foundation of the revealed order of the Church and the unique role of the prophet.

Joseph Smith recognized Hiram Page's revelations as a more serious challenge than simple differences of opinion or fascination with false revelation. For the Church to remain true to founding principles, the keys of revelation and Church government needed to remain with those who were called and ordained. The apparent failure of some to understand this principle greatly concerned Joseph. But because of the emotions surrounding the situation, Joseph "thought it wisdom not to do much more than to converse with the brethren on the subject."[14] Nevertheless, this strategy did not prove adequate, and as support for Hiram's revelations grew, Joseph felt prompted to inquire of the Lord.

Newel Knight recorded the anguish the Prophet felt: "Joseph was perplexed and scarcely knew how to meet this new exigency," he wrote. "That night I occupied the same room that he did and the greater part of the night was spent in prayer and supplication."[15] Later, Joseph spoke with those involved and labored to convince them of their error. Newel Knight recorded: "They were convinced of their error, and confessed the same, renouncing the revelations as not being of God, but acknowledged that Satan had conspired to overthrow their belief in the true plan of salvation."[16] During this time Joseph received the revelation now known as Doctrine and Covenants 28. The revelation confirmed the false nature of Hiram Page's revelations and reinforced the role of the prophet in the revealed government of the Church.

Doctrine and Covenants 28 addressed Oliver Cowdery and reminded him of his role as the second presiding elder. Because of his prominent role in encouraging Hiram Page to seek revelations, the Lord gave Oliver the responsibility to restore confidence in revealed principles of Church government. By accepting the Lord's revelation, Oliver became part of the solution rather than remaining part of the problem.

The Lord instructed Oliver in three areas: the unique role of a prophet, his mission call to the land of Zion, and the nature of Hiram Page's error. As the second elder of the Church, Oliver had great responsibility to defend the revealed truths of the gospel, but his acceptance of the Page revelations manifested his lack of understanding. Doctrine and Covenants 28 gave Oliver sufficient instruction to correct his error and to help restore harmony in the Church.

The Lord reminded Oliver that "no one shall be appointed to receive commandments and revelations in this church excepting my servant Joseph Smith" (D&C 28:2). Oliver was authorized not to receive revelation but rather to teach the revealed truths.[17] Like Aaron of old, his authority included being "heard by the church in all things whatsoever thou shalt teach them by the Comforter, concerning the revelations" (D&C 28:1). As a modern Aaron, Oliver could "declare faithfully the commandments and the revelations, with power and authority unto the church," doing so "by wisdom" as directed by the Spirit and not "by way of commandment" (D&C 28:3, 5). Finally the Lord reproved Oliver for his attempts to correct the Prophet and encouraging others to receive revelations: "Thou shalt not command him who is at thy head, and at the head of the church; for I have given him the keys of the mysteries, and the revelations which are sealed" (D&C 28:6–7). In his calling as second elder, Oliver was to use his influence to correct misunderstanding among Church members.[18]

After reproving him, the Lord gave him a great opportunity: "I say unto you that you shall go unto the Lamanites and preach my gospel" (D&C 28:9). This mission had special implications for Oliver because of his interest in the false revelations Hiram Page received about the location of the city of Zion. The Lord's revelation reminded Oliver of Hiram Page's error by saying, "No man knoweth where the city Zion shall be built" (D&C 28:8). In correcting the speculations, the revelation identified the location of the city of Zion as being "on the borders by the Lamanites" (D&C

28:9). Perhaps the contrast between the reality of the Lamanite mission and the speculations of Hiram Page enabled Oliver to regain his focus as second elder.

The Lord next instructed Oliver to inform his friend Hiram Page "that those things which he hath written from that stone are not of me and that Satan deceiveth him" (D&C 28:11). The results of Hiram's deception had encouraged some to question the order of the Church, and because of his involvement in the deception, Oliver needed to act in his office to help Hiram understand the deception.

The September 1830 conference proved most important in the development of the Church. During the conference Joseph raised the matter of Hiram Page's revelations and found that some still did not understand how revelation comes to the Church.[19] Those present discussed the matter at length as the Prophet taught how the "Articles and Covenants" (now D&C 20 and 22), accepted at the June conference, applied to this situation. He referred to the revelation received before the September conference (D&C 28) and taught the danger of conflicting revelations. Joseph treated the matter as a principle of Church government and in doing so emphasized that "all things must be done in order, and by common consent in the church, by the prayer of faith" (D&C 28:13). Newel Knight recorded, "It was wonderful to witness the wisdom that Joseph displayed on this occasion, for truly God gave unto him great wisdom and power, and . . . none who saw him administer righteousness under such trying circumstances, could doubt that the Lord was with him, as he acted—not with the wisdom of man, but with the wisdom of God. The Holy Ghost came upon us and filled our hearts with unspeakable joy."[20] After the discussion, "Brother Page, as well as the whole Church who were present, renounced the said stone, and all things connected therewith."[21] Those present then partook of the sacrament and participated in confirmations and ordinations with a spirit of charity and peace. The minutes of the meeting simply record: "Brother Joseph Smith, Jr. was appointed by the voice of the Conference to receive and write Revelations & Commandments for this Church."[22]

The experience with the Hiram Page revelations marked an important point in the doctrinal development of the Church. The issue was one of Church government because the false revelations challenged the unique role of the anointed prophet. The conference established a clear precedent in defining the process of revelation and the central role of the prophet as the one "given . . . the keys of the mysteries, and the revelations" (D&C 28:7). From that time forth this principle has remained central in the governing principles of the Church. Of this matter the Prophet later said, "I will inform you that it is contrary to the economy of God for any member of the Church, or any one, to receive instructions for those in authority, higher than themselves . . . for the fundamental principles, government, and doctrine of the Church are vested in the keys of the kingdom."[23]

Even after several generations, the Hiram Page incident remains a landmark example of an important principle in Church government. In the October 1972 general conference, President Harold B. Lee read from a 1913 letter by the First Presidency: "From the days of Hiram Page . . . at different periods there have been manifestations from delusive spirits to members of the Church. . . .

"When visions, dreams, tongues, prophecy, impressions or an extraordinary gift of inspiration convey something out of harmony with the accepted revelations of the Church or contrary to the decisions of its constituted authorities, Latter-day Saints may know that it is not of God, no matter how plausible it may appear."[24]

The Hiram Page experience prepared Church members for the coming revelations that would require them to leave their homes in New York and participate in the gathering in Ohio. Joined by a growing number of converts, the faithful gave heed to the Prophet Joseph Smith and worked to build a community of Saints and to raise a temple in expectation of a divine endowment. Led by the Prophet, the Saints overcame great adversity as they learned the lessons about building Zion. Their faith in receiving the Lord's word through Joseph Smith, "as if from mine own mouth, in all patience and faith," enabled many to receive the promised blessing that "the gates of hell shall not prevail against you; yea, and the Lord God will disperse the powers of darkness from before you, and cause the heavens to shake for your good, and his name's glory" (D&C 21:4–6).

Hiram Page accepted the Lord's revelation and the Prophet's counsel and responded obediently to the call to move first to Kirtland and then to Missouri. He suffered the expulsion from Missouri and worked to resettle in Clay County.[25] During that time he became disappointed with the Saints' failure to establish Zion and, with Oliver Cowdery and the Whitmers, began to question the Prophet's leadership. Improper handling of Church lands and funds led to the excommunication of Oliver and the Whitmers. At that time Hiram chose to denounce the Church and the Prophet.[26] He moved to Ray County, Missouri, and lived there until his death in 1852. Yet even after his dissociation from the Church, Hiram Page continued to testify of the reality of the gold plates and the divinity of the Book of Mormon.

NOTES

1. For a comprehensive discussion of the Hiram Page incident, see Bruce G. Stewart, "Hiram Page: An Historical and Sociological Analysis of an Early Mormon Prototype" (M.A. thesis, Brigham Young University, 1987). For a discussion of folk traditions of early members of the Church, see Ronald W. Walker, "The Persisting Idea of American Treasure Hunting," *BYU Studies* 24 (fall 1984): 429–61.

2. Contemporaries of Hiram Page, critical of the Church, commented on Hiram's use of the stone. E. D. Howe, *Mormonism Unvailed* (Painesville, Ohio: E. D. Howe, 1834), 215–16.

3. Andrew Jenson, *Latter-day Saint Biographical Encyclopedia,* 4 vols. (Salt Lake City: Andrew H. Jenson History Company, 1935), 1:277–78.

4. For comment on Joseph Smith's seerstone, see Joseph Fielding

Smith, *Doctrines of Salvation,* comp. Bruce R. McConkie, 3 vols. (Salt Lake City: Bookcraft, 1956), 3:225–226.

5. Joseph Smith, *History of The Church of Jesus Christ of Latter-day Saints,* ed. B. H. Roberts, 2d ed. rev., 7 vols. (Salt Lake City: The Church of Jesus Christ of Latter-day Saints, 1932–51), 1:109–10.

6. Ibid., 1:110.

7. Ibid., 1:77.

8. Donald Q. Cannon and Lyndon W. Cook, eds., *Far West Record* (Salt Lake City: Deseret Book, 1983), 1.

9. Richard L. Bushman, *Joseph Smith and the Beginnings of Mormonism* (Chicago: University of Illinois Press, 1984), 166. See also A. Gary Anderson, "The Prophet, Seer, and Revelator," in Robert L. Millett and Kent P. Jackson, eds., *The Doctrine and Covenants,* Studies in Scripture Series, vol. 1 (Salt Lake City: Randall Book, 1984), 148–151.

10. Smith, *History of the Church,* 1:105.

11. Ibid., 1:105.

12. For comment on the reaction of some to Joseph's decision to refrain from using his seerstone, see David Whitmer, *An Address to All Believers in Christ, by a Witness to the Divine Authenticity of the Book of Mormon* (Richmond, Mo.: David Whitmer, 1887; photo reprint, Concord, Calif.: Pacific Publishing, 1959), 32.

13. It is important to understand that although a difference of perspective existed, Oliver Cowdery and the Whitmers did not lose their affection and respect for the Prophet Joseph. During the Hiram Page affair they invited the Prophet to move to the Whitmer home to continue his work. The Whitmer family supported his work, and welcomed him with great joy. Newel Knight commented on the feelings of good will that all expressed when Joseph arrived in Fayette. "Newel Knight's Journal," in "Scraps of Biography," *Classic Experiences and Adventures* (Salt Lake City: Bookcraft, 1969), 63–67.

14. Smith, *History of the Church,* 1:110.

15. Knight, "Journal," 65.

16. Ibid., 65.

17. Hyrum M. Smith and Janne M. Sjodahl, *Doctrine and Covenants Commentary,* rev. ed. (Salt Lake City: Deseret Book, 1972), 141.

18. Sidney B. Sperry, *Doctrine and Covenants Compendium* (Salt Lake City: Bookcraft, 1960), 131.

19. Although some suggest that the meeting was a "stormy affair" that resulted in a confidence crisis settled only by a vote of the members (see Donna Hill, *Joseph Smith, the First Mormon* [Midvale, Utah: Signature Books, 1977], 117), that opinion stands in marked contrast

to the observations of Newel Knight, a participant in the conference (see Knight, "Journal," 65).

20. Knight, "Journal," 65.

21. Smith, *History of the Church,* 1:115.

22. Cannon and Cook, *Far West Record,* 3. For further discussion, see Larry C. Porter, "A Study of the Origins of The Church of Jesus Christ of Latter-day Saints in the States of New York and Pennsylvania, 1816–1831" (Ph.D. dissertation, Brigham Young University, 1971), 273–76.

23. Smith, *History of the Church,* 1:338.

24. Harold B. Lee, in Conference Report, October 1972, 125–26.

25. Jenson, *Biographical Encyclopedia,* 278.

26. Stewart, "Hiram Page," 152–54.

CHAPTER EIGHT

THE POWER TO PREVENT DECEPTION

H. DEAN GARRETT

From the very beginning of the Church, the Saints struggled with the problem of being deceived by false spirits, impostors, doctrines of the devil, and doctrines of men. The Lord supplied many revelations and insights through the Prophet Joseph Smith to assist the Saints in their efforts to avoid being deceived. The Lord emphasized following the living prophets as well as understanding the gifts of the Spirit and the doctrines of the gospel to equip an individual to prevent deception. These helps, combined with understanding the edification that comes from God and the pattern given to judge righteousness, protect the Saints just as much today as during the time of Joseph Smith.

FOLLOW THE LIVING PROPHET

On 6 April 1830, the day the Church was formally organized, the Lord gave the Saints directions that would prevent anyone from being deceived by false prophets or false revelations. The Lord explained to them the relationship the members of the Church should have with the prophet of God. The Lord called Joseph Smith a "seer, a translator, a prophet, an apostle of Jesus Christ, an elder of the church" (D&C 21:1). The members of the Church were commanded to "give heed unto all his words and commandments

H. Dean Garrett is professor and associate chair of the Department of Church History and Doctrine at Brigham Young University.

which he shall give unto you as he receiveth them, walking in all holiness before me" (D&C 21:4).

The most vital step in preventing deception is to follow the prophet of God. Note that a member is to give heed to "all" the words the prophet gives and do so by walking in all holiness before the Lord. The Lord understood that this was not an easy commandment. He gave each of us the ability to think for ourselves and the agency to act on our thoughts. He understood that we would need "patience and faith" (D&C 21:5). It is not always easy to follow the Lord's chosen mouthpiece. Sometimes his counsel is contrary to our desires or way of thinking. Sometimes it goes against professional training or philosophy we hold dear. It is easy to follow the prophet when we agree with him, but it becomes a real challenge to "give heed to *all* his words" when we disagree with him (emphasis added). Moreover, our obedience most often does not produce immediate results. It takes patience and faith to follow prophets of God. It always has, and it always will.

But the Lord blesses those who are faithful in following the counsels of his prophets. The revelation in Doctrine and Covenants 21 states three promises for those who are obedient: the gates of hell shall not prevail against them, the Lord will disperse the powers of darkness from before them, and the Lord will cause the heavens to shake for their good and his name's glory (D&C 21:6). These promises are long-term and sometimes hard to recognize. Consequently, it really does take faith and patience to follow the prophets.

The early Saints had a difficult time staying focused on Joseph Smith and refusing to heed the counsel of others who claimed to have had revelation. The first such challenge came while the Prophet Joseph Smith was visiting family members in Harmony, Pennsylvania. Oliver Cowdery, the second elder of the Church (D&C 20:2), was staying in Fayette, New York, with the Whitmer family. One of the Whitmers' sons-in-law, Hiram Page, had a peep stone through which he claimed to have received revelations concerning the future Zion. Oliver and other associates believed the revelations. When Joseph returned to Fayette, he was faced with the question of who was entitled to receive revelation for the Church. The Lord revealed that "no one shall be appointed to receive commandments and revelations in this church excepting my servant Joseph Smith, Jun., for he receiveth them even as Moses" (D&C 28:2). The Lord again instructed the members to focus on his called prophet to protect them from deception.

Six months later, shortly after the Saints arrived in Kirtland, Ohio, they had problems again discerning the truth. A woman by the name of Hubble claimed to have received revelations, which she began to preach to members of the Church. Little is known about these revelations other than that some of the members began to believe and preach them. The Lord reminded the Saints that Joseph was "appointed unto you to receive commandments and revelations until he be taken if he abide in me" (D&C 43:3). Sister Hubble was not the one appointed by the Lord to receive revelation for the Church, and her revelations were not acceptable.

The Lord will always have only one person in the Church called and designated to be his spokesman. Through that spokesman, the Lord will reveal his will for the Church. This principle prevents confusion among the Saints about whom they should follow and helps to avoid a Tower of Babel effect, with many speaking by different languages of revelation. The Church has only one language of revelation, spoken through God's prophet. Therefore, to prevent deception, we must follow the living prophet and those who are called to assist him. The *Millennial Star* records how we can tell who these leaders are: "The Prophet [Joseph Smith] declare[d] to the people how they might always know where to find the true church. He gave it as a guide for them ever afterwards and said the day would come when they would need it. He said: 'Factions and parties will arise out of this Church, and apostates will lead away many. But in the midst of all this, keep with the majority, for the true leaders of God's people will always be able to have a majority, and the records of the Church will be with them.'"[1]

GIFTS OF THE SPIRIT

Not only did those claiming to receive revelation confuse some of the early Saints but so did those who claimed to have the gifts of the Spirit. The Lord warned against evil spirits and the doctrine of men, "for some are of men, and others of devils" (D&C 46:7). To assist the Saints, the Lord taught that the gifts of the Spirit are given for the "benefit of those who love me and keep all my commandments, and him that seeketh so to do" (D&C 46:9). He reminded the Saints that the gifts of the Spirit were not to be used as a sign nor to add to one's lust (D&C 46:9). Everyone has at least one gift so that the whole Church can benefit (vv. 10–11).

The many different gifts listed in Doctrine and Covenants 46 range from the gift of administration to the gift of speaking in tongues, thus showing the diversity of the gifts of the Spirit. The gift of speaking in tongues is one gift in which deception is easily possible. The Prophet Joseph Smith warned about the use of the gift of tongues: "Be not so curious about tongues, do not speak in tongues except there be an interpreter present; the ultimate design of tongues is to speak to foreigners, and if persons are very anxious to display their intelligence, let them speak to such in their own tongues."[2] The purpose of speaking in tongues is to interpret or speak another language in order to help others understand the gospel message. The Prophet Joseph Smith warned: "The gifts of God are all useful in their place, but when they are applied to that which God does not intend, they prove an injury, a snare and a curse instead of a blessing."[3] Consequently, to the bishop is given the gift "to discern all those gifts lest there shall be any among you professing and yet be not of God" (D&C 46:27). Thus, there is safety and protection for the Saints in that a bishop can declare whether an apparent expression of the Spirit is of God, of man, or of the devil.

THE DOCTRINE OF THE GOSPEL

Just as the misuse of gifts of the Spirit can mislead the Saints, so can the misunderstanding or misuse of the doctrines of the gospel. The Lord's warning about the doctrines of men was addressed when the Saints began to interact with the United Society of Believers in Christ's Second Appearing, more commonly known as the Shakers. The Shakers held unique doctrines concerning God and the Second Coming. They believed that "Christ's second coming had already occurred and he had appeared in the form of a woman, Ann Lee; baptism by water was not considered essential; the eating of pork was specifically forbidden, and many did not eat any meat; and a celibate life was considered higher than marriage" (D&C 49, headnote). Leman Copley, a convert from the Shakers, wanted to return and visit them. The Lord warned him that he was not to be taught by them but rather was to teach the gospel as it had been revealed and as he had been taught by the servants of the Lord (D&C 49:1–4). The Lord then revealed through his prophet the true doctrine concerning the Second Coming, ordinances of the gospel, the eating of meat, and the ordinance of marriage.

The safety of the Saints lies in following the prophets for protection not only from false revelations but also from false doctrines of the devil and the doctrines of men. In all aspects of our lives, we are faced with discussions and intellectual challenges that seem to contradict the principles of the gospel as we understand them. The key is not to compromise the doctrine but to keep our eyes on the standard works, the First Presidency, and the Quorum of the Twelve Apostles as they exercise their keys to declare the doctrines of the kingdom (D&C 124:126). The Lord counsels us through the example of Leman Copley that we should not take our teaching from men nor accept their doctrine but rather take our doctrine from him and his servants (D&C 49:4).

EDIFICATION FROM GOD

Just as some false ideas and concepts are hard to detect, so is the misuse of truth. In fact, truths can be misused and misunderstood to such a degree that deception takes place. The Lord declared that truth had to be taught by the Spirit of truth if it was of him. If it is taught in any other way, it is not of him. The process of teaching and learning truth is very simple. To prevent deception, we must teach and receive the truth by the Spirit of truth (D&C 50:17–20). By this method both the teacher and learner "understand one another, and both are edified and rejoice together" (D&C 50:22).

The Lord gave the early Saints another key to prevent deception: "And that which doth not edify is not of God, and is darkness. That which is of God is light; and he that receiveth light, and continueth in God, receiveth more light; and that light groweth brighter and brighter until the perfect day" (D&C 50:23–24). The word *edify* means "to instruct or benefit, esp. morally or spiritually."[4] So we should ask, Does this material instruct me or make me better morally? Note that the issue is not whether it is truth, for truth can be used in many ways, including ways that take a person away from God. Instead, the issue is whether or not I feel edified. Satan's work will never benefit us spiritually. Whereas Satan's work feels like darkness because of lack of spiritual and moral light, God's work is uplifting and leads to joy. Thus, the fruits of the truth and the actions encouraged by the use of that truth are more important than the truth itself.

THE PATTERN TO JUDGE

Often the early Saints were dealing not with philosophical ideas and truths but with individuals and their personalities. Despite their efforts, some Saints were still deceived by individuals who appeared to be righteous and acceptable to the Lord when in reality they were wicked and not accepted by him. The Lord warned that in the Church there were deceivers and hypocrites "which [had] given the adversary power" (D&C 50:7). The Lord gave a pattern to prevent individuals from being deceived by such persons, "for Satan is abroad in the land, and he goeth forth deceiving the nations" (D&C 52:14). This pattern is used to compare an individual's personality and behavior with a standard or outline, as when a pattern is used to cut a piece of cloth to fit a certain size. In this case, the Saints had to judge the person to determine if that person was a hypocrite or deceiver. Therefore, the pattern given by the Lord as a set of criteria should be used to judge individuals.

The Lord's pattern involved five questions to be used to detect a deceiver or hypocrite. The first question is, Does the individual pray? (D&C 52:15). An individual who presents himself as a righteous person and yet does not pray to the God of Israel is not righteous. Consistently throughout the Doctrine and Covenants the command is given to pray vocally and in secret. That is such an important part of a person's spiritual growth that the Lord decreed: "He that observeth not his prayers before the Lord in the season thereof, let him be had in remembrance before the judge of my people" (D&C 68:33). Furthermore, even if a person prays, what kind of prayer does he or she offer? A person can learn a lot about another individual's spirituality by listening to his or her prayers.

The next question in the pattern asks, Is the person's spirit contrite? (D&C 52:15). A person with a contrite spirit is humble and dependent upon God. Such a person shows godly sorrow for sins and has a deep appreciation and understanding of the Atonement. Having a contrite spirit allows one to seek a closeness to God and to understand that with him, nothing is impossible. Above all, a person whose spirit is contrite will do whatever the Lord commands him or her to do.

The third question in the pattern is, Is the person obedient to the ordinances of God? The answer to this question appears to be a critical part of the pattern because it is referred to twice, in verses 15 and 16. The attitude a person has towards making and keeping covenants is an important barometer of that person's spiritual strength. Anyone who is casual in obeying the conditions of the ordinances is usually also casual in developing spiritual goals and reaching them, no matter how spiritual that person may appear on the surface to be. A classic example is the way a person feels, talks, and acts concerning the sacred clothing that is worn after having participated in the endowment of the temple. If a person is casual about wearing sacred clothing, that person probably is also casual about living and obeying other commandments of God.

The fourth question the pattern asks is, Is the individual's language meek and edifying? (D&C 52:16). For language to "edify," it must instruct and improve the listener morally. Thus we should ask, Is there lowliness of heart and humility in this person's attitude and life? Do I feel good about myself after conversing with this person? One's language is often a window to the soul.

The fifth question is, Does the person tremble under the power of God? (D&C 52:17). How does a person tremble under the power of God? The answer may be hard to determine. Every individual has developed a feeling towards our Father in Heaven. If a person sees the hand of God in all aspects of his or her life (D&C 59:21), that person will understand the power and love of God in everyone's life. That will create a feeling of awe and trembling as that person contemplates his or her own total dependence upon God. The Lord makes a promise associated with this characteristic: a person will "be made strong, and shall bring forth fruits of praise and wisdom, according to the revelations and truths which I have given you" (D&C 52:17). The Lord declared that anyone who is "overcome and bringeth not forth fruits, even according to this pattern, is not of me. Wherefore, by this pattern ye shall know the spirits in all cases under the whole heavens" (D&C 52:18–19).

CONCLUSION

The Lord knew when we came to this earth that we would face the challenges of devils and men before we could return to him. He has not left us alone in that process of striving to follow truth. He gave us not only scriptures but also prophets and apostles to guide us in the decision-making processes of our lives. Also, the Lord bestows gifts of the Spirit to assist us in developing our own spiritual strength and calls leaders to guide us in the proper use of those gifts. Moreover, he has given us the Spirit of truth to assist in determining the proper use of truth. A divine pattern has also been revealed whereby we can judge ourselves and others to determine proper use of truth and the spiritual intent and strength of the individuals with whom we are dealing. Thus, we are not left alone and are without excuse in our quest for exaltation. As much as Satan would like to deceive us and misguide us, he cannot—as long as we are faithful to the guidelines God has given. As we study the revelations of the Lord found in the Doctrine and Covenants, we can learn not only how these guidelines were used and misused by the early Saints but also how we must use them in our own lives to prevent our being deceived.

NOTES

1. *Millennial Star* 45 (18 June 1883): 389.

2. Joseph Smith, *Teachings of the Prophet Joseph Smith,* sel. Joseph Fielding Smith (Salt Lake City: Deseret Book, 1965), 247–48.

3. Ibid., 248.

4. *Random House College Dictionary* (New York: Random House, 1990), 424.

CHAPTER NINE

TEACHING BY THE POWER OF THE SPIRIT

RICHARD R SUDWEEKS

Teaching has been part of The Church of Jesus Christ of Latter-day Saints since the day it was organized in April 1830. The individuals present on that occasion voted to accept Joseph Smith and Oliver Cowdery as "their teachers in the things of the kingdom of God."[1] Less than a year later, in February 1831, the Lord commanded the members of the Church that when they assembled together they should "instruct and edify each other" (D&C 43:8). The Lord reiterated that charge in December 1832, when he commanded the members of the Church to "teach one another the doctrine of the kingdom" (D&C 88:77).

Teaching has become a pervasive activity in the Church as the members attempt to "instruct and edify each other" (D&C 43:8). A large proportion of the active, adult men and women in the Church have accepted callings to serve as teachers in a priesthood quorum or auxiliary organization. They serve as scoutmasters, den mothers, MIA Maid advisors, and Gospel Doctrine instructors and in a host of other teaching roles. Members called to serve in such leadership positions as quorum presidents, Primary presidents, Relief Society presidents, bishops, stake presidents, mission presidents, area authorities, and general authorities are also called upon to teach others. In addition, there are tens of

Richard R Sudweeks is associate professor of instructional science at Brigham Young University.

thousands of missionaries and hundreds of thousands of home teachers and visiting teachers called to teach families or individuals in less formal settings. Parents too are charged with the responsibility of teaching their children the basic principles of the gospel (D&C 68:25–28). As President David O. McKay stated, "We are a Church of teachers."[2]

Much of the teaching done by Church leaders is in the form of speeches delivered in large meetings. Most teaching and public speaking in the Church is done live by persons on site, but there is an increasing use of recorded speeches by Church leaders and scripted instruction in various formats, especially videotapes.

Church members called to serve in teaching and leadership positions generally have little, if any, formal training in the art of teaching or the art of public speaking. So President McKay's statement could reasonably be extended to say, "We are a Church of teachers, but we rely upon lay members who lack formal training to do the teaching and expect them to succeed."

An examination of the scriptures in the Doctrine and Covenants will help us gain a better understanding of what it means to teach by the power of the Holy Ghost and to identify actions that individual teachers can take so that their teaching can be enhanced by that power.

THE TEACHER'S RESPONSIBILITY

An assignment to teach the gospel is a serious responsibility. Evidence of the seriousness of this responsibility is given in Doctrine and Covenants 42:12–14, in which the Lord directs the elders, priests, and teachers of the Church that their teaching should be "directed by the Spirit" (v. 13). The Lord promises them that "the Spirit shall be given unto you by the prayer of faith" (v. 14). Then he warns, "If ye receive not the Spirit ye shall not teach" (v. 14). This warning may be read as a declaration meaning that a person who attempts to teach without the power of the Spirit will be ineffective and unsuccessful.

Inspiration and confirmation. The Holy Ghost is a revelator. To teach by the power of the Holy Ghost is to teach by revelation. The teaching process includes two different forms of revelation. First, the teacher or speaker must receive revelation to know what message the Lord would have him or her teach on that occasion to the particular person or audience at hand. Second, the message must be accompanied by a confirming witness revealed to the recipient (D&C 18:2; 2 Nephi 33:1). For the sake of distinguishing between these two forms of revelation, we will label the first as *inspiration* and the second as *confirmation*. The main point is that teaching by the Spirit is a communicative process between a sender and a receiver that involves both inspiration and confirmation.

To the degree that a teacher or speaker receives inspiration, he or she will be guided by the Holy Ghost in deciding what ideas to teach and how to present these ideas in ways that will be meaningful and instructive to the intended learners. The teacher or speaker may also be prompted with new insights about the meaning of relevant scriptural passages or incidents in his or her own experience. The Holy Ghost may dictate the very words to be used, or the inspiration may consist of thoughts placed in the mind of the teacher or speaker by the Holy Ghost that are subsequently expressed in the individual's own words.

The recipients' response. Because the Lord usually does not impose knowledge of truth on individuals, the message sent by an inspired teacher may be recognized and accepted by some of the intended recipients and not by others. Hence, whether an individual receives a manifestation confirming the truthfulness of a teacher's message depends upon the hearer's receptiveness to the influence of the Holy Ghost (2 Nephi 33:2). When the teaching process is successful, the truthfulness of the sender's message is manifest to the recipient by the power of the Holy Ghost (Moroni 10:5).

Teaching by the Spirit is a collaborative and synergistic endeavor that occurs when both the sender (the teacher or speaker) and the receiver (the student or hearer) are influenced by the Holy Ghost. When the teacher is inspired and the learner is receptive to the confirming witness manifest by the Holy Ghost, then "he that preacheth and he that receiveth, understand one another, and both are edified and rejoice together" (D&C 50:21–22). Note the result. Not only do the teacher and learner communicate well enough that they understand one another but both are *edified.* The use of the verb *edified* implies that the teacher and the learner are mutually uplifted and that the faith of each is strengthened.

PREPARE TO RECEIVE THE GUIDANCE OF THE SPIRIT

Before a teacher can receive revelation from the Holy Ghost to enhance teaching, he or she must prepare to receive this blessing. The Doctrine and Covenants identifies at least four different characteristics that an individual should possess to be prepared: personal purity, humility, scripture knowledge, and faithful obedience.

Personal purity. The Doctrine and Covenants is consistent with the other standard works in teaching the need for repentance and personal purity before an individual may qualify to receive inspiration from the Holy Ghost continually (D&C 1:31–33; 76:52). The need for purity is emphasized in section 76, which states that God bestows the Holy Spirit "on those who love him, and purify themselves before him" (D&C 76:116).

A recurring warning in the Doctrine and Covenants is that the privilege of enjoying the guidance of the Holy Ghost is a conditional blessing that can be withdrawn (D&C 1:33; 70:14; 121:37; 130:23). The Lord taught Martin Harris that lesson when He withdrew His Spirit from him (D&C 19:20). A person who desires to enjoy the inspiration of the Holy Ghost continually must live worthy of this blessing continually.

Humility. Individuals cannot be taught by the Spirit unless they are humble. Evidence of the need for humility as a prerequisite to being taught by the Spirit is given in

Doctrine and Covenants 136:32–33: "Let him that is igno-rant learn wisdom by humbling himself and calling upon the Lord his God, that his eyes may be opened that he may see, and his ears opened that he may hear; for my Spirit is sent forth into the world to enlighten the humble and con-trite, and to the condemnation of the ungodly." "Ignorant" individuals are those who, regardless of how much school-ing they have completed, are ignorant of the limits of their knowledge and lack of wisdom regarding spiritual matters. Before such individuals can "learn wisdom," they must humble themselves through prayer so that their spiritual blindness and deafness can be healed and they can perceive the things of the Spirit. Arrogance, conceit, and haughti-ness are all forms of pride, which lessens an individual's sensitivity to promptings of the Spirit and can cause the Spirit to withdraw. For example, in Doctrine and Covenants 63:55 we read that Sidney Rigdon "grieved" the Spirit because "he exalted himself in his heart."

The Lord specifically instructed Thomas B. Marsh, the first president of the Quorum of the Twelve Apostles, and the other apostles not to exalt themselves (D&C 112:14–15). The Lord's promise to Thomas in verse 10 of section 112 also illustrates the need for humility as a pre-requisite to receiving inspiration. We often quote or refer to this beautiful passage without thinking of the condi-tional nature of the promise given. I have paraphrased this passage to emphasize the "if . . . , then . . ." nature of this promise.

Doctrine and Covenants 112:10 (quoted version): "Be thou humble; and the Lord thy God shall lead thee by the hand, and give thee answer to thy prayers."

Doctrine and Covenants 112:10 (paraphrased version): "If you will humble yourself, then I will guide you and give you answers to the matters you have prayed about."

Knowledge of the scriptures. A person who desires to be enlightened by the Spirit must first prepare by studying and pondering the truths of the gospel that the Lord has already revealed in available scripture. This principle is clearly taught in the revelation given to Hyrum Smith and recorded in Doctrine and Covenants 11. Late in May 1829 Hyrum traveled to Harmony, Pennsylvania, to visit his younger brother Joseph and Oliver Cowdery, who were engaged in translating the Book of Mormon. Hyrum wanted to find out how he could assist in the Lord's work— before the translation was completed and more than ten months before the organization of the Church. He was apparently very anxious to assist in the Restoration by preaching the gospel. In this revelation, Hyrum was commanded that he should not suppose that he had been called to preach until he was actually called. Further, he was directed to "wait" (v. 16), to "hold your peace" (v. 18), and to "be patient" (v. 19). In addition, he was told what he should do to prepare himself to assist in the work: "Seek not to declare my word, but first seek to obtain my word, and then shall your tongue be loosed; then, if you desire, you shall have my Spirit and my word, yea, the power of God unto the convincing of men. But now hold your peace; study my word which hath gone forth among the children of men, and also study my word which shall come forth among the children of men, or that which is now translating" (D&C 11:21–22).

Hyrum was specifically told that before he made any attempt to teach the gospel, he should first seek to "obtain" the Lord's word by studying the Bible (the word that had already gone forth) and the Book of Mormon (the word that would come forth but was still being translated). Verse 21 describes the Lord's twofold promise to Hyrum. First, his tongue would be "loosed," suggesting that his ability to express himself orally would be enhanced. Second, "then if you desire, you shall have my Spirit and my word, yea, the power of God unto the convincing of men." The word "yea" performs an important function in this sentence: it introduces an emphatic phrase that reaffirms and amplifies the meaning of the preceding statement. In this context, "yea" means *indeed* or *not only this but even*. Hence, Hyrum was promised that he would be blessed not only with the

Lord's "Spirit" and his "word" but also with "the power of God unto the convincing of men."

The Lord's advice to Hyrum should be instructive to all of us. If we desire to teach with the Spirit and have the power of God unto the convincing of others, we must first acquire an understanding of the gospel through thoughtful, persistent study of the scriptures.

Faithful obedience. When the Lord counseled "the elders, priests, and teachers of this church" in Doctrine and Covenants 42:12–14 about the need to teach by the Spirit, he included this charge in verse 13: "And they shall observe the covenants and church articles to do them." President Harold B. Lee stressed the verb *do* in this verse as a way of emphasizing that teachers or speakers who desire to have the influence of the Spirit accompany their teachings must first be obedient to the principle they are attempting to teach.[3]

President Heber J. Grant was even more emphatic regarding the need to live the gospel in one's personal life as a prerequisite to having the influence of the Holy Ghost guide and enhance one's teaching: "No man can teach the Gospel of Jesus Christ under the inspiration of the living God and with power from on high unless he is living it."[4]

PREPARING THE MESSAGE TO BE PRESENTED

Impromptu versus prayerfully planned messages. One issue that a teacher or speaker must consider when preparing to fulfill a teaching or speaking assignment is to what extent to plan the message. The pivotal scripture in the Doctrine and Covenants related to this issue comes from the revelation on priesthood to Joseph Smith in Kirtland in September 1832: "Neither take ye thought beforehand what ye shall say; but treasure up in your minds continually the words of life, and it shall be given you in the very hour that portion that shall be meted unto every man" (D&C 84:85).

One way to interpret this verse is to conclude that teachers and others who speak in the Church should avoid planning what message they will present and how they will present it. Instead of preparing a specific message, they should focus their attention on studying the scriptures and then rely upon the Holy Ghost to direct their thoughts and give them ideas to present in an impromptu speech or lesson.

Elder Neal A. Maxwell has suggested a more correct interpretation. He explained that preparation is necessary and that the Holy Ghost influences teachers and speakers during their preparation as they compose their thoughts and organize their presentation: "When we speak about teaching by the Spirit it is not about a mystical process which removes responsibility from the missionary or teacher for prayerful and pondering preparation. Teaching by the Spirit is not the lazy equivalent of going on 'automatic pilot.' We still need a carefully worked out 'flight plan.'"[5]

Treasure up the words of life. Doctrine and Covenants 84:85 directs the Saints to "treasure up in your minds continually the words of life." We typically think of the word *treasure* as being a noun, but in verse 85 it is used as a transitive verb. The verb *treasure up* has two meanings. In one sense, it means to collect objects of value and store them up for future use. In the other sense, it means to value, cherish, or prize an object. To "treasure up . . . the words of life" means more than just to stockpile information from the scriptures. To "treasure up" suggests the need to be discerning and to exercise judgment in distinguishing between trivial tidbits and more significant ideas. This appraisal process involves prayerfully pondering ideas we encounter as we study the standard works and the teachings of the modern prophets to gain an understanding of their meaning and to assess their significance.

Pondering should not be confused with daydreaming. Productive pondering is a focused and directed activity. President Joseph F. Smith's description of the activities he engaged before receiving the vision of the redemption of the dead recorded in section 138 illustrates what focused pondering includes. Notice the verbs used by President Smith to describe his experience. In the first three verses, he tells us that while he sat in his room *"pondering* over the scriptures,"* he *reflected* upon "the great atoning sacrifice that was made by the Son of God" and the love manifest by Christ's coming into the world. Then according to verse 5, his mind *reverted* to two scriptural passages he had previously read in 1 Peter. In an attempt to further understand these two passages, he opened his Bible and *read* each of them again. Although he had previously studied both of these passages, on this occasion, "[he] *was greatly impressed,* more than [he] had ever been before" with their contents (emphasis added).

Why was he so impressed? Apparently because he gained new insights into the meaning and significance of the two passages. But whatever new insights he had acquired from this rereading of the scriptures was just the beginning of what was to come, because in verse 11 he states that while he was engaged in this process of pondering, "the eyes of my understanding were opened, and the Spirit of the Lord rested upon me, and I saw the hosts of the dead, both small and great." This experience of President Joseph F. Smith illustrates that productive pondering is an active search process aimed at discovering meaning or resolving some puzzling issue and that such pondering is an essential part of what it means to "treasure up . . . the words of life."

Contrast the active mental effort needed to conduct this search process with Oliver Cowdery's cursory attempt to receive inspiration as described in Doctrine and Covenants 9. After Oliver unsuccessfully attempted to translate, the Lord told him that the privilege of translating would be taken from him because he "feared" (v. 11) and "did not continue as [he] commenced" (v. 5). Then the Lord explained that he had not understood what he must do to receive inspiration: "Behold, you have not understood; you have supposed that I would give it unto you, when you took no thought save it was to ask me. But, behold, I say unto you, that you must study it out in your mind; then you must ask me if it be right" (D&C 9:7–8).

Study it out in the mind. According to Elder Neal A.

Maxwell, the process of thoughtfully preparing to teach a lesson or present a talk is an invitation to the Holy Ghost to guide one's thinking. Elder Maxwell said further that the enlightened mind that results from having studied out an issue or topic is better prepared to receive additional insights when the talk or lesson is presented: "Studying out something in one's own mind is, in itself, an invitation to the Spirit in our preparations as well as in our presentations. We must not err, like Oliver Cowdery, by taking no thought except to ask God for his Spirit (D&C 9:7). The Lord is especially willing to take the lead of an already informed mind in which things have been 'studied out.' Additionally, if we already care about those to be taught, the Lord can inspire us with any customized counsel or emphasis which may be needed."[6]

Because inspiration typically comes piecemeal, inspired insights are often not fully developed or clearly articulated when they first come to mind. Instead, they emerge gradually, "line upon line, precept upon precept" (D&C 98:12) and "revelation upon revelation, knowledge upon knowledge" (D&C 42:61). Emerging insights typically need to be studied out.

Prayer is a necessary part of the process of eliciting this developing knowledge, but the Lord's message to Oliver Cowdery indicates that prayer by itself is insufficient. One further way to study out a topic in preparation for a teaching or speaking assignment is for the teacher or speaker to write about what it means to him or her personally. The act of writing is a process of discovery that enables the writer to ponder on paper or on the screen of a computer terminal. Writing displays the writer's thoughts so they can be seen and evaluated. The process of reviewing one's writing stimulates the writer to think further. This process is generative, because it leads the writer to elaborate the emerging idea and to develop other, related ideas. The process of trying to articulate one's ideas and feelings in written words and sentences reveals one's thoughts in a manner that permits one to see them, to evaluate them, and to refine them.

Donald Murray described the advantages of writing as a way of thinking: "Writing, in fact, is the most disciplined form of thinking. It allows us to be precise, to stand back and examine what we have thought, to see what our words really mean, to see if they stand up to our own critical eye, make sense, and will be understood by someone else."[7]

Thus, the process of writing about ideas that emerge as teachers and speakers attempt to study out an issue or a topic enables them to engage in disciplined pondering. Disciplined pondering is not only focused and directed but more precise and more productive of significant insights. When I prepare a lesson or a speech, I frequently write about some parts of the subject to better understand it and to find out what the Lord wants me to say. I may set aside the manuscript when I present the lesson or talk, but having written about the subject helps me speak with greater clarity and with increased confidence.

Disciplined pondering can help teachers acquire the understanding needed to speak with conviction and assurance. The disciplined pondering that results from writing about the subject is one especially helpful way to "treasure up . . . the words of life" (D&C 84:85).

Seek confirmation. Frequent prayer should be part of the process of "studying out" a subject or principle that the teacher or speaker is preparing to teach or speak about. The procedure that the Lord outlined for Oliver Cowdery includes two steps: "You must study it out in your mind; then you must ask me if it be right" (D&C 9:8). The pronoun *it* in the first clause refers to the subject or principle that the teacher or speaker needs to study. The *it* in the second clause refers to the plan that the teacher has tentatively decided on. The process is not complete until the teacher has tested the proposed plan by taking it to the Lord and inquiring if "it be right." The Lord specified to Oliver Cowdery the criteria for understanding the Lord's answer in such a case: "And if it is right I will cause that your bosom shall burn within you; therefore, you shall feel that it is right. But if it be not right you shall have no such feelings, but you shall have a stupor of thought that shall cause you to forget the thing which is wrong; therefore, you cannot write that which is sacred save it be given you from me" (D&C 9:8–9).

Attempting to resolve a problem or issue by studying it out in one's mind is a process of reasoning. Based on the Lord's response to Oliver Cowdery in Doctrine and Covenants 9:7–9, Elder Dallin H. Oaks has suggested two general principles about the relationship between reason and revelation. First, he declares, "That relationship is *sequential*. Study and reason come first. Revelation comes second" (emphasis in original).[8] Then he explains that reason without revelation is insufficient. Although study and reason may lead to a correct solution, only revelation can confirm it. Hence, reason and revelation are both necessary.[9] Oliver failed because "he took no thought" (v. 7) except to ask for revelation. He could not receive confirmation, because he had neglected first to study the prolem out in his mind and then to develop a proposed solution.

Focus on an edifying message. According to the late Lowell Bennion, a good lesson is focused on one main idea or a single controlling purpose.[10] Emerson Roy West claims that a good speech is similarly focused and uses an interesting analogy to illustrate this point. He suggests that speakers who have trouble focusing on a particular topic are "like a disorganized gardener[:] they pull out a few radishes, then some carrots, and then start picking beans, never completing any one task."[11]

Speeches and lessons that lack focus tend to ramble. Rather than concentrating on a focal idea and developing it, the teacher or speaker glosses over a series of ideas without adequately developing any of them. Consequently, the presentation tends to be filled with clichés or half-baked abstractions that lack substance and concreteness.

The key question the teacher or speaker needs to answer is, To what extent is the message edifying? A speaker or teacher who desires to teach by the power of the Spirit must focus on a message that will "edify" the audience and strengthen their commitment to live the gospel; the Lord made this point very clear in Doctrine and Covenants 50:23: "And that which doth not edify is not of God, and is darkness."

The best way for a teacher to ensure that the message is edifying is to focus on basic principles taught in the standard works and in the writings of the modern prophets. Scriptural principles may be illustrated with inspirational examples from other good literature or from personal experience, but the focus should be on the scriptural principle and examples should be spiritually uplifting rather than just emotionally appealing. To ensure that the message is edifying, a teacher or speaker should avoid speculating about esoteric questions or dwelling on fringe topics.

PRESENTING THE MESSAGE BY THE POWER OF THE SPIRIT

Improvise as moved upon by the Spirit. Before teachers or speakers begin to present the message, they should pray in faith that the guidance of the Holy Ghost will be present throughout the duration of their lesson or speech (D&C 19:38; 42:14). The teacher or speaker might ask the Lord specifically for help in identifying and responding to the needs of the class or audience and then be flexible and willing to improvise as guided by the Spirit. This responsiveness to the Spirit might mean departing from the planned presentation by skipping some parts, by making impromptu substitutions, or by elaborating on some points with new insights that come at the moment (D&C 100:6). This Spirit-guided spontaneity is a distinguishing characteristic of what it means to speak as one is "moved upon by the Holy Ghost" (D&C 68:3). Such spontaneity helps the teacher provide the "customized counsel or emphasis" to which Elder Maxwell referred.[12]

Pray for utterance. Teachers and speakers should humbly pray for the Holy Ghost to inspire their thinking and give them utterance. The Lord's promise to David Whitmer recorded in Doctrine and Covenants 14:8 is applicable in this situation: "If you shall ask the Father in my name, in faith believing, you shall receive the Holy Ghost, which giveth utterance, that you may stand as a witness of the things of which you shall both hear and see and also that you may declare repentance unto this generation." This promise is based on the condition that David Whitmer ask for the Lord's help in a prayer of faith. If he does so, he is promised that he will receive the Holy Ghost, "which giveth utterance." Utterance is the ability to articulate thoughts and to express feelings in words and sentences that communicate clearly and effectively. This expressive ability is a blessing which comes from the Holy Ghost and is given in answer to prayer.

Avoid pedantry. The Lord's injunction that "every man [should] esteem his brother as himself" (D&C 38:24) applies to teachers just as much as it does to other members of the Church. Consequently, teachers and speakers should avoid using the opportunity to teach as a means of parading their knowledge. Arrogance hinders learning. The Lord warned against using position as a means of gratifying one's own pride or vain ambitions (D&C 121:36–37). Persons who desire to teach by the Spirit must avoid the intellectual smugness that sometimes leads teachers or speakers to respond in a disdainful or condescending manner to students or members of the audience they consider to be less knowledgeable than themselves. Such put-downs offend learners and cause the Spirit of the Lord to withdraw.

Testify. When called upon to teach a lesson or present a talk in church, a teacher has responsibility to bear witness of the truthfulness of the specific gospel principle being taught. To testify is to bear one's own witness of the truth. It is to publicly declare and attest that one has received revelation from the Holy Ghost certifying that that principle is true. The teacher should simply but boldly proclaim what he or she personally believes or knows to be true about that principle (D&C 80:4).

If moved by the Spirit, the teacher may briefly relate a spiritual experience that helped him or her gain a testimony of the principle being taught. In such a case, the teacher or speaker must refrain from exaggerating or embellishing the incident in any way and also from becoming so involved in retelling the experience that he or she forgets to bear testimony. The teacher should also be sensitive to the constraining influence of the Spirit: "Remember that that which cometh from above is sacred, and must be spoken with care, and by constraint of the Spirit; and in this there is no condemnation, and ye receive the Spirit through prayer; wherefore, without this there remaineth condemnation" (D&C 63:64).

Let the Spirit do the convincing. In the last verse of his preface to the Doctrine and Covenants the Lord states, "For behold, and lo, the Lord is God, and the Spirit beareth record, and the record is true, and the truth abideth forever and ever. Amen" (D&C 1:39). In the middle of this statement, the Lord declares that "the Spirit beareth record." To *bear record* is to give testimony that substantiates and establishes the truth. One function of the Holy Ghost is to manifest the truthfulness of gospel principles as they are taught by humble servants of the Lord (Moroni 10:5). The evidence provided by the Holy Ghost is usually detectable not by the human senses of sight, hearing, touch, smell, or taste but by an additional spiritual sense. Spiritually manifested evidence provides the confirming witness that enables a receptive recipient to know for a surety that a principle is true and of God.

In their attempts to teach the gospel, teachers or speakers need not, and indeed should not, attempt to contrive emotional responses for their students or listeners. Elder Loren C. Dunn emphasized that teaching by the Spirit is much more than "telling inspirational stories or relating experiences that appeal to the emotions."[13] He warned teachers not to confuse emotional appeals with the influence of the Spirit. To paraphrase Elder Dunn, the confirming influence of the Spirit may not be emotionally appealing, but it will be edifying and uplifting. Conversely, that which is emotionally appealing will not necessarily be edifying.[14]

Doctrine and Covenants 100 contains a revelation given to Joseph Smith and Sidney Rigdon when they visited the small town of Perrysburg in western New York in October 1833. The Lord directed them to "lift up their voices" to the people in that area and to "speak the thoughts that I shall put into your hearts" (v. 5). Then the Lord added the following "commandment" and "promise": "But a commandment I give unto you, that ye shall declare whatsoever thing ye declare in my name, in solemnity of heart, in the spirit of meekness, in all things. And I give unto you this promise, that inasmuch as ye do this the Holy Ghost shall be shed forth in bearing record unto all things whatsoever ye shall say" (D&C 100:7–8).

I believe that the promise given to the Prophet and Sidney Rigdon applies to all who are called to teach the gospel to others. Inasmuch as we comply with the conditions of this promise, the Holy Ghost will "be shed forth in bearing record" of the truthfulness of the ideas we have taught.

Avoid being so self-reliant that the Spirit is excluded. During preparation and presentation, teachers or speakers must be careful not to exclude the Spirit by attempting to teach solely with their own learning (2 Nephi 28:4) or solely by the power of human reasoning and persuasion (1 Corinthians 2:1–5, 11–14). Teachers or speakers must recognize the limitations of human wisdom and reasoning as they apply to spiritual matters. They must acknowledge dependence on the Lord (D&C 59:21) and ask for his help in overcoming weaknesses in their reasoning and in their presentation skills. Teachers or speakers should pray to be able to speak with conviction while presenting the message the Lord wants presented.

Two verses near the end of section 46 present helpful advice that should help teachers and speakers prevent themselves from getting in the way when attempting to teach by the Spirit. First, whatever is attempted in the Spirit "must be done in the name of Christ" (D&C 46:31).

Second, the teacher or speaker must "give thanks unto God in the Spirit" for any success experienced (D&C 46:32).

CONCLUSION

Teaching by the Spirit is a collaborative process that includes inspiration received by the teacher or speaker and confirmation experienced by the learner. Both are forms of revelation from the Holy Ghost. For the learning process to occur, both the teacher and the learner must have prepared themselves to be sensitive to the promptings of the Spirit through personal purity, humility, and obedience to the Lord's commandments. In addition, the teacher or speaker should seek to know and treasure up the word of the Lord.

Teachers and speakers should work to develop prayerfully prepared messages that will edify learners. They should present their message with Spirit-guided spontaneity and rely upon the Spirit to do the convincing. In making their presentation, they should take precautions to avoid pedantry and any form of self-reliance that might exclude the Spirit.

Members of the Church who serve in teaching assignments can and do receive revelation to guide their preparation and enhance their teaching. Learners can and do receive the witness of the Holy Ghost confirming that what they have been taught is true. These miracles happen day after day, week after week throughout the Church.

Members of the Church can increase their teaching effectiveness if they prepare themselves spiritually, put more effort into prayerfully preparing messages that edify, and rely upon the Lord to give them utterance.

NOTES

1. Joseph Smith, *History of The Church of Jesus Christ of Latter-day Saints,* ed. B. H. Roberts, 2d ed. rev., 7 vols. (Salt Lake City: The Church of Jesus Christ of Latter-day Saints, 1932–51), 1:77.

2. David O. McKay, "That You May Instruct More Perfectly," *Improvement Era,* August 1956, 59, 557.

3. Harold B. Lee, *The Teachings of Harold B. Lee,* comp. Clyde J. Williams (Salt Lake City: Bookcraft, 1996), 456.

4. Heber J. Grant, in Conference Report, April 1938, 15.

5. Neal A. Maxwell, *That Ye May Believe* (Salt Lake City: Bookcraft, 1992), 40.

6. Ibid., 41.

7. Donald M. Murray, *Write to Learn,* 3d ed. (Fort Worth: Holt, Rinehart & Winston, 1990), 3.

8. Dallin H. Oaks, *The Lord's Way* (Salt Lake City: Deseret Book, 1991), 64.

9. Ibid., 64–66.

10. Lowell L. Bennion, *Jesus the Master Teacher* (Salt Lake City: Deseret Book, 1981), 52.

11. Emerson Roy West, *How to Speak in Church* (Salt Lake City: Deseret Book, 1976), 17.

12. Maxwell, *That Ye May Believe*, 41.

13. Loren C. Dunn, "Teaching by the Power of the Spirit," *Ensign,* September 1984, 11.

14. Ibid.

CHAPTER TEN

REAL COVENANTS AND REAL PEOPLE

CRAIG J. OSTLER

The Doctrine and Covenants contains many well-known revelations. Among them are the three degrees of glory, the ministry of the Savior in the spirit world following his crucifixion, revelations on the priesthood, and the signs of the Second Coming. Within them we find the answers to many of life's questions. There are also, however, some lesser-known revelations and passages that provide valuable insights and also have answers to questions. In some cases the questions and answers are of a more individual nature. A characteristic of these lesser-known revelations is that they are usually shorter, or the passages are quoted less often. They were often given for individuals who are also less known to members of the Church today. As a result, we may tend to give less attention to these revelations in our personal study and class discussions and thus miss the important insights they provide. Indeed, there may even be those who question why such revelations are included in the Doctrine and Covenants. An examination of a few of these "lesser-known" revelations and passages illustrates their value and suggests a few keys that we might apply to our study of other lesser-known revelations.

Craig J. Ostler is assistant professor of Church history and doctrine at Brigham Young University.

DOCTRINE AND COVENANTS 79 AND 80

The revelations recorded in Doctrine and Covenants 79 and 80 were received by the Prophet Joseph Smith in March 1832. They are calls to missionary service. Section 79 was directed to Jared Carter, and section 80 to Stephen Burnett. The insight gained from these revelations comes from the contrast in the mission calls. Jared Carter was called specifically to "go again into the eastern countries" (D&C 79:1). He had just returned from serving as a missionary for nearly six months in that very same area a few weeks before this revelation was received. In contrast, Stephen Burnett was told "go ye and preach my gospel, whether to the north or to the south, to the east or to the west, it mattereth not, for ye cannot go amiss" (D&C 80:3).

The first missionary was given a specific area of assignment, and the second missionary was told he could go anywhere. Apparently there are times and circumstances in which it matters very much where an individual is called to serve and other times when the area of assignment is not as important. I have seen this truth in my own life. For example, there have been occasions when it was very important that I be assigned as a home teacher to a particular family—I was so informed by my priesthood leaders. On other occasions, I was informed that it really did not matter where I gave my service; as my priesthood leader felt that I could serve just about anywhere, or, in the words of the Lord to Stephen Burnett, "it mattereth not, for you cannot go amiss."

The experience of Jared Carter when he responded to the Lord's call to return to the eastern countries illustrates the importance of that assignment. He accepted the call to return to the area of his previous mission with enthusiasm. After his service in this call came to an end, he recorded in his journal: "Now while I make this record, I remember the goodness of the Lord to me in the mission that I have lately been to in the East. I have enjoyed my health continuely and the Lord, not withstanding the great opposition to the glorious work, he has blessed me . . . in this mission in which I have been gone six months and two days. The Lord has permitted me to administer the gospel to 79 souls and many others by my instrumentality have been convinced of this most glorious work, where I have been in this mission." [1]

The importance of serving a second time in the same calling is demonstrated by the many individuals who received the gospel due to Jared Carter's repeat service. This revelation reminds those who are called to the same callings more than once that the Lord is aware of their lives and talents and is mindful of those whom they may bless in their repeat service.

DOCTRINE AND COVENANTS 96

Doctrine and Covenants 96 contains another lesser-known passage that provides important insight. In verses 6 through 9, John Johnson was told by the Lord that his offering was accepted and that his prayers were heard. Before this revelation, the Prophet Joseph Smith and his wife, Emma, had lived with John and his wife, Elsa, on their farm in Hiram, Ohio. On this farm the leading elders of the Church met in conference and determined to publish a selection of the revelations that had been received. They called that collection the Book of Commandments. [2] Here Joseph and Sidney Rigdon received the vision of the three degrees of glory while they were engaged in the translation of the Bible.

The Lord instructed Joseph the Prophet that "it is expedient in me that he [John Johnson] should become a member of the order" (D&C 96:8). The order of which he was to become a member was a business firm composed of some of the leading elders of the Church and was referred to as the United Order or United Firm. Members of this order covenanted to consecrate their surplus property and business profits for the poor and needy of the Church. [3] At this time, as indicated in section 96, the order had negotiated the purchase of a farm from Peter French that included a house, or inn. As a member of the order, John was instructed by the Lord that he was to "seek diligently to take away incumbrances that are upon the house named among you" (D&C 96:9).

This simple passage in the Doctrine and Covenants had a profound influence in the life of John Johnson and the history of the Church. John sold his home and farm in Hiram, Ohio, as part of honoring the covenant he had made as a member of the order. The large frame home is still standing today, along with several other buildings on the property. In fact, the home is used as a visitors center for the Church. It is evident that John was a prosperous farmer in the community. The proceeds from the sale of his farm in Hiram were combined with the money of the order to pay the mortgage on the Peter French farm.[4] It was on a part of this land that the Kirtland Temple was built. This temple and the blessings received in it (among them the preparatory ordinances of the endowment), many great spiritual manifestations, and the long-awaited restoration of priesthood keys held by Moses, Elias, and Elijah were made possible in part by this one man's offering. Therefore, an obscure commandment in the Doctrine and Covenants to an individual not commonly known shows the importance of the covenants made by real people of the 1830s. Further, the implication is that members today who keep their covenant of consecrating their worldly wealth and time may someday be given the same promise the Lord gave to John Johnson, "Unto whom I give a promise of eternal life inasmuch as he keepeth my commandments from henceforth" (D&C 96:6).

DOCTRINE AND COVENANTS 108

Doctrine and Covenants 108, addressed to Lyman Sherman, illustrates a valuable personal application for many Saints today. Little is known about why this section was given. Also, unlike the revelations previously discussed, our insight into its value is not enhanced by an understanding of the life of Lyman Sherman as we have record of it today. In fact, it has been my own experience as a bishop that has helped me understand this revelation. I have found that the Lord's words to Brother Sherman offer hope for those within the Church who may be prompted by the Spirit of the Lord to visit with their bishop concerning their standing before the Lord. On account of similar spiritual promptings, Lyman Sherman went to the Prophet Joseph Smith and expressed his feelings: "I have been wrought upon to make known to you my feelings and desires, and was promised that I should have a revelation which should make known my duty."[5] As a result, Joseph received the following: "Verily thus saith the Lord unto you, my servant Lyman: Your sins are forgiven you, because you have obeyed my voice in coming up hither this morning to receive counsel of him whom I have appointed. Therefore, let your soul be at rest concerning your spiritual standing" (D&C 108:1–2).

This may not have been the first time Lyman was prompted to visit with his priesthood leader concerning his spiritual standing. The Lord admonished Lyman to "resist no more my voice" (D&C 108:2). How long he had been receiving promptings from the Lord to visit with the Prophet is not known. It is evident, however, that his anxiety over his spiritual standing could have been of a shorter length if he had not earlier resisted the Lord's voice to go to the Prophet. In like manner, there are members today who resist visiting with their priesthood leaders concerning their spiritual standing, even though the Lord has prompted them to do so many times. How sweet is the comforting solace that comes from meeting with one's bishop and receiving the assurance that one can be at peace concerning his or her spiritual standing before the Lord. That peace may not come during the initial interview, but, as Lyman Sherman learned, as the individual is able to "receive counsel of him whom I [the Lord] have appointed," forgiveness will come. Additional strength will come as the member follows the further counsel given to Lyman in this revelation: "And arise up and be more careful henceforth in observing your vows, which you have made and do make, and you shall be blessed with exceeding great blessings" (D&C 108:3).

DOCTRINE AND COVENANTS 117

When I was teaching a class on the Doctrine and Covenants, one of the students related that she had been approached by a friend of another faith, who asked, "Do you know who Oliver Granger was?" She simply answered that she had never heard of him. The friend's reaction took her by surprise: "Well, that just proves that Joseph Smith was a false prophet!" The friend then referred to the revelation contained in Doctrine and Covenants 117:12: "And again, I say unto you, I remember my servant Oliver Granger; behold, verily I say unto him that his name shall be had in sacred remembrance from generation to generation, forever and ever, saith the Lord."

It appeared obvious to the friend that because the student did not know who Oliver Granger was, this revelation was not true. A closer reading of the passage reveals that more important than having any other individual remember Oliver Granger is that the Lord indicated that he remembered his servant Oliver Granger. No doubt through the succeeding generations, the Lord still remembers Oliver and holds his name in sacred remembrance. Who was Oliver Granger and what covenant did he make to be held in sacred esteem by the Lord?

"Oliver Granger was a man of faith and business ability—two qualities which form a rare combination. . . . When the Prophet fled from Kirtland, he appointed Granger his business agent, and so well did he perform this duty that he was commended by business men."[6] This information concerning Oliver Granger makes the following instructions from the Lord easier to understand: "Therefore, let him contend earnestly for the redemption of the First Presidency of my Church, saith the Lord; and when he falls he shall rise again, for his sacrifice shall be more sacred unto me than his increase, saith the Lord" (D&C 117:13).

The covenant that Oliver Granger made to put his

business talents to work on behalf of the First Presidency later led to another blessing. "At a conference held at Quincy, (Illinois), May 4th to 6th, 1839, he was appointed to return to Kirtland and take charge of the Temple and Church there."[7] Thus he also fulfilled the Lord's command in this same revelation: "Verily I say unto you, let all my servants in the land of Kirtland remember the Lord their God, and mine house also, to keep and preserve it holy, and to overthrow the moneychangers in mine own due time, saith the Lord." (D&C 117:16).

The story of this man and the lessons we can learn for our own lives are revealed in the sacrifice he made to be the Prophet's business agent. Being a man of sound business sense and reputation, Oliver might have become a very wealthy man. Indeed, his name might be more commonly known among members of the Church had he become a man of immense wealth. The Lord recognizes the sacrifice of opportunity for wealth made by his servants. The Lord assured Oliver that "his sacrifice shall be more sacred unto me than his increase" (D&C 117:13), and it is true in the lives of Saints today. Throughout the Church are those who could obtain more wealth, but that might require less service in the kingdom. The Lord, however, does not count the value of his children according to the amount of tithes and offerings they contribute to the kingdom. The Lord may receive their sacrifice as being more sacred to him than their increase.

The answers to difficult decisions concerning wealth versus service may be found in this revelation. Oliver Granger was a man who paved the way for those who sacrifice worldly wealth to give service in the kingdom. Therefore, with the Lord, I feel to exclaim, "Let no man despise my servant Oliver Granger, but let the blessings of my people be on him forever and ever" (D&C 117:15).

DOCTRINE AND COVENANTS 99

Doctrine and Covenants 99 is another revelation that might be classified as a lesser-known section. This revelation was a call for John Murdock to proclaim the gospel. An understanding of the historical background and the individual to whom the revelation was addressed may help the reader to apply the principles found in this section. The first verse elicits our interest because Brother Murdock was called to preach the gospel "in the midst of persecution and wickedness" (D&C 99:1). In a later verse, the Lord counseled John to send his children to "the bishop in Zion" (D&C 99:6).

John Murdock, at the time of this missionary call, was a widower left to bring up five children at the death of his wife. Two of his children had been given to Joseph the Prophet and his wife, Emma, to rear as their own. John's beloved wife, Julia, had died in giving birth to twins. About the same time Emma Smith had also given birth to twins, both of whom died within hours of their birth. John, having no relatives who had accepted the fulness of the restored gospel and to whom he could entrust the babies,[8] took his motherless babies to Emma. The twins, a boy and a girl, were named Joseph and Julia.

By the time this revelation was received, in August 1832, the baby Joseph had become the first martyr for the gospel. At the time of the baby's death, Joseph and Emma resided with John Johnson and his wife, Elsa, on their farm in Hiram, Ohio. On the evening of 24 March 1832, a mob entered the Johnson home and dragged the Prophet Joseph from his room. Emma and Joseph had been taking turns caring for the eleven-month-old twins, who were seriously ill with measles. Emma had nursed the children, and Joseph was sleeping in the trundle bed with little Joseph lying on his chest. The mob took the Prophet but left little Joseph behind to the ravages of the cold that swept into the room. On March 29, on account of the cold and the measles, the not-quite-year-old baby boy died.[9] John Murdock was on a mission at the time. When he returned he recorded in his journal: "[I] arrived in Ohio, in the Church in the month of June, about 12 months after leaving my children. . . . arrived there about the 1st of June, found my little son Joseph had died. I had left my eldest son Orrice with Benjamin Bragg and John with Philo Judd and Phebe with Syrenus Burnet. I had to pay them all full price for keeping my children during my absence. But my daughter was still doing well with Bro. Joseph, the Prophet."[10]

At this time Orrice was seven years old; John, six; and Phebe, four. These were the children whom, in obeying the instructions contained in the revelation, John Murdock was to send to Zion to stay with the family of Bishop Edward Partridge. Again we read from John's journal: "I then continued with the church preaching to them and strengthening them and regaining my health till the month of Aug. when I received the Revelation recorded in the Book of Covenants [D&C], page 206, at which time I immediately commenced to arrange my business and provide for my children and send them up to the Bishop in Zion, which I did by the hand of Bro. Caleb Baldwin in Sept. I gave him ten dollars a head for carrying up my 3 eldest children."[11]

In addition to clarifying the instructions concerning the children to be sent to Zion, John's journal also gives examples of the doctrine of the "law of representation" in which the Lord had told John that "thou art called to go into the eastern countries from house to house, from village to village, and from city to city, to proclaim mine everlasting gospel unto the inhabitants thereof, in the midst of persecution and wickedness. . . . And who receiveth you receiveth me. . . . And whoso rejecteth you shall be rejected of my Father and his house; and you shall cleanse your feet in the secret places by the way for a testimony against them" (D&C 99:1–2, 4).

He recorded: "I then settled my business and on the 24th of Sept. I visited Father Clapp's family [his deceased wife's father and family] preached the gospel to them. They were very unbelieving and hard. I returned to the brethren in Kirtland on the 25th and on the 27th started, in company with Brother Zebedie Coltrin, and on that day called on Mr. Conning's family, Father Clapp's family and Benjamin

Blich's family; all unbelieving. Stayed with Bro. Kingsbury, in Painesville, Preached in the evening. He gave each of us 75¢ God bless him. Met with a Dr. Matthews, a very wicked man, and [he] reviled against us, the Book of Mormon, and the Doctrine we taught. We bore testimony according to the Commandment and the Lord helped us in tending to the ordinance."[12]

These revelations were given to real people who made real covenants with the Lord to serve him. These revelations profoundly influenced the lives of these people. The Lord was mindful of John Murdock's faithfulness in keeping the commandments given to him in the revelation. He had truly sacrificed to bring forth the kingdom of God.

The placement of section 99 in the Doctrine and Covenants positions it in the chronological context of the Saints' persecutions in and expulsion from Jackson County, Missouri, during 1833. Actually, the revelation was received a year earlier, in August 1832. But, the placement of this section directs our attention to the fact that John Murdock had sent his children to Zion and they had been there without father or mother during that troubled time. As recorded in Doctrine and Covenants 103, the Lord called for an army to march to Missouri to redeem the Saints who had been driven from their homes and property. John Murdock had a double interest in going with the army (which became known as Zion's Camp). He had not seen his three eldest children in more than a year. What had happened to these children sent to Zion at the instructions of the Lord? At the end of the journey to Zion, the little army of Saints was disbanded at Fishing River. John wrote concerning his little daughter: "On the 30th [of June 1834], word came to me that my daughter Phebe was sick nigh unto Death, of Cholera, and Bro. A. [Algernon] S. [Sidney] Gilbert, with whom she lived was dead. I immediately went and took care of her till July 6th when the Spirit left the body just at the break of day, being 6 years, 3 months, 27 days old."[13]

His journal continues with the names of two young

men, Reid Peck and Henry Rawlins, being blessed for their help as they "assisted me and we buried her by little after sun rise in the morning. She was decently laid out, and they dug a grave and we laid 2 split shakes in the bottom and one each side and laid in some straw, and laid the corpse on it, laid 2 sticks across and covered it over, and that was her coffin."[14]

What may have been passed over as insignificant verses of the Doctrine and Covenants mean more to us when we understand the real people involved and the influence their real covenants had in their lives.

DOCTRINE AND COVENANTS 88

John Murdock was involved in another covenant which the Lord made with the elders in the School of the Prophets at Kirtland. In the revelation known as the Olive Leaf (D&C 88), the Lord gave the elders gathered the following promise:

"And if your eye be single to my glory, your whole bodies shall be filled with light, and there shall be no darkness in you; and that body which is filled with light comprehendeth all things.

"Therefore, sanctify yourselves that your minds become single to God, and the days will come that you shall see him; for he will unveil his face unto you, and it shall be in his own time, and in his own way, and according to his own will.

"Remember the great and last promise which I have made unto you; . . . And I give unto you, who are the first laborers in this last kingdom, a commandment that you assemble yourselves together, and organize yourselves, and prepare yourselves, and sanctify yourselves; yea, purify your hearts, and cleanse your hands and your feet before me, that I may make you clean;

"That I may testify unto your Father, and your God, and my God, that you are clean from the blood of this wicked generation; that I may fulfil this promise, this great and last promise, which I have made unto you, when I will" (D&C 88:67–69, 74–75).

This revelation was given for real people. These were not idle promises to be passed over lightly. They were and are real covenants that the Lord made with his Saints. A fulfill-ment of this "great and last promise" was recorded by John Murdock in his journal. Referring to a prayer meeting held in the Prophet Joseph Smith's quarters at the Newell K. Whitney store in Kirtland, Ohio, Brother Murdock wrote: "In one of these meetings the Prophet told us, if we could humble ourselves before God, and exercise strong faith, we should see the face of the Lord. And about midday the visions of my mind were opened, and the eyes of my understanding were enlightened, and I saw the form of a man, most lovely, the visage of his face was sound and fair as the sun. His hair a bright silver grey, curled in most majestic form, His eyes a keen penetrating blue, and the skin of his neck a most beautiful white and he was covered from the neck to the feet with a loose garment, pure white, whiter than any garment I have ever before seen. His coun-tenance was most penetrating, and yet most lovely. And while I was endeavoring to comprehend the whole person-age from head to feet it slipped from me, and the vision was closed up. But it left on my mind the impression of love, for months, that I never before felt to that degree."[15]

CONCLUSION

The lesser-known revelations and passages of the Doctrine and Covenants illustrate how wise it is to include such sections in this important book of answers. A few moments of pondering their messages will bring us renewed commitment to live the restored gospel and an appreciation for the real people with whom the Lord made real covenants. Thus we see that as we study and teach the Doctrine and Covenants, it is important to give attention to revelations that are lesser known as well as those with which we are more familiar. Understanding the lives and circumstances of those individuals who were addressed in the revelations brings a greater appreciation of the influence these revelations had in the lives of early Church members as well as the understanding and strength they offer for students of the Doctrine and Covenants today.

NOTES

1. Journal of Jared Carter, typescript, Special Collections, Harold B. Lee Library, Brigham Young University, Provo, Utah, 20.

2. Joseph Smith, *History of The Church of Jesus Christ of Latter-day Saints,* ed. B. H. Roberts, 2d ed. rev., 7 vols. (Salt Lake City: Deseret Book, 1973), 2:224–25.

3. For a further study of the United Firm, see Lyndon W. Cook, *Joseph Smith and the Law of Consecration* (Provo, Utah: Grandin Book, 1985), 57–67.

4. Milton V. Backman Jr., *The Heavens Resound: A History of the Latter-day Saints in Ohio 1830–1838* (Salt Lake City: Deseret Book, 1983), 144. Keith W. Perkins, "Land Ownership in Kirtland," in *Historical Atlas of Mormonism,* ed. S. Kent Brown, Donald Q. Cannon, and Richard H. Jackson (New York: Simon & Schuster, 1994), 24.

5. Smith, *History of the Church,* 2:345.

6. Hyrum M. Smith and Janne M. Sjodahl, *Doctrine and Covenants Commentary* (Salt Lake City: Deseret Book, 1958), 746.

7. Ibid.

8. John Murdock to Julia Murdock Smith Dixon Middleton, 20 January 1859, in John Murdock Journal, typescript, Special Collections, Harold B. Lee Library, Brigham Young University, 154–59.

9. Smith, *History of the Church,* 1:261–65.

10. John Murdock Journal, 20.

11. Ibid.

12. Ibid.

13. Ibid., 25.

14. Ibid., 25–26

15. Ibid., 21.

CHAPTER ELEVEN

WHEN WILL ZION BE REDEEMED?

MONTE S. NYMAN

When will Zion be redeemed? From the very beginning of the history of the Church when the concept of the building of a Zion society was introduced, there has been much speculation, much misinformation, and many ideas put forth about when and how Zion will be redeemed. The Lord invites the members of the Church to search the scriptures and avoid the confusion of speculation. As we seek an answer to our question, we must first determine the meaning of the term *Zion*.

President David O. McKay said, "Zion means, literally, a 'sunny place,' or 'sunny mountain.' It first designated an eminence in Palestine on which Jerusalem is built. In the Doctrine and Covenants, Zion has three designations: first, the land of America; second, a specific place of gathering; and third, the pure in heart."[1] Each one of these Doctrine and Covenants definitions given by President McKay will be briefly analyzed, but the redemption of Zion, the "specific place of gathering," or city of the New Jerusalem, will be emphasized.

ZION AS THE LAND OF AMERICA

The Prophet Joseph Smith said: "You know there has been great discussion in relation to Zion—where it is, and

Monte S. Nyman is professor of ancient scripture at Brigham Young University.

where the gathering of the dispensation is, and which I am now going to tell you. The Prophets have spoken and written upon it; but I will make a proclamation that will cover a broader ground. The whole of America is Zion itself from north to south, and is described by the Prophets, who declare that it is the Zion where the mountain of the Lord should be, and that it should be in the center of the land. When Elders shall take up and examine the old prophecies in the Bible, they will see it."[2]

The whole of North and South America is Zion. General Mormon also understood this definition of Zion. In Alma we read, "And it came to pass that when he had poured out his soul to God, he [General Mormon] named all the land which was south of the land Desolation, yea, and in fine, all the land, both on the north and on the south—a chosen land, and the land of liberty" (Alma 46:17). As the Prophet Joseph Smith said, when elders will take up the scriptures and the prophecies and look at them, they will find that to be the case.[3] When we accept this definition of Zion, we can understand the prophecies spoken by the ancient prophets in a new light.

A SPECIFIC PLACE OF GATHERING

The Lord revealed to the Latter-day Saints that the specific place of gathering was Independence, Jackson County, Missouri, the center place of Zion (D&C 57:3). The center place introduces another scripture related to the gathering of the Saints. The prophet Isaiah spoke of enlarging the tent of Israel—of lengthening its cords and strengthening its stakes (Isaiah 54:2). At the time of Moses, the tabernacle was a tent, which was picked up and carried. It was, in effect, a portable temple. After that time, the concept of Israel being gathered into a tent was familiar among the prophets.

The "tent of Israel" has great importance to Latter-day Saints. No other group in the Christian world uses the term *stake,* but we speak of the thousands of stakes of Zion. This term has direct reference to the tent of Israel. To set up a tent, particularly a large tent, you must have at least one large center pole held up by cords or ropes secured to stakes driven into the ground. The center pole, or the center place, cannot be set up until there are stakes established all the way around it. Similarly, Zion must have stakes all the way around the New Jerusalem (Independence, Missouri) before the tent of Israel will be established.

We now have many places of gathering, stakes established all around Jackson County, and are coming to the time of establishing a center place. Every state in the United States has one or more stakes, and there are stakes in Canada, Mexico, and Central American countries. Stakes are also established throughout other parts of the world, but the Lord defined Independence, Missouri, as the center of "the land which I have appointed . . . for the gathering of the saints . . . the land of promise, and the place for the city of Zion" (D&C 57:1–2). Therefore, it seems that the tent concept refers to the Americas and specifically to North America, which was the initial place appointed for the gathering. Now, as the Church, or the tent of Israel, is enlarged, it will be necessary, as Isaiah says, to "lengthen [the] cords and strengthen [the] stakes." This strengthening will enable Zion to be established successfully.

THE PURE IN HEART

The Doctrine and Covenants describes the people who inhabit the land of Zion as the pure in heart (D&C 97:21). Earlier the Lord had given the formula for becoming pure in heart: "And if your eye be single to my glory, your whole bodies shall be filled with light, and there shall be no darkness in you; and that body which is filled with light comprehendeth all things. Therefore, sanctify yourselves that your minds become single to God, and the days will come that you shall see him; for he will unveil his face unto you, and it shall be in his own time, and in his own way, and according to his own will" (D&C 88:67–68).

The people who had gathered to Jackson County, Missouri, and were driven out were commanded to build a temple in Kirtland, Ohio (D&C 95:8), where they could work toward perfection and becoming pure in heart. The Lord declared in a revelation to Joseph Smith that the house of Zion was to be "For a place of thanksgiving for all saints, and for a place of instruction for all those who are called to the work of the ministry in all their several callings and offices; that they may be perfected in the understanding of their ministry, in theory, in principle, and in doctrine, in all things pertaining to the kingdom of God on the earth, the keys of which kingdom have been conferred upon you" (D&C 97:13–14).

Becoming pure in heart is a process. Through the instruction received in the temple and through serving in various callings, the people would become perfected in understanding. The perfection of understanding and an eye single to the glory of God would help them become pure in heart. If the temple was built and not defiled, the Lord's glory would rest upon it. "Yea, and [the Lord's] presence shall be there, for [he] will come into it, and all the pure in heart that shall come into it shall see God" (D&C 97:16). Thus will be fulfilled the beatitude: "Blessed are all the pure in heart, for they shall see God" (3 Nephi 12:8; Matthew 5:8).

To establish a center place of Zion, the Lord must have a Zion people. Therefore, the place to begin to establish Zion is in the individual. The whole idea of the gospel is to make ourselves pure in heart. Then when enough people seeking to become pure in heart gather together in a designated place, a stake of Zion is established. When a center place is established, surrounded by stakes of Zion, the stakes will be strengthened and the cords will be lengthened to include North and South America and even the whole world as part of the Zion of our God.[4] The Lord promised these blessings to the people gathered in Ohio in 1833: "And, now, behold, if Zion do these things she shall prosper, and spread herself and become very glorious, very great, and very terrible. And the nations of the earth shall honor her, and shall say: Surely Zion is the city of our God, and surely

Zion cannot fall, neither be moved out of her place, for God is there, and the hand of the Lord is there; and he hath sworn by the power of his might to be her salvation and her high tower" (D&C 97:18–20).

Those people failed; therefore, this promise is to be fulfilled later. Zion's extension to North and South America and the whole world may not be completely fulfilled until the end of the Millennium, but we should work toward this goal.

OUR GREATEST OBJECT

With the restoration of the gospel and the establishment of the Church in 1830, the Prophet Joseph Smith received numerous revelations for various individuals to "seek to bring forth and establish the cause of Zion" (D&C 6:6; 11:6; 12:6; 14:6). On one occasion, the Prophet said, "We ought to have the building up of Zion as our greatest object."[5] Every dispensation in the history of the world has been given the same commandment: to seek to bring forth and establish the cause of Zion. It will be accomplished in this dispensation, although the early members of the Church were given the opportunity and failed.

NEW JERUSALEM OF THE SEED OF JOSEPH

Regarding the city of the New Jerusalem in America, the Lord talked about the day of calling and the day of choosing (D&C 105:35). The day of calling seems to be the one that was issued in Doctrine and Covenants 58. The members of the Colesville Branch had just moved to the land of Independence, Missouri, the center place of Zion (D&C 57) and were given further information concerning the future glory of Zion. The Lord revealed: "Ye cannot behold with your natural eyes, for the present time, the design of your God concerning those things which shall come hereafter, and the glory which shall follow after much tribulation. For after much tribulation come the blessings. Wherefore the day cometh that ye shall be crowned with much glory; the hour is not yet, but is nigh at hand" (D&C 58:3–4).

A careful reading shows that the Lord told the Saints that they were not going to establish the city of Zion at that time but that a great period of tribulation yet awaited them. The Lord further stated their purposes in going to Jackson County at this time: "Behold, verily I say unto you, for this cause I have sent you—that you might be obedient, and that your hearts might be prepared to bear testimony of the things which are to come" (D&C 58:6). It was an individual test for these people to go into Jackson County to see if they would be obedient to the things the Lord had commanded. Also, it was important that their "hearts might be prepared to bear testimony." To establish Zion in the future, the Lord needed individuals who had been there, to bear testimony of the land.

The second purpose of the Saints' going to Independence was that the Saints "might be honored in laying the foundation, and in bearing record of the land upon which the Zion of God shall stand" (D&C 58:7). Though the Saints failed to comprehend their immediate purpose in going to the land, they were told that they were only going to lay the foundation of Zion.

The third and final reason for sending the Saints to Missouri was "that a feast of fat things might be prepared for the poor; yea, a feast of fat things, of wine on the lees well refined, that the earth may know that the mouths of the prophets shall not fail. Yea, a supper of the house of the Lord, well prepared, unto which all nations shall be invited" (D&C 58:8–9). Two questions arise from this statement. First, what is the feast of fat things? and second, what prophets foretold it?

Searching the scriptures reveals that the feast of fat things is related to the law of consecration and stewardship. It is a law that will bless the poor and eliminate poverty (D&C 42:30–34; 51:7–15). It is a law that will bring about an equality among the Saints—not in the sense that we usually think of but an equality in which all are equal because there is "no respect to persons as to those who [stand] in need" (Alma 1:30). It is a law which will allow the Saints to "prosper and become far more wealthy than those who [do] not belong to [the] church" (Alma 1:31). It is the law that will be lived in Zion, the only law upon which Zion can be built (D&C 51:2–3; 104:15–18; 105:3–5, 34). It is a privilege for the Saints, said the Lord to Edward Partridge, to establish this law (D&C 51:15).

What prophets foretold the feast of fat things? Although all of the prophets spoke generally of Zion as North and South America,[6] Isaiah was the prophet who specifically foretold of the feast of fat things. He prophesied that the Lord will reign in Mount Zion (Isaiah 24:23) and the strong people shall glorify the Lord (Isaiah 25:3). "For thou hast been a strength to the poor, a strength to the needy in his distress, a refuge from the storm, a shadow from the heat, when the blast of the terrible ones is as a storm against the wall" (Isaiah 25:4).

The law of consecration was to eliminate poverty. The places of refuge for the Saints were the stakes of Zion, as the Lord revealed in the Doctrine and Covenants (D&C 115:5–6; 124:36). The strangers (Gentiles) are to be brought low (Isaiah 25:5), and then, the Lord said: "And in this mountain (of Zion or America) shall the Lord of hosts make unto all people a feast of fat things, a feast of wines on the lees, of fat things full of marrow, of wines on the lees well refined" (Isaiah 25:6).

Isaiah said "all people" would be invited to the feast. In the Doctrine and Covenants, the Lord said "all nations shall be invited" (D&C 58:9), but the invitations are to be extended to the nations in a certain order. "First, the rich and the learned, the wise and the noble; and after that cometh the day of my power; then shall the poor, the lame, and the blind, and the deaf, come in unto the marriage of the Lamb, and partake of the supper of the Lord, prepared for the great day to come" (D&C 58:10–11).

The first invited to the feast are the rich and the learned, the Gentile nations of the earth. The word *nations* is often translated "Gentiles."[7] In the revelation in which he intro-duced the law of consecration to remember the poor (D&C

42:30–38), the Lord declared: "For it shall come to pass, that which I spake by the mouths of my prophets shall be fulfilled; for I will consecrate of the riches of those who embrace my gospel among the Gentiles unto the poor of my people who are of the house of Israel"(D&C 42:39). Again the Lord referred to what he spake by the mouths of the prophets, and he equated the Gentiles with riches. After the rich and the learned are invited, the "poor of [the Lord's] people who are the house of Israel" (D&C 42:39) are to be invited. One purpose of the revelation of the gospel in the latter days was "that it might be fulfilled, which was written by the prophets" (D&C 1:18). The Lord's use of the exact words of the prophets in his revelations to the Latter-day Saints is not coincidental. It is given to us to be able to interpret the prophets and to verify the revelation. As Nephi said, "In the days that the prophecies of Isaiah shall be fulfilled men shall know of a surety, at the times when they shall come to pass" (2 Nephi 25:7).

As the Colesville Branch moved into Jackson County in 1831, the inhabitants of Missouri (the Gentiles) were given the opportunity to accept the gospel, come in and be numbered with Israel, and help build Zion. They rejected that opportunity by driving out the Saints; when the rejection is full, the fulness of the Gentiles will have come to pass (3 Nephi 16:10; D&C 45:28–29). Nevertheless, the mission of the Saints was not a total failure. The Lord said that he had spoken to the Saints "that the testimony might go forth from Zion, yea, from the mouth of the city of the heritage of God" (D&C 58:13). The mission of the early Saints who went to Missouri in 1831 was to bear testimony of the land. They were now qualified to bear that testimony.

The Saints were driven out of Jackson County in 1833. A revelation was given to them concerning why they had been driven out. They had not been a people who were pure in heart. "There were jarrings, and contentions, and envyings, and strifes, and lustful and covetous desires among them; therefore by these things they polluted their inheritances. They were slow to hearken unto the voice of the Lord their God; therefore, the Lord their God is slow to hearken unto their prayers, to answer them in the day of their trouble. In the day of their peace they esteemed lightly my counsel; but, in the day of their trouble, of necessity they feel after me" (D&C 101:6–8).

Two months later, the Lord gave the early members of the Church the opportunity to go back and endeavor to redeem their brethren who were driven from Zion (D&C 103:1–2). He decreed then that if they would hearken unto his counsel, they should "begin to prevail against mine enemies from this very hour" (D&C 103:6). Zion's Camp was organized to redeem Zion. Four months later, after they had failed in their attempt, the Lord gave them additional counsel. In that revelation (D&C 105), he repeats that they had not been obedient (v. 3), they had been full of all manner of evil (v. 3), they would not impart of their substance to the poor (v. 3), and they had not been united according to the law of the celestial kingdom, as was required (v. 4). He further stated that the only way that Zion will ever be built up is upon the principles of the law of the celestial kingdom (v. 5).

PREREQUISITES FOR REDEEMING ZION

The Lord revealed that his elders must wait for a little season before Zion will be redeemed. He did not define the length of a "little season" but outlined eight things that must be accomplished before that redemption will come to pass. Actually nine events must occur; the Lord had revealed another in a revelation previously received. The Lord promised those who would gather to return to Missouri (Zion's Camp) that "the redemption of Zion must needs come by power; therefore, I will raise up unto my people a man, who shall lead them like as Moses led the children of Israel. For ye are the children of Israel, and of the seed of Abraham, and ye must needs be led out of bondage by power, and with a stretched-out arm" (D&C 103:15–17).

The man like unto Moses is the president of the Church,

the president of the high priesthood (D&C 107:91–92). That man is the mouthpiece of the Lord, as was Moses. Other men may receive personal revelation, but the one to whom the Lord speaks directly to guide his Church is its president (Numbers 12).

Elder John A. Widtsoe has verified scripturally that the man like unto Moses is the president of the Church: "In the early days of the Church, persecution raged against the Saints in Jackson County, Missouri. For the comfort of the people, the Lord gave several revelations. In one, he promised, 'I will raise up unto my people a man, who shall lead them like as Moses led the children of Israel' (D&C 103:16). There have been many conjectures concerning this statement. There have even been misguided men who have declared themselves to be this man 'like as Moses.'

"Yet, the meaning as set forth in the scriptures is very simple. In modern revelation, the President of the Church is frequently compared to Moses. Soon after the organization of the Church, the Lord said, 'no one shall be appointed to receive commandments and revelations in this church excepting my servant Joseph Smith, Jun., for he receiveth them even as Moses' (D&C 28:2). In one of the greatest revelations upon Priesthood, this is more specifically expressed: 'The duty of the President of the office of the High Priesthood is to preside over the whole church, and to be like unto Moses' (D&C 107:91).

"The discussion of this question among the Saints, led to the following statement in the *Times and Seasons* (6:922) by John Taylor, then the editor: 'The President [of the Church] stands in the Church as Moses did to the children of Israel, according to the revelations.'"[8]

The Lord will raise up the man who will lead the children of Israel back to build up the city of the New Jerusalem (D&C 103:16). That man is the President of the Church. He may be the present president of the Church or any one of his successors.

Doctrine and Covenants 105 outlines the rest of the nine prerequisites for the redemption of Zion. The people must receive and be taught through their temple endowment. The Lord instituted the endowment "that [the elders] themselves may be prepared, and that my people may be taught more perfectly, and have experience, and know more perfectly concerning their duty, and the things which I require at their hands. And this cannot be brought to pass until mine elders are endowed with power from on high" (D&C 105:10–11). Zion will never be established except by a people who receive and live up to their temple endowment, which is to help them become pure in heart (D&C 97:12–16). This revelation was given in 1834, and the Kirtland Temple was completed two years later, in 1836. The dedication of the temple on 3 April 1836 was a great historical incident spoken of by the prophets. The collective outpouring of the Spirit accompanied this dedication.[9] Yet that endowment of spiritual power does not fulfill the prophecy; each member must be personally endowed as well.

The people must also be taught the fulness of the gospel of Jesus Christ more perfectly at the temple of the Lord. The temple is the Lord's university. It is a degree-granting university, fully accredited in every aspect, in which we prepare ourselves for the celestial degree. Therefore, when the Lord stated that the Saints must be taught more perfectly, he was referring to the building of the temple and the receiving of personal endowments. In the temple endowment, we are instructed how to live; then we covenant to live as we have been instructed. Doing work for our dead also brings us personal blessings of increased knowledge. It is true that to bring our ancestors out of the spirit world, we must vicariously perform their temple ordinances. That is a vital and integral doctrine of the gospel. But we are also beneficiaries because we have a constant reminder of those covenants, better enabling us to know how to live and what the Lord requires at our hands. With this knowledge, we may become a pure people, a Zion people, ready to establish the center place of Zion in the tent of Israel. If the relatively few Saints in 1833 who had not received their temple endowments could have redeemed Zion had they hearkened to the Lord, certainly we now have enough temples built and people endowed for Zion to be redeemed if the rest of the Lord's prerequisites are met.

The third prerequisite of the redemption of Zion is that when the people are prepared, the Lord will fight the Saints' battles for them. To the elders of the Church, he says: "For behold, I do not require at [your] hands to fight the battles of Zion; for, as I said in a former commandment [D&C 98:37], even so will I fulfil—I will fight your battles" (D&C 105:14). Zion's Camp had been offered divine intervention but had not been faithful (D&C 105:15–19). The Lord had told Zion's Camp four months earlier that from that very day he would give them power to prevail over their enemies (D&C 103:6). The same promise is applicable to us. From this very day, if we will become the Zion people that we have the potential of being, the Lord will fight our battles. But if we again let jarrings and contentions and the designs of the world enter our lives, the Lord will not redeem Zion.

We occasionally hear that Heber C. Kimball prophesied that there would not be a yellow dog left to wag its tail in resistance to the Saints' return to Jackson County.[10] This prophecy has been tied to another prophecy—that Zion will be swept clean. These are actually two separate prophecies and should not be linked together. The sweeping clean of Missouri may have already been fulfilled. During the Civil War, opposing factions called the Bushwhackers and the Jayhawkers battled in Missouri. Through these and other battles, Zion, or Missouri, was swept clean, leaving only chimneys in place of farms and houses.[11] The yellow dog prophecy may be referring to another kind of resistance. The return of specified Saints to Missouri will come about in a natural way; they will have no resistance from the inhabitants. Today, many members live happily in Missouri without resistance. The Lord said he would fight our battles; he will take care of whatever resistance is raised if we trust him.

The fourth prerequisite for redeeming Zion is the establishment of stakes around the center place, New Jerusalem. The Lord commanded: "that as many as have come up hither, that can stay in the region round about, let them stay; and those that cannot stay, who have families in the east, let them tarry for a little season, inasmuch as my servant Joseph shall appoint unto them" (D&C 105:20–21).

The people dwelling in the regions round about as appointed seems to refer to the establishment of stakes around the New Jerusalem for the center place, or center pole, of the tent of Israel to be put in place. Earlier, when the members of the Church were under great persecution, the Lord had declared that Zion would "not be moved out of her place, notwithstanding her children are scattered" (D&C 101:17). The pure in heart would return "that the prophets might be fulfilled" (D&C 101:19). Then he would appoint other places of gathering, which would "be called stakes, for the curtains or the strength of Zion" (D&C 101:21). (Note again the association with the tabernacle of Moses.) The Lord then admonished, "And let all my people who dwell in the regions round about be very faithful, and prayerful, and humble before me, and reveal not the things which I have revealed unto them, until it is wisdom in me that they should be revealed. Talk not of judgments, neither boast of faith nor of mighty works, but carefully gather together, as much in one region as can be, consistently with the feelings of the people" (D&C 105:23–24).

To understand the Lord's instructions not to disclose or boast of the revelation concerning Zion, we must know the background of what had taken place there. In 1831, the Saints arrived in Independence in the midst of a rough group of settlers. There, they boasted of building up Zion and implied that they were going to drive out all of the inhabitants. This attitude undoubtedly contributed to their being driven out. The Lord chastised the Saints for their behavior and admonished them to go about their future building up of stakes quietly, without conceit, living the gospel and preparing themselves for the Second Coming.

The Lord instructs the people to "find favor in the eyes of the people, until the army of Israel becomes very great" (D&C 105:26). This is the fifth prerequisite of the redemption of Zion. Estimates of the number of people driven out of Missouri range from approximately three thousand to twelve thousand. The total membership of the Church at the time is not known, but lower estimates seem more correct. Still, when we compare the larger number (twelve thousand) to our present Church membership (nearly ten million), we can see that the army of Israel has become very great. We do not know how many soldiers the Lord requires in his army of Israel, but it's obvious that his ranks have grown tremendously. As Church membership continues to skyrocket, we need not fear that the Lord will have sufficient men and women to bring to pass his great work of redeeming Zion.

The sixth prerequisite of the redemption of Zion concerns the purchase, not conquest, of the land of New Jerusalem. The Lord will "soften the hearts of the people, as [he] did the heart of Pharaoh, from time to time, until [his] servant Joseph Smith, Jun., and [his] elders, whom [he has] appointed. . . . [will send] wise men, to fulfil that which I have commanded concerning the purchasing of all the lands in Jackson county that can be purchased, and in the adjoining counties round about" (D&C 105:27–28).

The Church has very quietly purchased land in Missouri. Much speculation has been made about how much land has been bought, but though the amount of land in Missouri that is owned by the Church is not known, we can be assured that the work is progressing.

A few years ago, the governor of Missouri issued a decree abolishing the extermination order issued by former Governor Lilburn W. Boggs, which had stated that no Mormon was welcome in Missouri. This is a noteworthy example of hearts being softened. Other events have taken place and will yet take place to that same effect. In our day, for instance, political leaders and dignitaries of the United States and of foreign countries who come to Utah visit the prophet and the First Presidency. Though some visits may be mere political moves, nonetheless, they are a recognition of the kingdom of Zion. Again, how much more is required will be known when the Lord reveals it.

Earlier, the Lord revealed that the only way Zion will be built up is by purchase or by blood, and the Lord forbade the shedding of blood (D&C 63:27–31). Therefore, the Lord instructed the Saints in other areas to send money to the land of Zion to make purchases. The faithful would receive an inheritance in Zion (D&C 63:37–41, 47–48). Just as David was forbidden to build the temple because he was a man of war (1 Chronicles 28:2–3), it seems that we, as a people, will also be forbidden to enter Zion if we attempt to obtain the land by force. The land in Missouri will be purchased, not conquered (D&C 105:28–29).

The Church and the kingdom of God will become banners to the world. That is the seventh prerequisite. The Lord's "army [will] become very great" and become pure and holy, or sanctified before the Lord, "that it may become fair as the sun, and clear as the moon, and that her banners may be terrible unto all nations" (D&C 105:31).[12] The banner of Zion, the ensign—the Book of Mormon and the Church—must be waved for the world to see. Eventually, the New Jerusalem will become the banner acknowledged by the Gentiles, or the world (Isaiah 60:3). When that happens, the army of Israel will become great and also become sanctified. "The kingdoms of this world [will] be constrained to acknowledge that the kingdom of Zion is in very deed the kingdom of our God and his Christ; therefore let us become subject unto her laws" (D&C 105:32). The character of the people of the Church both individually and collectively will lead other nations to recognize the hand of God upon Zion (D&C 45:64–71). Although this prophecy is not yet fulfilled, the recognition of the Church and kingdom by the people and nations of the world is coming to pass.

The reinstitution of the law of consecration in Zion, the New Jerusalem, is prerequisite number eight. The Lord commanded the Saints to "let those commandments which [he has] given concerning Zion and her law be executed and fulfilled, after her redemption" (D&C 105:34). The Lord commanded the early Saints called to move to Missouri to covenant to live the law of consecration (D&C 72). The Lord then declared: "There has been a day of calling, but the time has come for a day of choosing; and let those be chosen that are worthy. And it shall be manifest unto my servant, by the voice of the Spirit, those that are chosen; and they shall be sanctified" (D&C 105:35–36).

Some have believed that all the members of the Church would leave their homes and go to Missouri; however, that concept is not clearly taught in the scriptures. We cannot establish the center place without having stakes. Those who will go to Jackson County will be called in an orderly manner. The call will come on an individual basis as people are needed to establish the center place of Zion. But there will be multitudes who will not be called. Bear in mind that those who are not called are not necessarily unworthy or less worthy than those who are called. The stakes must be maintained, and leadership will be needed in those stakes. The call to Jackson County is simply a different stewardship that a person will be given for establishing the Zion society there. Those people will be united in living the principles of the law of the celestial kingdom, including the law of consecration.

The ninth prerequisite requires us to do missionary work in the meantime. The Lord admonishes us to "sue for peace, not only to the people that have smitten [us], but also to all people; and lift up an ensign of peace, and make a proclamation of peace unto the ends of the earth" (D&C 105:38–39). Those who preach the gospel are the publishers of peace (Mosiah 15:13–18). The Latter-day Saints are to preach the gospel to the world. Today we have about fifty thousand missionaries in many countries of the world. Still other countries are being prepared by the Lord. Missionary work will continue into the Millennium, and the Lord will proclaim when enough people have heard the gospel message for Zion to be established.

Of the nine prerequisites outlined by the Lord for the redemption of Zion, all have been met to one degree or another; and many Saints are prepared to meet further requirements. To prepare for the redemption of Zion on an individual basis, we must make ourselves a Zion people, live the principles of the gospel to fulfill our temple covenants, and preach the gospel to all the world. May we prepare ourselves further and become a Zion people, pure in heart.

NOTES

1. David O. McKay, "Zion Shall Flourish," *Instructor,* February 1959, 33.

2. Joseph Smith, *Teachings of the Prophet Joseph Smith,* sel. Joseph Fielding Smith (Salt Lake City: Deseret Book, 1976), 362.

3. Ibid.

4. Brigham Young taught that "Zion will extend, eventually, all over the world"; in *Journal of Discourses,* 26 vols. (London: Latter-day Saints' Book Depot, 1854–86), 9:138. Because this is a millennial condition and will happen following the establishment of the city of the New Jerusalem, it is only mentioned here.

5. Smith, *Teachings of the Prophet Joseph Smith,* 160.

6. Ibid., 362.

7. See James Hastings, *Dictionary of the Bible,* ed. Frederick C. Grant and H. H. Rowley, rev. ed. (New York: Charles Scribner's Sons, 1963), 689–90.

8. John A. Widtsoe, *Evidences and Reconciliations,* arr. G. Homer Durham (Salt Lake City: Bookcraft, 1960), 248.

9. Joseph Smith, *History of The Church of Jesus Christ of Latter-day Saints,* ed. B. H. Roberts, 2d ed. rev., 7 vols. (Salt Lake City: The Church of Jesus Christ of Latter-day Saints, 1932–51), 2:427–28.

10. *Deseret News,* 23 May 1931, as cited in Roy W. Doxey, *Zion in the Last Days* (Salt Lake City: Olympus Publishing, 1965), 55.

11. The destruction of Missouri fulfilled a prophecy of Joseph Smith to General Doniphan. See B. H. Roberts, *A Comprehensive History of The Church of Jesus Christ of Latter-day Saints, Century One,* 6 vols. (Salt Lake City: Deseret News Press, 1930), vol. 1, chapter 39.

12. This is an allusion to the Song of Solomon. Most people are aware that Joseph Smith said the Song of Solomon was not inspired; they may wonder why the Lord used it here. Perhaps the author of the Song of Solomon was quoting from something else or perhaps some things in it are inspired.

CHAPTER TWELVE

MARRIAGE AND FAMILY: "ORDAINED OF GOD"

GUY L. DORIUS

The importance of marriage and family in the great plan of happiness has been emphasized by the Lord through prophets for most of this dispensation. As recently as 23 September 1995, the First Presidency and the Quorum of the Twelve Apostles issued a proclamation on the family. President Gordon B. Hinckley stated: "We, the First Presidency and the Council of the Twelve Apostles of The Church of Jesus Christ of Latter-day Saints, solemnly proclaim that marriage between a man and a woman is ordained of God and that the family is central to the Creator's plan for the eternal destiny of His children."[1]

The need for this proclamation is evidenced by the increase in marital dissolution and unhappy families. Many people seem to take lightly the important doctrine of marriage. The importance of marriage and family is not new doctrine but a reiteration of doctrine taught by many leaders of the Church. In 1970 Elder Bruce R. McConkie taught: "From the moment of birth into mortality to the time we are married in the temple, everything we have in the whole gospel system is to prepare and qualify us to enter that holy order of matrimony which makes us husband and wife in this life and in the world to come.

"Then from the moment we are sealed together by the

Guy L. Dorius is assistant professor of Church history and Doctrine at Brigham Young University.

power and authority of the holy priesthood—the power to bind on earth and have it sealed eternally in the heavens—from that moment everything connected with revealed religion is designed to help us keep the terms and conditions of our marriage covenant, so that this covenant will have efficacy, virtue, and force in the life to come.

"Thus celestial marriage is the crowning ordinance of the gospel, the crowning ordinance of the house of the Lord. Thus the family unit is the most important organization in time or in eternity.

"And thus we should have more interest in and concern for our families than for anything else in life."[2]

Because of the great emphasis on marriage and family, it is fundamental for Latter-day Saints to consider the historical and doctrinal foundations of these teachings. Although principles pertaining to marriage and family are taught throughout the scriptures, the most specific instructions are found in the Doctrine and Covenants, which provides a scriptural framework of marriage and family relations.

THE HISTORY

The central role that marriage has in the gospel plan is presented in the recent proclamation to the Church. In it we read: "The family is ordained of God. Marriage between man and woman is essential to His eternal plan."[3]

This latest affirmation of the importance of marriage has its roots early in the history of the Church. Joseph had strong family ties and always viewed his own family as crucial to his happiness. Yet alternative views concerning marriage were taught among religious sects in the early nineteenth century. When the Saints were instructed to move from New York State to the Kirtland, Ohio, area, they came into contact with the Shakers. The Shakers taught that to receive a higher degree of salvation, one had to be celibate. The Lord gave a revelation to be read to the Shaker community (D&C 49), in which he refuted the Shaker doctrine that taught against marriage. The Lord stated: "And again, verily I say unto you, that whoso forbiddeth to marry is not ordained of God, for marriage is ordained of God unto man" (D&C 49:15). Therefore, in the early days of the Restoration, the doctrine of marriage was firmly established as a God-ordained ordinance. Additionally, the Lord addressed the objection the Shakers had to the intimate relationship between a husband and wife in bringing children into the world. The revelation continued: "Wherefore, it is lawful that he should have one wife, and they twain shall be one flesh, and all this that the earth might answer the end of its creation; and that it might be filled with the measure of man, according to his creation before the world was made"(D&C 49:16–17). Therefore, not only marriage, or the companionship of a husband and wife, was revealed to be ordained of God but also the bringing of children into the world was revealed as an essential part of God's plan in the very creation of the earth.

At the same time, the Lord gave instruction (known as "the law") to the brethren in Ohio in which he reiterated the commandments. He then stated: "Thou shalt love thy wife with all thy heart, and shalt cleave unto her and none else. And he that looketh upon a woman to lust after her shall deny the faith, and shall not have the Spirit; and if he repents not he shall be cast out. Thou shalt not commit adultery; and he that committeth adultery, and repenteth not, shall be cast out" (D&C 42:22–24). Not only was the Lord commanding unity and complete fidelity in marriage but he connected fidelity and having the Spirit and characterized lust as denying the faith and losing membership in the kingdom. At approximately the same time the Lord declared that marriage was "ordained of God," he was developing the doctrine that marriage was crucial in the spiritual development of Church members.

Other evidence suggests that the brethren were teaching the importance of marriage early in Church history. The first edition of the Doctrine and Covenants (1835) included an article titled "Marriage." Elder B. H. Roberts stated: "When the Book of Doctrine and Covenants was presented to the several quorums of the priesthood of the Church for acceptance in the general assembly of that body, the 17th of August, 1835, an article on 'Marriage' was presented by W. W. Phelps, which for many years was published in the Doctrine and Covenants. It was not a revelation, nor was it presented as such to the general assembly of the priesthood. It was an article, however, that represented the views of the assembly on the subject of marriage at that time."[4]

This article addressed the issue of civil marriage and instructed that marriage should be "celebrated with prayer and thanksgiving."[5] It is obvious that the Church taught that marriage was positive and desirable. Joseph was not present at the conference when the article was presented, but it remained in the Doctrine and Covenants until it was replaced by section 132 in 1876.

There is evidence that Joseph had received earlier revelations that gave him insights concerning future laws and keys that would seal a husband and wife in the covenant of marriage after the resurrection. Elder Roberts wrote that there is good reason to believe that Joseph had received the information in section 132 of the Doctrine and Covenants, the section on eternal marriage, as early as 1831.[6] Why was the revelation not written until 1843? One obvious answer is that the keys, or authorization, needed to seal marriages for eternity had not yet been restored. That which was revealed to Joseph Smith at such an early date emphasized the keys of the priesthood being used to perform marriage. Earlier, the Lord revealed that the keys of baptism were needed for the ordinance of baptism to be recognized by God (see D&C 13; 22). Joseph Smith and Oliver Cowdery learned from the translation of the Book of Mormon plates that authority to perform baptisms was necessary. Following their sincere prayer inquiring about baptism, John the Baptist restored the keys of the Aaronic Priesthood, including the keys of baptism.

Similarly, while Joseph Smith and Sidney Rigdon were translating the Bible, they had questions concerning the teachings on marriage, and they sought the Lord's guidance. The Lord revealed to Joseph the essential elements of the law and the authority necessary to be married in eternity. Although the Prophet may have understood, the Church had not had sufficient time to understand such important doctrine nor had the keys been restored.

THE RESTORATION

It is quite well known that on 3 April 1836 in the Kirtland Temple, Joseph Smith received important keys to the fulness of priesthood ordinances. Less well known is that after the appearances of the Savior and Moses and before the appearance of Elijah, Elias appeared and committed the dispensation of Abraham. Joseph recorded: "After this, Elias appeared, and committed the dispensation of the gospel of Abraham, saying that in us and our seed all generations after us should be blessed" (D&C 110:12). This was an important event in the unveiling of eternal, or celestial, marriage. Elder Bruce R. McConkie taught: "Now what was the *gospel of Abraham?* Obviously it was the commission, the mission, the endowment and power, the message of salvation, given to Abraham. And what was this? It was a divine promise that both in the world and out of the world his seed should continue 'as innumerable as the stars; or, if ye were to count the sand upon the seashore ye could not number them.' (D. & C. 132:30; Gen. 17; Abra. 2:1–12.)

"Thus the gospel of Abraham was one of celestial marriage. . . . It was a gospel or commission to provide a lineage for the elect portion of the pre-existent spirits, a gospel to provide a household in eternity for those who live the fulness of the celestial law. This power and commission is what Elias restored, and as a consequence, the righteous among all future generations were assured of the blessings of a continuation of the seeds forever, even as it was with Abraham of old."[7] Further emphasis was given to the importance of children and family in the implications of eternal marriage.

Elias restored the dispensation in which the Abrahamic covenant was made, thus restoring the doctrine of celestial marriage. This restoration was still not enough for celestial marriage to last through the eternities. It was therefore necessary for Elijah to return with keys of the priesthood. Why was Elijah's return so necessary? Joseph Smith answered: "Why send Elijah? Because he holds the keys of the authority to administer in all the ordinances of the Priesthood; and without the authority is given, the ordinances could not be administered in righteousness."[8]

Through those keys and authority Joseph Smith was now able to officiate in all of the ordinances necessary for the salvation and exaltation of men and women. Elijah restored the keys that seal all blessings to us for time and all eternity. President Ezra Taft Benson taught: "Elijah brought the keys of sealing powers—that power which *seals* a man to a woman and *seals* their posterity to them endlessly, that which *seals* their forefathers to them all the way back to Adam. This is the power and order that Elijah revealed—that *same order* of priesthood which God gave to Adam and to all the ancient patriarchs which followed after him."[9]

THE LAW

Joseph Smith was then prepared to instruct the Saints in celestial marriage. Not until 1843 were the revelations issued that teach the doctrine of celestial marriage. Joseph gave the following instructions to the Church: "In the celestial glory there are three heavens or degrees; and in order to obtain the highest, a man must enter into this order of the priesthood [meaning the new and everlasting covenant of marriage]; and if he does not, he cannot obtain it. He may enter into the other, but that is the end of his kingdom; he cannot have an increase" (D&C 131:1–4). This section introduces to the Church the need to have the new and everlasting covenant of marriage to be exalted. It also defines what is meant by exaltation when it indicates that those who do not receive this covenant will not have an increase. This sounds much like the promise made to Abraham that his seed would be innumerable not only in this life but throughout all eternity. Therefore, the restoration of the blessings of Abraham enable Saints in this dispensation to enjoy a continuation of the promises made to him.

The Lord continued to clarify the doctrine of marriage in Doctrine and Covenants 132. The revelation first exhorts those reading to "prepare thy heart to receive and obey the instructions which I am about to give unto you; for all those who have this law revealed unto them must obey the same" (D&C 132:3). Why prepare our hearts? With increasing divorce rates, it is understandable that the Lord teaches that successful marriages take a prepared heart. He is also about to reveal that not only do certain marriages continue through eternity but that some will not.

The revelation then gives the law of marriage and the conditions of the law: "For behold, I reveal unto you a new and an everlasting covenant; and if ye abide not that covenant, then are ye damned; for no one can reject this covenant and be permitted to enter into my glory. For all who will have a blessing at my hands shall abide the law which was appointed for that blessing, and the conditions thereof, as were instituted from before the foundation of the world. And as pertaining to the new and everlasting covenant, it was instituted for the fulness of my glory; and he that receiveth a fulness thereof must and shall abide the law, or he shall be damned, saith the Lord God" (D&C 132:4–6). The idea of a "new and everlasting covenant" was familiar doctrine for the Saints. In section 22 of the Doctrine and Covenants they learned of the new and everlasting covenant of baptism. The covenant of baptism initiates our salvation and exaltation, but to enter into God's glory, one must accept the new and everlasting covenant of marriage. Those who do not will be damned, or in other words, denied eternal increase.

The revelation then teaches the conditions that make this law binding: "And verily I say unto you, that the conditions of this law are these: All covenants, contracts, bonds, obligations, oaths, vows, performances, connections, associations, or expectations, that are not made and entered into and sealed by the Holy Spirit of promise, of him who is anointed, both as well for time and for all eternity, and that too most holy, by revelation and commandment through the medium of mine anointed, whom I have appointed on the earth to hold this power (and I have appointed unto my servant Joseph to hold this power in the last days, and there is never but one on the earth at a time on whom this power and the keys of this priesthood are conferred), are of no efficacy, virtue, or force in and after the resurrection from the dead; for all contracts that are not made unto this end have an end when men are dead" (D&C 132:7).

Stated simply, covenants made in this life must be sealed by the Holy Spirit of Promise to be recognized in the next life. At the time of the revelation Joseph held the keys, or the power that Elijah had committed to him, to initiate covenants that would be valid after death. Those included the new and everlasting covenant of marriage, or celestial marriage. In the Church today, we sustain the present prophet as the only one authorized to exercise those keys. Though the keys may be delegated to such others as sealers in the temple, they are always used under the direction of the living prophet.

The Lord reiterates this point by reminding us that anything of this world, "whether it be ordained of men, by thrones, or principalities, or powers, or things of name, whatsoever they may be, that are not by me or by my word, saith the Lord, shall be thrown down, and shall not remain after men are dead, neither in nor after the resurrection, saith the Lord your God" (D&C 132:13).

The revelation clarifies which marriages do not endure through eternity and provides two examples of marriage that do not fall under the eternal nature of the new and everlasting covenant of marriage. The first of these involves a man who marries a woman "not by me nor by my word" (D&C 132:15). This marriage union is not of force after death. These marriages are civil marriages which generally do not pretend to have eternal consequence.

The ser   of marriage is discussed in verse 18 which has ι   ·e. A man may "make a covenant with her for ι.   ·l eternity," but without the proper authority,   vill not exist beyond death. These marriages ma,   ʿormed by well-meaning individuals who belie   marriage but do not understand the necessity ι   thority. These may also include marriages in wι.   may write their own vows and include eternal ι   ·ther of these marriages is valid after death. Aι   ιas stated: "Therefore, when they are out of thι   . they neither marry nor are given in marriage; but are .ppointed angels in heaven, which angels are ministering servants, to minister for those who are worthy of a far more, and an exceeding, and an eternal weight of glory. For these angels did not abide my law; therefore, they cannot be enlarged, but remain separately and singly, without exaltation, in their saved condition, to all eternity; and from henceforth are not gods, but are angels of God forever and ever" (D&C 132:16–17).

Finally, the Lord teaches us of the only marriage that will exist beyond death. He states: "And again, verily I say unto you, if a man marry a wife by my word, which is my law, and by the new and everlasting covenant, and it is sealed unto them by the Holy Spirit of promise, by him who is anointed, unto whom I have appointed this power and the keys of this priesthood; and it shall be said unto them—Ye shall come forth in the first resurrection; and if it be after the first resurrection, in the next resurrection; and shall inherit thrones, kingdoms, principalities, and powers, dominions, all heights and depths—then shall it be written in the Lamb's Book of Life, that he shall commit no murder whereby to shed innocent blood, and if ye abide in my covenant, and commit no murder whereby to shed innocent blood, it shall be done unto them in all things whatsoever my servant hath put upon them, in time, and through all eternity; and shall be of full force when they are out of the world; and they shall pass by the angels, and the gods, which are set there, to their exaltation and glory in all things, as hath been sealed upon their heads, which glory shall be a fulness and a continuation of the seeds forever and ever" (D&C 132:19).

From this verse we understand that to be exalted and have eternal increase, eternal marriage must be sealed upon us under the new and everlasting covenant of marriage by him who has the authority. It must be noted that part of this verse alludes to having one's calling and election made sure. Sidney B. Sperry stated: "It should be made clear that the part of verse 19 beginning with 'it shall be said unto them—Ye shall come forth in the first resurrection . . . ' does not pertain to marriage, but to having one's calling and election made sure."[10] It is interesting that in both sections 131 and 132, following the revelation of the new and everlasting covenant of marriage, there is a discussion of having one's calling and election made sure. That gives added emphasis to the doctrine of marriage as an important step toward our exaltation. Indeed, exaltation can only be enjoyed by those who are married and sealed as man and wife, to live together eternally.

It is also important to consider the language of the Lord as he discusses civil marriages in contrast to celestial marriage. As he taught us of civil marriage, in both instances he refers to a man making a "covenant with her," meaning his wife (D&C 132:15, 18). In verse 19 the idea of a man covenanting with a woman is conspicuously missing. In eternal marriage, the covenants are made with God. This covenant includes another person and involves promises and covenants with each other, but eventually it comes back to a covenant relationship between us and God. In all other forms of marriage, the vows are made to another person. We know from sad experience that covenants between individuals are easily negotiated and broken. We know that covenants with God are not negotiable. In referring to teachings of Heber C. Kimball, Hugh Nibley stated:

"As Heber C. Kimball reminded the Saints, there are no covenants made between individuals in the Church. All promises and agreements are between the individual and our Father in Heaven; all other parties, including the angels, are present only as witnesses. Therefore whether anybody else observes and keeps the promise is not my concern, but if I do not do what I have promised, what blessings can I expect?"[11]

This reminds us that if we break our marriage covenant, we are not just breaking covenants with a person, we are breaking covenants with God. It is ironic that people would hold on carefully to their baptismal covenant, but the idea of a broken marriage does not hold the same fear. The exalting power of the new and everlasting covenant of marriage must not be overlooked. The Lord invites us to consider that as he teaches us that when we accept this covenant and abide in it, "then shall they be gods, because they have no end; therefore shall they be from everlasting to everlasting, because they continue; then shall they be above all, because all things are subject unto them. Then shall they be gods, because they have all power, and the angels are subject unto them. Verily, verily, I say unto you, except ye abide my law ye cannot attain to this glory. For strait is the gate, and narrow the way that leadeth unto the exaltation and continuation of the lives, and few there be that find it, because ye receive me not in the world neither do ye know me. But if ye receive me in the world, then shall ye know me, and shall receive your exaltation; that where I am ye shall be also. This is eternal lives—to know the only wise and true God, and Jesus Christ, whom he hath sent. I am he. Receive ye, therefore, my law" (D&C 132:20–24).

The Lord ties our exaltation directly to our willingness to receive his law and abide in it. That law includes this sacred order of marriage. It is interesting that the scriptures here invite us to think of "eternal lives" in contrast with "eternal life" (John 17:3). Exaltation is experienced as couples and families, not as individuals. We also learn that to receive this law is to receive the Savior. It may be concluded that to truly know Christ, we must experience marriage under the new and everlasting covenant.

Many suppose that we do not have the fulness of the law because we don't practice plural marriage. Indeed, the remaining verses of section 132 deal with the plural marriage application of this law. But we would be wise to remember that this law is administered through the living prophet and the Lord directs him as to its current application. On 6 October 1890, President Wilford Woodruff issued a manifesto declaring the revealed end of the practice of plural marriage in The Church of Jesus Christ of Latter-day Saints. Since that time, the law of celestial marriage has been applied to the marriage of one man and one living woman at a time. Elder Bruce R. McConkie stated:

"Plural marriage is not essential to salvation or exaltation. Nephi and his people were denied the power to have more than one wife and yet they could gain every blessing in eternity that the Lord ever offered to any people. In our day, the Lord summarized by revelation the whole doctrine of exaltation and predicated it upon the marriage of one man to one woman. (D. & C. 132:1–28.) Thereafter he added the principles relative to plurality of wives with the express stipulation that any such marriages would be valid only if authorized by the President of the Church. (D. & C. 132:7, 29–66.)"[12]

CONCLUSION

In the official proclamation on the family we read: "The divine plan of happiness enables family relationships to be perpetuated beyond the grave. Sacred ordinances and covenants available in holy temples make it possible for individuals to return to the presence of God and for families to be united eternally."[13]

We are blessed to have this modern revelation to guide us in our return to our Father in Heaven and to remind us of the sacred obligation we have to keep the covenants we have made. We must realize that our marriages and families play an important role in our relationship with Christ and therefore take seriously the commitment we have made to build celestial families.

NOTES

1. Gordon B. Hinckley, "The Family," *Ensign,* November 1995, 102.

2. Bruce R. McConkie, "Salvation Is a Family Affair," *Improvement Era,* June 1970, 43–44.

3. Hinckley, "Family," 102.

4. B. H. Roberts, Introduction to *History of The Church of Jesus Christ of Latter-day Saints,* by Joseph Smith, ed. B. H. Roberts, 2d ed. rev., 7 vols. (Salt Lake City: The Church of Jesus Christ of Latter-day Saints, 1932–51), 5:xxx.

5. 1835 edition of the Doctrine and Covenants, 251.

6. Roberts, Introduction, xxix–xxx. Elder Roberts taught: "There is indisputable evidence that the revelation making known this marriage law was given to the Prophet as early as 1831. In that year, and thence intermittently up to 1833, the Prophet was engaged in a revision of the English Bible text under the inspiration of God, Sidney Rigdon in the main acting as his scribe. As he began his revision with the Old Testament, he would be dealing with the age of the Patriarchs in 1831. He was doubtless struck with the favor in which the Lord held the several Bible Patriarchs of that period, notwithstanding they had a plurality of wives. What more natural than that he should inquire of the Lord at that time, when his mind must have been impressed with the fact—Why, O Lord, didst Thou justify Thy servants, Abraham, Isaac and Jacob; as also Moses, David, and Solomon, in the matter of their having many wives and concubines (see opening paragraph of the Revelation)? In answer to that inquiry came the revelation, though not then committed to writing.

"Corroborative evidences of the fact of the revelation having been given thus early in the Prophet's career are to be found in the early charges against the Church about its belief in 'polygamy.'"

Elder Roberts continues: "In this article on marriage the following sentence occurs:

"'Inasmuch as this Church of Christ has been reproached with the crime of fornication and polygamy, we declare that we believe that one man should have one wife, and one woman but one husband, except in case of death, when either is at liberty to marry again.'

"From this it is evident that as early at least as 1835 a charge of polygamy was made against the Church. Why was that the case unless the subject of 'polygamy' had been mooted within the Church? Is it not evident that some one to whom the Prophet had confided the knowledge of the revelation he had received concerning the rightfulness of plural marriage—under certain circumstances—had unwisely made some statement concerning the matter?"

7. Bruce R. McConkie, *Mormon Doctrine,* 2d ed. (Salt Lake City: Bookcraft, 1966), 219–20.

8. Joseph Smith, *Teachings of the Prophet Joseph Smith,* sel. Joseph Fielding Smith (Salt Lake City: Deseret Book, 1976), 172.

9. Ezra Taft Benson, "What I Hope You Will Teach Your Children about the Temple," *Ensign,* August 1985, 10.

10. Sidney B. Sperry, *Doctrine and Covenants Compendium* (Salt Lake City: Bookcraft, 1960), 723.

11. Hugh Nibley, *Approaching Zion,* ed. Don E. Norton (Salt Lake City: Deseret Book and Foundation for Ancient Research and Mormon Studies, 1989), 385. The reference from Heber C. Kimball may come from *Journal of Discourses,* 26 vols. (London: Latter-day Saints' Book Depot, 1854–86), 6:127.

12. McConkie, *Mormon Doctrine,* 578–79.

13. Hinckley, "Family," 102.

CHAPTER THIRTEEN

BIBLICAL LANGUAGE AND IMAGERY IN THE DOCTRINE AND COVENANTS

D. KELLY OGDEN

Modern revelations compiled in the Doctrine and Covenants, the only book of scripture given originally in English, contain some fascinating similarities to the language used in ancient revelations in the Holy Bible. Although the one record is distanced from the other in time and space—thousands of years and thousands of miles apart—there are remarkable parallels in language style and expression. What follows is an examination of this unique phenomenon: throughout history God has spoken through his prophets and apostles and his Son using analogies and figurative expressions that are timeless and fit a wide divergence of cultural and geographical settings.

There is a plausible rationale for the similarities of language between the ancient and the modern revelations. Joseph Smith, the receiver of most of the latter-day revelations, grew up in the revivalist culture of western New York in the early 1800s and was known to be a student of the Bible. Certainly Bible-style language could then appear in his own writings. But in addition to that, if the author of the revelations in both cases is the same Person, shouldn't some similarities be apparent? Would an author, even God,

D. Kelly Ogden is associate professor of ancient scripture at Brigham Young University.

use similar kinds of expressions addressing such different peoples in such disparate settings? God himself has said: "Know ye not that the testimony of two nations is a witness unto you that I am God, that I remember one nation like unto another? Wherefore, *I speak the same words unto one nation like unto another.* And when the two nations shall run together the testimony of the two nations shall run together also. . . . For I command all men, both *in the east and in the west* . . . that they shall write the words which I speak unto them" (2 Nephi 29:8, 11; emphasis added).

We may expect, therefore, to see similarities in phraseology and figures of speech used in the two scriptural records. Indeed, there are many familiar-sounding words and expressions. Not only are such actual Hebrew terms as *amen, Satan, sabaoth, seraph,* and *hosanna* employed in modern scripture, but many standard idiomatic phrases are represented, such as "children of men," "children of Israel," "house of Israel," "house of David," and "house of Judah." *House* is often used with its metaphorical meaning of "posterity," as "the house of Aaron" (D&C 84:27), "their house shall be left unto them desolate" (D&C 84:115), and storms, winds, and rains "beat upon their house" (D&C 90:5). Other phrases include "anger or wrath kindled," "stirred up to anger," and "Lord of hosts" ("Lord of *Sabaoth*" occurs several times; the word has nothing to do with the Sabbath; *tzvaot* in Hebrew means "hosts").

Another example of biblical phraseology evident in the Doctrine and Covenants is that of the Lord "visiting" his people with blessing or punishment: "in the day of visitation and of wrath" (D&C 56:1); "I may visit them in the day of visitation. . . . I will visit and soften their hearts" (124:8–9). People in the ancient Semitic world did not just die; they "taste[d] of death," a much more graphic expression perpetuated in modern revelation (D&C 42:46, 47). Time is measured with the phrase "for the space of . . ." five years, a thousand years, half an hour, or a season (D&C 64:21; 71:2; 88:95, 110). Rather than a single verb, a series of verbal expressions is typical of Hebraic writing; for example, "Arise and shine forth" (D&C 115:5); "awake, and arise, and come forth" (D&C 117:2); and "arise and come up and stand" (D&C 124:103).

As in the Bible, so the Doctrine and Covenants refers to the coming of the Bridegroom in terms of a fig tree, a thief in the night, and a woman in travail.

As in the Bible world in the east, so the modern revelations in the west speak of taking up your cross (D&C 23:6), girding up your loins (D&C 27:15; 36:8), having your lamps trimmed and burning (D&C 33:17), putting on armor (D&C 27:15), gathering in tares (D&C 38:12), pruning the vineyard (D&C 24:19), and being laden with many sheaves (D&C 75:5).

Following are three dramatic examples of biblical expressions used again in this modern day in similar but enhanced context.

THREE BIBLICAL EXPRESSIONS IN MODERN REVELATION

"They are as grass" (D&C 124:7). From a psalmist and from the prophet Isaiah, we learn the symbolism of grass. "As for man, his days are as grass: as a flower of the field, so he flourisheth. For the wind passeth over it, and it is gone; and the place thereof shall know it no more." (Psalm 103:15–16.) "All flesh is grass, and all the goodliness thereof is as the flower of the field: The grass withereth, the flower fadeth: because the spirit of the Lord bloweth upon it: surely the people is grass. The grass withereth, the flower fadeth: but the word of our God shall stand for ever." (Isaiah 40:6–8.)

Grass was a physical similitude of the transitoriness of man. With the heavy rains of wintertime, grass flourishes and spreads its velvety green carpet even over the barren wilderness; but with the wisp of the hot desert wind, it is gone. The blades are vivacious and vigorous one day, vanished the next. So is the life of man.

The same image appears also in Doctrine and Covenants 124:2–3, 7. The Lord commanded the Prophet Joseph Smith to "make a solemn proclamation of my gospel. . . .

This proclamation shall be made to all the kings of the world . . . to the honorable president-elect, and the high-minded governors of the nation in which you live, and to all the nations of the earth. . . . Call ye, therefore, upon them with loud proclamation, and with your testimony, fearing them not, for *they are as grass,* and all their glory as the flower thereof which soon falleth."

"Stand by the wall" (D&C 121:15). To twentieth-century English ears the phrase "pisseth against the wall" (1 Samuel 25:22, 34; 1 Kings 14:10) is a vulgar, even offensive expression. It is, however, a superb illustration of the lusty, down-to-earth figures of speech used by ancient Hebrew writers, who were, in a very vivid sense, literary artists, painters of powerful mental pictures that conjured up lasting images and impressions. The phrase "any that pisseth against the wall"—that is, any male who urinates on a wall (which for females is a physical impossibility)—involves the concept of *exterminating a family.* The same idiom (without the offensive term) occurs, with the same meaning, in Doctrine and Covenants 121:15: "And not many years hence, that they and their posterity shall be swept from under heaven, saith God, that not one of them is left to stand by the wall."

"As the dews of Carmel" (D&C 128:19). Dew was of vital importance to agriculture in the ancient Holy Land during a five- to six-month period with no rain. Great humidity produces moisture during the dry season resulting in dew at night. In Hosea 14:5 the Lord says: "I will be as the dew unto Israel" (also Genesis 27:28; Deuteronomy 33:28; Zechariah 8:12). Doctrine and Covenants 128:19 contains another extraordinary illustration of how prophetic imagery used in the land of the Bible carries over even into latter-day revelation. Mount Carmel is a mountain range in the northwest of the Holy Land and is used in Old Testament writings as a symbol of richness and fruitfulness. Hebrew *Kerem-El* means "Garden of God" (Isaiah 33:9; 35:2; Jeremiah 50:19). The Lord uses this mountain in Israel and its unique climatic condition to voice prophecy: "As the dews of Carmel, so shall the knowledge of God descend upon [the Latter-day Saints]." The power of God's reference is realized when one learns that Mount Carmel averages 250 dew-nights a year! This fact is impressive testimonial of the divine provenance of modern scripture—the Prophet Joseph Smith certainly would not have known that geographical detail. But it was not Joseph Smith speaking in the revelation; it was the Lord drawing an image from the Old Land and dropping it into a modern revelation to teach a truth.

OTHER ANCIENT LITERARY DEVICES IN MODERN SCRIPTURE

Other figurative language and literary devices are also evident in modern scripture as in the old. Following are numerous examples.

A favorite and effective way that ancient Semitic writers taught was by comparing phenomena in nature with the human experience. The key word is *comparison.*

Simile

The modern revelations feature many examples of one thing resembling another, that is, explicit comparisons (employing the words *like* or *as*). People or things are "as stubble" (D&C 64:24), "as the stars" or "as the sand upon the seashore" (D&C 76:109), "as a scroll" (D&C 88:95), "as salt" (D&C 103:10), "as a flame of fire," "like the pure snow," "as the sound of the rushing of great waters" (D&C 110:3), "as serpents" (D&C 111:11), "as the dews from heaven" (D&C 121:45), "like wolves" (D&C 122:6), "as watchmen" (D&C 124:61), "like a refiner's fire, and like fuller's soap" (D&C 128:24), "as an oven" (D&C 133:64), and "like a lamb to the slaughter" (D&C 135:4).

Metaphor

The revelations feature many declarations that one thing is, or represents, another, that is, implicit comparisons. The Lord refers to "vessels of wrath" (D&C 76:33), "the lake of fire and brimstone" (D&C 76:36), "the wine-press of the fierceness of the wrath of Almighty God" (D&C 76:107), "the mother of abominations" (D&C 88:94), "the sword of mine indignation" (D&C 101:10), and "a generation of vipers" (D&C 121:23). The Savior declared, "I have trodden the wine-press alone" (D&C 133:50). Joseph Smith alluded to "the storm [that] is fully blown over" (D&C 127:1). Of course the Lord and the Prophet are not referring to physical vessels, lakes, wine-presses, swords, vipers, and storms and so forth—these images are called up to illustrate a principle or to give vivid expression to something happening in life.

Personification

In the latter-day revelations various inanimate objects or things are represented as persons or as having human characteristics. "Their eyes are full of greediness" (D&C 68:31), "the sun shall hide his face . . . and the moon shall be bathed in blood; and the stars shall become exceedingly angry" (D&C 88:87). The Lord refers to "warm hearts and friendly hands" (D&C 121:9), the "jaws of hell" (D&C 122:7), and making "hell itself shudder" (D&C 123:10). "The mountains shout for joy, and . . . valleys cry aloud. . . . The woods and all the trees of the field praise the Lord; . . . solid rocks weep for joy . . . and . . . the sun, moon, and the morning stars sing" (D&C 128:23).

Neutral objects are sometimes given masculine and feminine gender: "The earth rolls upon her wings, and the sun giveth his light by day, and the moon giveth her light by night" (D&C 88:45). "Zion shall escape if she observe to do all things whatsoever I have commanded her . . . I will visit her according to all her works . . . if she sin no more" (D&C 97:25–27). "The sun shall hide his face in shame" (D&C 133:49).

Polyptoton

The latter-day revelations feature fascinating examples of verbs used together with a cognate noun (cognate accusative). Biblical examples are "vowed a vow" (Genesis 28:20), "shouted with a great shout" (1 Samuel 4:5), "sacrificed sacrifices" (1 Samuel 11:15), "devised devices"

(Jeremiah 11:19), "divine divinations" (Ezekiel 13:23), "preach . . . the preaching" (Jonah 3:2), "lament . . . [a] lamentation" (Micah 2:4), "work a work" (Acts 13:41), and "fought a good fight" (2 Timothy 4:7). Parallels in the Doctrine and Covenants are "work a marvelous work" (D&C 18:44), "crowned with the crown" (D&C 76:108), "vex . . . with a sore vexation" (D&C 87:5), "sinned . . . a very grievous sin" (D&C 95:3), "bless her with blessings, and multiply a multiplicity of blessings upon her" (D&C 97:28), "decreed a decree" (D&C 103:5), "cursed them with a . . . curse" (D&C 104:4), and "I desired, with exceedingly great desire" (D&C 127:10).

Geographical Imagery

One who is well acquainted with the Bible knows how attached biblical writers were to their homeland. The Lord revealed his will through the minds of these prophets and historians using many images from their natural surroundings. Even if the reader of modern revelation does not expect it, he still finds an amazing number of references to images of nature, some even carried over to the western world from their native oriental milieu. It is the same God who speaks, and he uses some of the same images in the different dispensations. He refers to the "coming forth of my church out of the wilderness" (D&C 5:14). He encourages the Saints to "partake of the waters of life freely" (D&C 10:66) and to "publish it [the good news] upon the mountains, and upon every high place" (D&C 19:29). "Zion shall rejoice upon the hills and flourish" (D&C 35:24). The modern (as well as the ancient) land of promise is "a land flowing with milk and honey" (D&C 38:18). The Lord refers to "valleys to be exalted, and . . . mountains to be made low" (D&C 49:23), "a well of living water, springing up unto everlasting life" (D&C 63:23), "the stone which is cut out of the mountain without hands" (D&C 65:2), "the voice of one crying in the wilderness" (D&C 88:66), "the ax [that] is laid at the root of the trees" (D&C 97:7), "the waste places of Zion" (D&C 101:18), "a refuge from the storm" (D&C 115:6), making "solitary places to bud and to blossom" (D&C 117:7), "dews from heaven" (D&C 121:45), and "in the barren deserts . . . pools of living water; and the parched ground shall no longer be a thirsty land" (D&C 133:29).

Flora and Fauna. Various flora and fauna appropriate to ancient and modern times are mentioned in the latter-day revelations: lilies of the field, fig trees, box trees, fir trees, and pine trees; chickens, dogs, swine, horses, mules, beasts of the field, fowls of the air, fish of the sea, creeping things, serpents, vipers, lions, wolves, lambs, and eagles.

Rock, stone. As in biblical literature, so in the modern revelations, rock and stone symbolize something solid, firm, immovable (i.e., dependable, trustworthy). The Lord says "you shall have my word, my rock" (D&C 11:16), "my rock, which is my gospel" (D&C 11:24), "my church, my gospel, and my rock" (D&C 18:4, 5), "the stone of Israel" (D&C 50:44). "From thence shall the gospel roll forth . . . as a stone which is cut out of the mountain without hands" (D&C 65:2), "this stake which I have planted to be a cornerstone of Zion" (D&C 124:2).

Harvest imagery. This world is represented as a field, which God, as the great Husbandman, is preparing to bring forth fruit for harvest. Those who have not been fruitful will be "cut off"—using the agricultural image—and destroyed. "The field is white already to harvest" and the laborer "thrusteth in his sickle" (D&C 4:4). "The world is ripening" (D&C 18:6), and "they shall be gathered in" (D&C 29:8). The Saints are commanded to "thrash the nations" (D&C 35:13) and "gather the tares" (D&C 38:12). "The rebellious shall be cut off" or "plucked out" (D&C 64:35, 36), "bound in bundles" to be burned (D&C 88:94), or sifted "as chaff" (D&C 52:12). Of the wicked, the Lord says, "their basket shall not be full . . . their barns shall perish" (D&C 121:20), but of the righteous: you shall "joy in the fruit of your labors" (D&C 6:31); "you shall be laden with sheaves upon your back, for the laborer is worthy of his hire" (D&C 31:5). "He that is faithful . . . shall be kept and blessed with much fruit" (D&C 52:34), "fruit meet for their Father's kingdom" (D&C 84:58). At that point, "the harvest [is] ended" (D&C 45:2).

Vine, vineyard. Viticulture figures significantly in scriptural symbolism, ancient and modern. This world is referred to as "the Lord's vineyard" (D&C 72:2, 5), and "the Lord of the vineyard" (D&C 103:21) often alludes to his hope of much "fruit of the vine" (D&C 27:5; 89:16). "I will bless all those," says the True Vine, "who labor in my vineyard" (D&C 21:9). He calls "faithful laborers into [his] vineyard, that it may be pruned for the last time" (D&C 39:17); they are called to "prune my vineyard with a mighty pruning" (D&C 24:19). Each of the laborers is "planted in the land of [his] inheritance" (D&C 55:5), but of one who is unfruitful, the Lord says, "another will I plant in his stead" (D&C 35:18). His watchmen are expected to be "found upon the watch-tower" (D&C 101:12), to raise the warning voice, to "throw down the towers of mine enemies, and scatter their watchmen" (D&C 105:16, 30). Of his own role, the Lord of the vineyard explains in viticultural terms, "I have trodden the wine-press alone . . . ; I have trampled them in my fury, and I did tread upon them in mine anger" (D&C 133:50–51).

Sheep, shepherd, flock, lamb. Sheep have been inextricably tied to the theology of God's people since the beginning. Although the pastoral economy of ancient Israel has less significant parallel in modern Church history, yet the symbolism and imagery continue in latter-day revelation. "I am the good shepherd" (D&C 50:44) says the Lord, who was also "the Lamb, who was slain" (D&C 76:39; cf. 135:4). He calls his followers his "little flock" (D&C 6:34). He commands undershepherds to, "feed my sheep" (D&C 112:14), and while we are engaged in that "feeding" his promise is "I will take care of your flocks" (D&C 88:72). The revelations personify the various functions of the Lamb of God by speaking of "the Lamb's Book of Life" (D&C 132:19), "the marriage of the Lamb" (D&C 58:11), "the supper of the Lamb" (D&C 65:3), and "the song of the Lamb" (D&C 133:56).

Anatomical Imagery

The human body is the greatest of all God's creations. It is not surprising, therefore, to find in ancient and modern revelation references to all parts of the body: head, face, mind, eye, ear, mouth, voice, tongue, teeth, neck, arm, hand, heart, bosom, bowels, bellies, loins, seed, knee, and foot. In the English language we use body parts to express numerous processes and phenomena: we face, we eye, we lick, we mouth, we shoulder, we hand, we thumb, we stomach, and we foot. We speak of the eye of a needle, a tongue of land, the mouth of a river, the neck of a bottle, the shoulder of a road, the belly of a ship, and the foot of a mountain. In the revelations, all parts of the body—from head to foot—have their own didactic purposes. Following are examples of the Lord and his servants using all parts of the body to illustrate their teachings.

Head(s). The head usually represents the whole person: "It shall be answered with a blessing upon their heads" (D&C 25:12), or curses "answered upon the heads of the rebellious" (D&C 56:4), "lest sore judgments fall upon your heads" (D&C 82:2), and "the sin be upon the heads of the parents" (D&C 68:25). The revelations speak of "songs of everlasting joy upon their heads" (D&C 66:11), "that he may administer blessings upon the heads of the poor" (D&C 124:21). "This anointing have I put upon his head . . . [and] upon the head of his posterity after him" (D&C 124:57).

Face. The face may represent surface, as "the face of the earth" (D&C 5:33), or the face may represent the Divine Presence: "preparing the way before my face" (D&C 39:20). Rather than "be chastened and stand rebuked before my face" (D&C 95:2), we are encouraged to "seek the face of the Lord always" (D&C 101:38).

Mind(s). The mind is the center of man's thoughts (cf. the heart as the center of emotions). Of Joseph Smith the Savior one time said, "your mind became darkened" (D&C 10:2). God describes the natural man as having a "carnal mind" (D&C 67:12). Contrariwise we are counseled to be of "one mind" (D&C 45:65), with a "willing mind" (D&C 64:34), remaining "steadfast in your minds" (D&C 84:61). "Sanctify yourselves that your minds become single to God" (D&C 88:68).

The mind may also refer to the center of God's thoughts: scripture is "the mind of the Lord" (D&C 68:4), "the mind and will of the Lord" (D&C 133:61).

Eye(s). Eyes signify sight and also estimation or judgment. "Mine eyes are upon you," the Lord declares (D&C 38:7), and "abominations shall be made manifest in the eyes of all people" (D&C 35:7). If we are righteous and forgiving, the Lord will touch "the eyes of our understanding" (D&C 76:19), and we "may be justified in the eyes of the law" (D&C 64:13). Jesus referred on one occasion to an ancient prophet who "had his eye fixed on the restoration" (D&C 128:17), and he warned on another occasion that he would "make bare his holy arm in the eyes of all nations" (D&C 133:3).

Ear(s). The ear is used in relation to man's hearing, in the sense of *hearkening* or obeying: "open ye your ears and hearken" (D&C 33:1), "give ear to the words which I shall speak" (D&C 43:1), "give ear, O earth" (D&C 76:1).

The ear is also used in relation to God hearing, in the sense of responding to human cries: "the cry of the saints . . . shall cease to come up into the ears of the Lord" (D&C 87:7); let "thine ear be penetrated . . . let thine ear be inclined" (D&C 121:2, 4).

Mouth(s). As eyes are opened to see, and ears are opened to hear, so the mouth is opened to *speak* ("and he spoke" is normal for us, but the ancients preferred "and he opened his mouth and spoke"). "He shall open his mouth and declare" (D&C 24:12); "open thy mouth at all times, declaring my gospel" (D&C 28:16); "open your mouths and they shall be filled" (D&C 33:8, 10).

The mouth is the instrument or agent of communication: "by the mouth of all the holy prophets" (D&C 27:6), "by the mouth of my servants" (D&C 43:25, 30), and "in the mouth of two or three witnesses" (D&C 128:3).

The mouth is also the source of God's pronouncements: "lest I smite you by the rod of my mouth" (D&C 19:15); "every word that proceedeth forth from the mouth of God" (D&C 84:44); "until the mouth of the Lord shall name" (D&C 90:20, 21).

Voice(s). The voice represents God himself: "Hearken unto the voice of the Lord" (D&C 25:1), "the still small voice" (D&C 85:6), "the voice of him who dwells on high" (D&C 1:1).

The voice also represents the word or the message of God: "the voice of the Lord is unto all men" (D&C 1:2); "mine elect hear my voice" (D&C 29:7); "scripture [is] . . . the voice of the Lord" (D&C 68:4); "whoso receiveth not my voice is not acquainted with my voice, and is not of me" (D&C 84:52); "hear my words, which are my voice" (definition by parallelism) (D&C 84:60).

Other uses of the voice are defined in terms of sound, testimony, and witness. The Doctrine and Covenants speaks of the voices of thunders, lightnings, tempests, earthquakes, and famines (D&C 43:21–25) and the voices of judgment, mercy, and glory and honor (D&C 43:25). The Lord talks about his elders, chosen "by the voice of his Spirit" (D&C 52:1). Joseph Smith is to "preside over the conference by the voice of it" (D&C 28:10), and others "shall be appointed by the voice of the church" (D&C 38:34). Revelations refer to "the voice of the conference" (D&C 72:7), "the voice of the council" (D&C 104:53), and the "voice of the [quorum]" (D&C 107:27). A familiar idiom is used in modern as well as in ancient scripture: "lift up the voice" occurs more than twenty times in the Doctrine and Covenants.

Tongue(s). The tongue represents language. "Every man shall hear the fulness of the gospel in his own tongue" (D&C 90:11); the message will spread to all "nations, kindreds, tongues, and people" (D&C 7:3); some would even "speak with tongues" and employ the "interpretation of tongues" (D&C 46:24, 25). The tongue is also used as the instrument of language articulation or the ability to articulate: "then shall your tongue be loosed" (D&C 11:21); of others, "their tongues shall be stayed" (D&C 29:19); and in the end, "every tongue shall confess" (D&C 76:110).

Teeth. Teeth are always used in connection with bitterness and remorse in the day of judgment: "weeping, wailing, and gnashing of teeth" (D&C 19:5 and five other occurrences).

Neck. The neck represents stubbornness, a stiff unyielding attitude toward godly things: "this unbelieving and stiffnecked generation" (D&C 5:8); "the stiffneckedness of my people" (D&C 56:6); "the bands of her neck" (D&C 113:9, 10).

Arm(s). The arm is an instrument of blessing or punishment: "the arm of the Lord shall be revealed" (D&C 1:14), "for mine arm is over all the earth" (a literal impossibility, but symbolically impressive) (D&C 15:2); "the arm of the Lord shall fall" (D&C 45:45), and "they shall know mine arm and mine indignation" (D&C 56:1, definition by parallelism); on the other hand, "he would have extended his arm and supported you" (D&C 3:8); "I will encircle thee in the arms of my love" (D&C 6:20), "whose arm of mercy hath atoned for your sins" (D&C 29:1); "I am God, and mine arm is not shortened" (D&C 35:8, cf. 2 Nephi 28:32: "mine arm is lengthened out all the day long"); his disciples may be "led out of bondage . . . with a stretched-out arm" (103:17).

Hand(s). The hand represents God himself: "receive a witness from my hand" (D&C 5:32); "punishment which is given from my hand" (D&C 19:10); "inquire for yourself at my hand" (D&C 30:3); "laws which ye have received from my hand" (D&C 58:23); "appointed by the finger of the Lord . . . and dedicated by the hand of Joseph Smith" (D&C 84:3); "you have inquired of my hand to know" (D&C 132:1); "all who will have a blessing at my hands" (D&C 132:5). Hands also represent men themselves: "I will require this at their hands" (D&C 10:23); "lift up the hands which hang down" (D&C 81:5); the kingdom of God was "set up without hands" (D&C 109:72); "the keys of this dispensation are committed into your hands" (D&C 110:16).

Hands represent power and control. "The land of Zion—
I, the Lord, hold it in mine own hands" (D&C 63:25); "all
flesh is in mine hand" (D&C 61:6); "the heavens and the
earth are in mine hands" (D&C 67:2; the above three references are literally absurd but symbolically significant);
"your families are well; they are in mine hands" (D&C
100:1); "I will give this city into your hands" (D&C 111:4);
"let not my servant Joseph put his property out of his
hands" (D&C 132:57).

Hands represent instrumentality and are also an agent of
discipline: "by your hands I will work a marvelous work"
(D&C 18:44); "ordained under his hand" (literally and figuratively) (D&C 20:3); "the church shall lift up their hands
against him" (D&C 42:81); "I, the Almighty, have laid my
hands upon the nations, to scourge" (D&C 84:96); "importune for redress . . . by the hands of those who are placed
as rulers" (D&C 101:76); "established the Constitution of
this land, by the hands of wise men" (D&C 101:80).

Right and left hands are used as symbols of favor and dis-
favor: "those who are found on my left hand" (D&C 19:5)
are opposite those who may "sit down on the right hand
of the Father" (D&C 20:24); "the righteous shall be gathered on my right hand . . . and the wicked on my left
hand" (D&C 29:27).

Hands sometimes are given human qualities (personifi-
cation). The revelations speak of "holy hands" (D&C 60:7),
"chastening hand" (D&C 87:6), "fostering hand" (D&C
109:69), "friendly hands" (D&C 121:9), "damning hand"
(D&C 123:7), and "iron hand" (D&C 123:9).

The idiom "at hand" means soon or near. "The day [is]
soon at hand when the earth is ripe" (D&C 29:9); "the
kingdom of heaven is at hand" (D&C 33:10); "speaking
after the manner of the Lord, they are now nigh at hand"
(D&C 63:53).

Heart(s). Of all anatomical imagery, the hand and the
heart are used most; "he that hath clean hands, and a pure
heart" (Psalm 24:4) epitomizes the most desired qualities.

The heart is the center of emotion and devotion. The

Doctrine and Covenants has poignant examples: "you cried unto me in your heart" (D&C 6:22); "cleave unto me with all your heart" (D&C 11:19); "with full purpose of heart" (D&C 17:1); "pray vocally as well as in thy heart" (D&C 19:28); "with singleness of heart" (D&C 36:7); "with one heart" (D&C 45:65). "He exalted himself in his heart" (D&C 63:55), and they "forgave not one another in their hearts" (D&C 64:8). "I, the Lord, require the hearts of the children of men. . . . The Lord requireth the heart and a willing mind" (D&C 64:22, 34); "they united their hearts" (D&C 84:1); "purify your hearts" (D&C 88:74); "for the purpose of subduing the hearts of . . . men" (D&C 96:5); "our hearts flow out with sorrow" (D&C 109:48).

The revelations refer to "hardened hearts" (D&C 5:18), sincere hearts (D&C 5:24), "honest hearts" (D&C 8:1), "corrupt hearts" (D&C 10:21), angry hearts (D&C 10:24), lifted hearts (D&C 19:39), "broken hearts" (D&C 20:37), "contrite heart[s]" (D&C 21:9), open hearts (D&C 23:2, 3), lowly hearts (D&C 32:1), unbelieving hearts (D&C 38:14), pure hearts (D&C 41:11), proud hearts (D&C 42:40), blinded hearts (D&C 58:15), "doubtful heart[s]" (D&C 58:29), "cheerful hearts" and "glad heart[s]" (D&C 59:15), "humble hearts" (D&C 61:2), "thankful heart[s]" (D&C 62:7), fearful hearts (D&C 67:3), murmuring hearts (D&C 75:7), "evil hearts" (D&C 84:76), troubled hearts (D&C 98:18), vain hearts (D&C 106:7), softened hearts (D&C 121:3, 4), and "warm hearts" (D&C 121:9). The revelations do indeed have an expansive array of emotions seated in the heart.

Bosom(s). The bosom represents the innermost part but also stands for the whole body or soul: "I will cause that your bosom shall burn within you" (D&C 9:8); "the scriptures . . . are in mine own bosom" (D&C 35:20); "[I] have taken the Zion of Enoch into mine own bosom" (D&C 38:4); "all these things shall be gathered unto the bosom of the church" (D&C 38:38).

Bowels. The bowels are a center of deep feeling—again, representing the innermost part: "truth is established in her bowels" (D&C 84:101); "his bowels shall be a fountain of truth" (D&C 85:7); "my bowels are filled with compassion" (D&C 101:9); "let thy bowels also be full of charity" (D&C 121:45).

Bellies. Bellies are a center of desire and gratification: "whose bellies are not satisfied" (D&C 56:17).

Loins. The idiom "gird up the loins" means to prepare oneself for action; *gird* means "to secure or strengthen." It is appropriate that we are encouraged to surround the body parts associated with one of our highest functions, procreation, with *truth* and *faithfulness.* "Gird up your loins" (D&C 27:15, and ten other occurrences), "having your loins girt about with truth" (D&C 27:16); "every man should take . . . faithfulness upon his loins" (D&C 63:37).

Seed(s). Hebrew *zer'a,* Greek *sperma,* and Latin *semen* all refer to offspring, or progeny: "Adam and . . . his seed" (D&C 29:42); "Aaron and his seed" (D&C 84:18); "the seed of Abraham" (D&C 84:34); "the chosen seed" (D&C 107:40); "continuation of the seeds forever" (D&C 132:19); "Abraham received promises concerning his seed, and of the fruit of his loins" (definition by parallelism) (D&C 132:30).

Knee(s). The knee represents the whole person: "These all shall bow the knee" (D&C 76:110); "strengthen the feeble knees" (D&C 81:5).

Foot, feet. The foot or feet represent the whole person: "their enemies shall be under their feet" (D&C 35:14); "trodden under the feet of men" (D&C 101:40); "the kingdoms of the world are subdued under my feet" (D&C 103:7); "the Lord set his foot upon this mount" (D&C 45:48); "appointed Michael your prince, and established his feet" (D&C 78:16); "importune at the feet of the judge" (D&C 101:86); "How beautiful upon the mountains are the feet of those that bring glad tidings" (D&C 128:19).

Royalty Imagery

As indicated earlier, the creation of spiritual and physical bodies for his children was Heavenly Father's crowning creation. With the potential of God's children to become like him, we may expect to see in the scriptural record

references to ruling and reigning with kingdoms, dominions, thrones, anointings, scepters, and crowns.

The Father, who is King above, is described in "heaven,
thy holy habitation, where thou sittest enthroned, with
glory, honor, power, majesty, might, dominion . . . with
those bright, shining seraphs around thy throne" (D&C
109:77, 79). His children may also attain such royal station.
The righteous "shall inherit the kingdom of heaven" (D&C
10:55); they "shall receive a crown of eternal life" (D&C
20:14); "a crown of righteousness" (D&C 25:15); "be
crowned with much glory" (D&C 58:4); and "crowned with
blessings" (D&C 59:4); "the blessings of the kingdom are
yours" (D&C 61:37). Some are "found worthy, and
anointed, and ordained . . . they may claim their anointing" (D&C 68:20, 21); anyone who is righteous "shall in
nowise lose his crown" (D&C 75:28); "they are they who
are priests and kings" (D&C 76:56). "Then shall he be
crowned with the crown of his glory, to sit on the throne
of his power to reign forever" (D&C 76:108); "come up
unto the crown prepared for you, and be made rulers over
many kingdoms" (D&C 78:15); "holding the scepter of
power" (D&C 85:7); "thrones, or principalities, or powers"
(D&C 132:13); "crowns of eternal lives in the eternal
worlds" (D&C 132:55); "thy scepter [shall be] an unchang-
ing scepter . . . and thy dominion shall be an everlasting
dominion" (D&C 121:46).

Those attaining such glorious status will enjoy royal
attire; they will be "clothed with robes of righteousness"
(D&C 29:12), "clothed with power and great glory" (D&C
45:44), and "clothed with light" (D&C 85:7). The
"anointed ones [shall be] . . . clothed with salvation" (D&C
109:80).

Battle Imagery

The war that began in heaven continues to be waged
here on earth; the battlefield has changed, but the conflict
goes on. In ancient scripture, modern revelations, and even
in the hymns we sing, we refer to armies, warriors, battles,

armor, weapons, swords, breastplates, shields, helmets, bucklers, and banners—all in a symbolic way.

Satan (Hebrew, *Adversary*) "maketh war with the saints of God, and encompasseth them round about" (D&C 76:29), but "I, the Lord, rule in the heavens above, and among the armies of the earth" (D&C 60:4); "I will fight your battles" (D&C 105:14). His people constitute "an army with banners" (D&C 5:14), "the strength of my house, even my warriors" (D&C 105:16). Our Leader commands: "take upon you my whole armor" (D&C 27:15), "having on the breastplate of righteousness" (D&C 27:16), "the shield of faith" (D&C 27:17), "the helmet of salvation, and the sword of my Spirit" (D&C 27:18). "I will be their shield and their buckler" (D&C 35:14), and "I will let fall the sword in their behalf" (D&C 35:14), "the sword of mine indignation" (D&C 101:10). "Let my army become very great" (D&C 105:31); and he assures us that "no weapon formed against [us] shall prosper" (D&C 109:25).

Marriage Imagery

One of the most sacred of covenant relationships is the marriage covenant, which requires the utmost fidelity, sacrifice, and commitment. God's marriage to his people is featured in the writings of Old Testament prophets and New Testament apostles and in latter-day revelations. The Lord is the Bridegroom (D&C 33:17; 65:3; 88:92; 133:10). The Church is the bride (D&C 109:73–74). The Lord's second coming is the festive marriage celebration (D&C 58:11; 133:19).

Summary

By examining hundreds of examples we have seen that God does indeed "speak the same words unto one nation like unto another" and that "the testimony of the two nations shall run together" (2 Nephi 29:8). Many of his timeless comparisons and figurative expressions drawn from the biblical world—its landscapes, flora and fauna, harvests, vineyards, shepherding, royalty, battle, and marriage images—are perpetuated in his revealed words in these latter days. He has given at least one reason for this consistent teaching style: "I do this that I may prove unto many that I am the same yesterday, today, and forever" (2 Nephi 29:9).

CHAPTER FOURTEEN

THE DAY OF JUDGMENT AS TAUGHT IN THE DOCTRINE AND COVENANTS

TERRY B. BALL

There are certain events through which every soul born to this earth must pass. Paul identified two when he wrote to the Corinthians, "For since by man came death, by man came also the resurrection of the dead. For as in Adam all die, even so in Christ shall all be made alive" (1 Corinthians 15:21–22). The newly converted Alma the Younger taught of a third certainty. He exclaimed, "all men shall stand to be judged of him" (Mosiah 27:31). Of these three certain events—death, resurrection, and the final Judgment—this last perhaps causes us the most concern. The universality of the Judgment causes each of us to consider the interrogatives, who? when? what? where? why? how? We wonder: Who will judge us? When will we be judged? What are the criteria upon which we will be judged? When must we prepare for the Judgment? Where will the Judgment place us? Why will we be judged? How will we be judged?

One manifestation of God's love for us is that he has provided answers to these important questions through the scriptures. The Doctrine and Covenants is an especially valuable scriptural source for finding such answers. Not

Terry B. Ball is assistant professor of ancient scripture at Brigham Young University.

only does the Doctrine and Covenants confirm those answers given in other scriptures but it also adds significant insights found nowhere else in the standard works. Those who study it carefully will be better able to prepare for the great day of judgment.

WHO WILL JUDGE US?

In a revelation on the degrees of glory the Lord revealed that "God and Christ are the judge of all" (D&C 76:68; see also 77:12; 82:23; 88:104). Some might question the role of the Father in the Judgment in light of Christ's teachings recorded in the Gospel of John in which he taught that "the Father judgeth no man, but hath committed all judgment unto the Son" (John 5:22). Christ later explained, however, that the Father does indeed play a role in the Judgment, for all the judgments the Son makes are according to the will of the Father (see John 8:15–16, 26, 50).

The Book of Mormon teaches that Christ will be assisted in the Judgment of the house of Israel by the twelve original apostles and that the twelve New World apostles would assist with the judging of the remnant of the descendants of Lehi (1 Nephi 12:9–10; Mormon 3:18–19). The Doctrine and Covenants clarifies that the assisting apostles would judge only the righteous (D&C 29:12). Elder Bruce R. McConkie summarized and clarified the roles of the Father, the Son, the Holy Ghost, and the apostles in the Judgment. "The scriptural assertion that all men 'shall be brought and be arraigned before the bar of Christ the Son, and God the Father, and the Holy Spirit, which is one Eternal God, to be judged according to their works, whether they be good or whether they be evil' (Alma 11:44) means simply that Christ's judicial decisions are those of the other two members of the Godhead because all three are perfectly united as one. The ancient Twelve and the Nephite Twelve, and no doubt others similarly empowered, will sit in judgment, under Christ, on selected portions of the house of Israel; but their decrees will be limited to those who love the Lord and have kept his commandments, 'and none else.' (D&C ˥9:12; 3 Ne. 27:27; Matt. 19:28)."¹

˥lthough apostles and others play a role in the ˥ent, Jacob testified that the final decision to allow ˥e into the kingdom ultimately belongs to the Savior ˥9:41). It is most appropriate that he who atoned foˑ ˑld make that judgment.

WHEN ˑ BE JUDGED?

Our juˑ ˑnt is both a process and an event. Throughout our existence we go through a process of partial and preparatory judgments, all leading up to the event of our final judgment. The Doctrine and Covenants teaches that one of the earliest judgments came in the premortal existence when those spirits who followed Lucifer and rebelled against our Heavenly Father's plan "were thrust down, and thus came the devil and his angels; and, behold, there is a place prepared for them from the beginning, which place is hell" (D&C 29:37–38). Jacob taught that there was also an early judgment passed upon man at the fall of Adam and that it would have been the final judgment were it not for the atonement of Christ: "Wherefore, it must needs be an infinite atonement—save it should be an infinite atonement this corruption could not put on incorruption. Wherefore, the first judgment which came upon man must needs have remained to an endless duration. And if so, this flesh must have laid down to rot and to crumble to its mother earth, to rise no more" (2 Nephi 9:7).

The Doctrine and Covenants further teaches that some judgments, especially those of chastening, are poured out upon men during mortality (e.g., D&C 84:58; 99:5; 109:30, 38; 124:52; 136:42). Joseph F. Smith explained that the purpose of such chastisement is to "bring mankind to a sense of his power and his purposes, that they may repent of their sins and prepare themselves for the second coming of Christ to reign in righteousness upon the earth."²

Alma taught that there will be a type of partial judgment immediately after death to determine our place in the spirit world (Alma 40:11–14). The Doctrine and Covenants teaches that there must also be a type of judgment at the Resurrection, for the wicked are to be resurrected after the righteous (D&C 63:17–18; 76:50–65; 88:97–101).

All of these early and partial judgments are not to be confused with the final judgment. Of the final judgment Jesus taught his disciples that "the Son of man shall come in the glory of his Father with his angels; and then he shall reward every man according to his works" (Matt. 16:27). The Doctrine and Covenants makes it clear that the coming in glory to which Jesus referred is at the end of the millennium, when the resurrection is to be completed, and the heaven and earth are about to pass away preparatory to the coming forth of the new heaven and new earth (D&C 29:22–28; see also 2 Nephi 9:15). The Doctrine and Covenants also suggests that the order of judgment will follow the order of resurrection, with the righteous being judged before the wicked (D&C 88:97–102; 86:1–7).

Although our judgment is not completed until the final judgment, Elder McConkie explained that "it is very evident that men will not have to await the day of final judgment—the formal occasion when every living soul will stand before the Judgment bar, an event that will not take place until the last soul has been resurrected—to learn their status and the degree of glory they are to receive in eternity. Those who are living a telestial law will be swept off the earth at the Second Coming. (D&C 101:24; Malachi 3; 4.) Those who come forth in the morning of the first resurrection, who 'are Christ's, the first fruits,' will have celestial bodies and go to a celestial kingdom. 'Those who are Christ's at his coming' will come forth with terrestrial bodies and go to a terrestrial kingdom. Similarly those coming forth in the beginning of the second resurrection will have telestial bodies and go to a telestial kingdom, while the sons of perdition, the last to be resurrected, will have bodies capable of receiving no glory and will be cast out with the devil and his angels forever. (D&C 88:98–102.)"[3]

WHAT ARE THE CRITERIA UPON
WHICH WE WILL BE JUDGED?

Our Father in Heaven wants us to be well prepared for the Judgment. That is one of the reasons he has revealed the standards by which we will be judged. In the Doctrine and Covenants we learn that the criteria by which we will be judged include our works, our desires, our scriptures, and our opportunities.

Works

While teaching Joseph Smith and Sidney Rigdon about the kingdoms to which man may be assigned at the Judgment, the Lord revealed that all men "shall be judged according to their works, and every man shall receive according to his own works, his own dominion, in the mansions which are prepared" (D&C 76:111; see also 19:3; 101:65; 121:24; 124:48; 128:6; 136:42; 137:9). Later it would be revealed that this is just, because God has given each of us moral agency, allowing us to individually "act in doctrine and principle," thus assuring that "every man may be accountable for his own sins in the day of judgment" (D&C 101:78).

Records are kept of our works and will be used at the Judgment. John the Revelator described the following vision: "And I saw the dead, small and great, stand before God; and the books were opened: and another book was opened, which is the book of life: and the dead were judged out of those things which were written in the books, according to their works" (Revelation 20:12).

In the Doctrine and Covenants Joseph Smith discussed what constitutes the books referred to in Revelation: "You will discover in this quotation that the books were opened; and another book was opened, which was the book of life; but the dead were judged out of those things which were written in the books, according to their works; consequently, the books spoken of must be the books which contained the record of their works, and refer to the records which are kept on the earth. And the book which was the book of life is the record which is kept in heaven; the principle agreeing precisely with the doctrine which is commanded you in the revelation contained in the letter which I wrote to you previous to my leaving my place—that in all your recordings it may be recorded in heaven.

"Now, the nature of this ordinance consists in the power of the priesthood, by the revelation of Jesus Christ, wherein it is granted that whatsoever you bind on earth shall be bound in heaven, and whatsoever you loose on earth shall be loosed in heaven. Or, in other words, taking a different view of the translation, whatsoever you record on earth shall be recorded in heaven, and whatsoever you do not record on earth shall not be recorded in heaven; for out of the books shall your dead be judged, according to their own works, whether they themselves have attended to the ordinances in their own *propria persona,* or by the means of their own agents, according to the ordinance which God has prepared for their salvation from before the foundation of the world, according to the records which they have kept concerning their dead" (D&C 128:7–8).

In Doctrine and Covenants 127 the Prophet explained again the importance of keeping accurate records of saving ordinances: "Verily, thus saith the Lord unto you concerning your dead: When any of you are baptized for your dead, let there be a recorder, and let him be eye-witness of your baptisms; let him hear with his ears, that he may testify of a truth, saith the Lord; that in all your recordings it may be recorded in heaven; whatsoever you bind on earth, may be bound in heaven; whatsoever you loose on earth, may be loosed in heaven" (D&C 127:6–7).

Apparently those works that are properly witnessed and recorded on earth will also be recorded in the book of life in heaven. Elder Orson Pratt described how these two records will be used at the Judgment: "The sacred books kept in the archives of eternity are to be opened in the great judgment day, and compared with the records kept on the earth; and then, if it is found that things have been done by the authority and commandment of the Most

High, in relation to the dead, and the same things are found to be recorded both on earth and in heaven, such sacred books will be opened and read before the assembled universe in the day of judgment, and will be sanctioned by Him who sits on the throne and deals out justice and mercy to all of his creation."[4]

In the Doctrine and Covenants we are taught that some works will receive special consideration at the Judgment. These include how we have forgiven, served, and judged others, as well as how we have responded to the opportunities and stewardships we have been given.

Forgiving others. At a general council of the Church held in April 1832, Bishop Edward Partridge and Elder Sidney Rigdon apparently resolved a misunderstanding between themselves.[5] The Lord showed his pleasure at their reconciliation by revealing "that inasmuch as you have forgiven one another your trespasses, even so I, the Lord, forgive you" (D&C 82:1). The doctrine that forgiving others is a requisite to obtaining forgiveness from God is also found in Doctrine and Covenants 64: "Wherefore, I say unto you, that ye ought to forgive one another; for he that forgiveth not his brother his trespasses standeth condemned before the Lord; for there remaineth in him the greater sin. I, the Lord, will forgive whom I will forgive, but of you it is required to forgive all men" (D&C 64:9–10; cf. Matthew 6:14–15; Mosiah 26:31).

These teachings suggest that those who come to the Judgment harboring grudges or malice against their fellow beings will not only find it difficult to obtain forgiveness for their own shortcomings but will also find that their refusal to forgive constitutes an additional sin for which they are accountable.

Serving others. While calling the Saints to repentance, the Lord said, "Wo unto you rich men, that will not give your substance to the poor, for your riches will canker your souls; and this shall be your lamentation in the day of visitation, and of judgment, and of indignation: The harvest is past, the summer is ended, and my soul is not saved" (D&C 56:16).

This passage suggests that another criteria by which we will be judged will be how we have served and ministered to the needs of our brethren. The truth is taught elsewhere in the Doctrine and Covenants as well: "Wherefore, be faithful; stand in the office which I have appointed unto you; succor the weak, lift up the hands which hang down, and strengthen the feeble knees. And if thou art faithful unto the end thou shalt have a crown of immortality, and eternal life in the mansions which I have prepared in the house of my Father" (D&C 81:5–6; cf. Matthew 25:31–46).

Doctrine and Covenants 4 teaches us that one of the most important services we can render to be deemed worthy of salvation at the Judgment is to teach others the gospel (D&C 4:4). In this section we also learn that such service to our fellowman is equated to serving God and that serving God "with all your heart, might, mind and strength" enables us to "stand blameless before God at the last day" (D&C 4:2–3; cf. Mosiah 2:17; Matthew 25:40).

Judging others. In the Sermon on the Mount Jesus taught that how we judge others will influence how we are judged: "Judge not, that ye be not judged. For with what judgment ye judge, ye shall be judged: and with what measure ye mete, it shall be measured to you again" (Matthew 7:1–2). The Joseph Smith Translation makes an important alteration to that passage, which helps us understand that the Savior's teaching is not a simple prohibition against any kind of judgment we might make. The Joseph Smith Translation reads, "Judge not *unrighteously,* that ye be not judged; *but judge righteous judgment.* For with what judgment ye shall judge, ye shall be judged; and with what measure ye mete, it shall be measured to you again" (JST, Matthew 7:2–3; emphasis added). The doctrine that righteous judgment is allowed without condemnation is in harmony with John's recording of the Savior's teachings: "Judge not according to the appearance, but judge righteous judgment" (John 7:24).

These teachings beg the question, How do we judge righteously? One answer is found in the Doctrine and Covenants in a revelation Joseph Smith received through the Urim and Thummim: "And now, verily, verily, I say unto thee, put your trust in that Spirit which leadeth to do good—yea, to do justly, to walk humbly, to judge righteously; and this is my Spirit" (D&C 11:12). The passage teaches that we can judge righteously by trusting in the Spirit and allowing it to inspire our judgments. Joseph F. Smith taught that there are some prerequisites to enjoying such inspiration: "The only safe way for us to do, as individuals, is to live so humbly, so righteously and so faithfully before God that we may possess his Spirit to that extent that we shall be able to judge righteously, and discern between truth and error."[6]

Desires

The Doctrine and Covenants makes it clear that we will be judged not only for what we do but also for what we desire. While explaining to Joseph Smith how his brother Alvin could be allowed into the celestial kingdom, even though he had died before the restoration of the gospel and its saving ordinances, the Lord declared, "All who have died without a knowledge of this gospel, who would have received it if they had been permitted to tarry, shall be heirs of the celestial kingdom of God; also all that shall die henceforth without a knowledge of it, who would have received it with all their hearts, shall be heirs of that kingdom; for I, the Lord, will judge all men according to their works, according to the desire of their hearts" (D&C 137:7–9).

Elder Dallin H. Oaks has also testified that we will be rewarded for our righteous desires, even if we may not have had opportunity to fulfill those desires in mortality: "We know that many worthy and wonderful Latter-day Saints currently lack the ideal opportunities and essential requirements for their progress. Singleness, childlessness, death, and divorce frustrate ideals and postpone the fulfillment of promised blessings. In addition, some women who desire

to be full-time mothers and homemakers have been literally compelled to enter the full-time work force. But these
frustrations are only temporary. The Lord has promised
that in the eternities no blessing will be denied his sons
and daughters who keep the commandments, are true to
their covenants, and desire what is right."[7]

The Book of Mormon prophet Alma confirmed that at
the Judgment we will not only be rewarded for our righteous desires (see Alma 41:3) but also be condemned for our
unrighteous desires and thoughts (see Alma 12:14; 29:4).

Our Scriptures

The Doctrine and Covenants makes it clear that the
scriptures constitute another standard by which we will be
judged; these include the Bible, the Book of Mormon (see
D&C 20:11–13; see also 2 Nephi 25:18; 33:14–15; 3 Nephi
27:25–27; Words of Mormon 1:11), and the Doctrine and
Covenants itself (D&C 41:12).

Opportunities

In 1832 the Lord revealed to Joseph Smith that at the
Judgment those who have been taught the gospel in mortality will not only be expected to have accomplished more
but also may be held more accountable for their sins than
those who never had the opportunity for such learning:
"Unto whom much is given much is required; and he who
sins against the greater light shall receive the greater condemnation. Ye call upon my name for revelations, and I
give them unto you; and inasmuch as ye keep not my say-
ings, which I give unto you, ye become transgressors; and
justice and judgment are the penalty which is affixed unto
my law" (D&C 82:3–4).

Once we understand this doctrine, some might conclude
that it would be better not to have access to greater light
and revelations and thereby avoid being a candidate for a
greater condemnation. Those making such a conclusion fail
to understand that though we cannot be as readily damned
if we are ignorant of the gospel, neither can we be exalted
without knowing and partaking of the gospel and its

saving ordinances (D&C 131:1–6). Moreover, we may be held accountable for refusing to accept the gospel if we have the opportunity (D&C 60:15; 75:21–22; 84:42, 114–115). This understanding raises some provocative questions. When must we accept the gospel and its ordinances to be prepared for the Judgment? Is there a deadline? What of those who never get the chance to hear the gospel? The revelations found in the Doctrine and Covenants answer these questions.

WHEN MUST WE PREPARE FOR THE JUDGMENT?

The Book of Mormon prophet Amulek declared, "This life is the time for men to prepare to meet God; yea, behold the day of this life is the day for men to perform their labors" (Alma 34:32). The Lord revealed to both Joseph Smith and to Nephite prophets that this life is a probationary state granted to us for the very purpose of preparing for the Judgment (D&C 29:42–43; 1 Nephi 10:21). The Doctrine and Covenants makes it clear, however, that any preparation for the Judgment that we did not have adequate opportunity or ability to accomplish in mortality may be completed through work in the spirit world and vicarious work in the temple (D&C 138:32–34; cf. D&C 76:72–73; 128:8). Elder Orson Pratt summarized why our Heavenly Father's plan makes the provision for those in the spirit world to hear and accept the gospel: "This was the object, then, that they [spirits in spirit world] might have the same Gospel that men have in the flesh. If we acknowledge they had not the opportunity of receiving it in the flesh, they must have it in the spirit world; for in the great judgment day all men are to be judged by the same Gospel, and consequently, in order to judge them, it was necessary that they should hear the same Gospel that was preached upon the earth, that they might have the privilege of entering into the presence of the Lord their God, or, if they rejected it, be justly condemned."[8]

Once we have accepted the gospel, we are given additional stewardships and opportunities to serve. At the

Judgment we will be expected to account for how we responded to those opportunities and will be rewarded or punished accordingly: "Wherefore, now let every man learn his duty, and to act in the office in which he is appointed, in all diligence. He that is slothful shall not be counted worthy to stand, and he that learns not his duty and shows himself not approved shall not be counted worthy to stand" (D&C 107:99–100; see also D&C 70:3–4; 104:13; Matthew 25:14–30).

WHERE WILL THE JUDGMENT PLACE US?

In speaking of where the Judgment will place us in the eternities, most of the standard works tend to focus on the extremes, the best and worst places to which one could be assigned. For example, in the Judgment parable of the sheep and goats, the wicked are simply damned and sent to hell, whereas the righteous are saved and sent to dwell with Christ (Matthew 25:31–46). The Book of Mormon also stresses the extremes. We learn that the punishments of the wicked include being cast off forever from the kingdom of God (1 Nephi 10:21; 15:33), remaining eternally in a filthy or unclean state (1 Nephi 15:33; Mormon 9:14) and in endless misery and unhappiness (Alma 41:4–5; Mormon 9:14), having died as to things pertaining unto righteousness (1 Nephi 15:33; Alma 12:16), suffering torment as a lake of fire and brimstone (2 Nephi 28:23; Mosiah 26:27; Alma 12:17; Moroni 8:21), and being captive to the devil (Alma 12:17). In contrast, the righteous will receive their just rewards, including the privilege of dwelling eternally with Christ (Mosiah 26:24; Alma 41:4; 3 Nephi 28:40; Mormon 7:7) in a state of righteousness and happiness (Alma 41:4; Moroni 9:13; Mormon 7:7).

The Doctrine and Covenants is perhaps the most thorough book of scripture in describing the places to which the Judgment may send us and what we can expect there. Not only does it discuss the maximum rewards and punishments to be given but it also addresses the question of what rewards or punishments are to be given to those who are worthy of something in between. That very question led Joseph Smith to receive Doctrine and Covenants 76. He explained: "Upon my return from Amherst conference, I resumed the translation of the Scriptures. From sundry revelations which had been received, it was apparent that many important points touching the salvation of man, had been taken from the Bible, or lost before it was compiled. It appeared self-evident from what truths were left, that if God rewarded every one according to the deeds done in the body the term 'Heaven,' as intended for the Saints' eternal home must include more kingdoms than one. Accordingly, on the 16th of February, 1832, while translating St. John's Gospel, myself and Elder Rigdon saw the following [D&C 76] vision."[9]

In the vision we first learn the fate of the extremely wicked, or sons of perdition, who "suffered themselves through the power of the devil to be overcome, and to deny the truth and defy my [God's] power" and who "denied the Holy Spirit after having received it, and having denied the Only Begotten Son of the Father, having crucified him unto themselves and put him to an open shame" (D&C 76:31, 35). We are taught that "these are they who shall go away into the lake of fire and brimstone, with the devil and his angels—and the only ones on whom the second death shall have any power; yea, verily, the only ones who shall not be redeemed in the due time of the Lord, after the sufferings of his wrath" (D&C 76:36–38).

Next we are told that those who were very faithful and righteous, who repented and accepted the gospel and the saving ordinances, and who were sealed by the Holy Spirit of Promise, will have celestial glory, living with God, as gods, having all godly attributes (D&C 76:50–70; see also D&C 88:19–20, 22; 131:1–3; 132:19–20; 137:1–3).

Then we are taught of the fate of those in between. We learn that those "who received not the testimony of Jesus in the flesh, but afterwards received it," who also were the "honorable men of the earth, who were blinded by the craftiness of men," yet still were "not valiant in the testimony of Jesus," will receive a terrestrial glory that differs from the celestial "as the moon differs from the sun." In this glory they are entitled to "the presence of the Son, but not of the fulness of the Father," and "obtain not the crown over the kingdom of our God" (D&C 76:71–79).

Finally we learn that there is a telestial glory in store for those "who deny not the Holy Spirit," but "received not the gospel of Christ, neither the testimony of Jesus" and who were "liars, and sorcerers, and adulterers, and whore-mongers, and whosoever loves and makes a lie." They are to suffer "the wrath of God," and are "cast down to hell," awaiting the time when "Christ shall have subdued all enemies under his feet, and shall have perfected his work." They will be the last to be "redeemed from the devil" and the last resurrected, after which they will receive the lowest degree of glory, one that differs from that of the terrestrial as the stars differ from the moon in brightness. There they will "receive not of his [Christ's] fulness" but "of the Holy Spirit" (D&C 76:81–86, 101–6).

Why Will We Be Judged?

We have been warned that in the last days some would suggest that there will be no judgment. They will profess that there is no sin, that God will not hold us accountable for our sins, or that God loves us so much that he will save us all regardless of our sins (2 Nephi 28:7–8). Such doctrine will cause some to question why we should be judged. Perhaps the simplest answer to the question can be found in the divine declaration that "I the Lord cannot look upon sin with the least degree of allowance" (D&C 1:31), or, as Nephi explained it, "Behold, I say unto you, the kingdom of God is not filthy, and there cannot any unclean thing enter into the kingdom of God" (1 Nephi 15:33–34). The Judgment will assure that only the righteous gain access to God's kingdom, thereby preserving its purity.

Others might question why it is so important for God's kingdom to be pure. Doctrine and Covenants 88 answers that there are certain laws associated with each kingdom and, in regard to God's kingdom, it is obedience to those laws that preserves, perfects, and sanctifies the kingdom and those in it (D&C 88:34–39). Accordingly, the celestial glory can be maintained only by righteousness. Moreover, the prohibition against evil in the celestial glory assures that only the righteous will have access to the powers of God. One can imagine the disastrous consequences should an evil and selfish being gain access to such power. The Judgment gives us the confidence that "the powers of heaven cannot be controlled nor handled only upon the principles of righteousness" (D&C 121:36).

How Will We Be Judged?

The principles upon which the Judgment will be based are outlined in Doctrine and Covenants 88. They include intelligence, wisdom, truth, virtue, light, mercy, and justice (D&C 88:40). An omniscient and loving God would judge no other way. When our judgment is completed, we will accept the decisions given, exclaiming, "Holy, holy are thy judgments, O Lord God Almighty" (2 Nephi 9:46). Those who are righteous will "have a perfect knowledge of their enjoyment, and their righteousness, being clothed with purity, yea, even with the robe of righteousness" (2 Nephi 9:14), whereas the wicked will be forced to acknowledge, "I know my guilt; I transgressed thy law, and my transgressions are mine; and the devil hath obtained me" (2 Nephi 9:46). Apparently, none of us will be taken away from the Judgment bar protesting, "It's unfair! I was framed! I demand a retrial! I want to appeal!" There will be no such nonsense. Rather, "every nation, kindred, tongue, and people shall see eye to eye and shall confess before God that his judgments are just" (Mosiah 16:1; see also Alma 41:7).

Conclusion

Through the Doctrine and Covenants and other scriptures, a just and loving Father in Heaven has revealed answers to important questions about the final day of judgment. Those questions include, Who will judge us? When will we be judged? What are the criteria upon which we will be judged? When must we prepare for the Judgment? Where will the Judgment place us? Why will we be judged? and, How will we be judged? As we study, understand, and teach these answers, we demonstrate both our gratitude to Father in Heaven and our willingness to follow his plan for our happiness.

NOTES

1. Bruce R. McConkie, *The Promised Messiah* (Salt Lake City: Deseret Book, 1978), 215–16. We understand that those who hold the office of bishop are also judges in Israel, but their stewardship applies to judgments rendered during mortality and not to the final judgment (D&C 58:17–18; 107:72–76).

2. Joseph F. Smith, *Gospel Doctrine* (Salt Lake City: Deseret Book, 1966), 55.

3. Bruce R. McConkie, *Mormon Doctrine*, 2d ed. (Salt Lake City: Bookcraft, 1966), 404.

4. Orson Pratt, in *Journal of Discourses*, 26 vols. (London: Latter-day Saints' Book Depot, 1854–86), 7:84.

5. Joseph Smith, *History of The Church Jesus Christ of Latter-day Saints,* ed. B. H. Roberts, 2d ed. rev., 7 vols. (Salt Lake City: The Church of Jesus Christ of Latter-day Saints, 1932–51), 1:267.

6. Smith, *Gospel Doctrine,* 45.

7. Dallin H. Oaks, *Ensign,* November 1993, 75.

8. Orson Pratt, in *Journal of Discourses,* 2:372.

9. Smith, *History of the Church,* 1:245.

CHAPTER FIFTEEN

THE SECOND COMING OF CHRIST: QUESTIONS AND ANSWERS

ROBERT L. MILLET

The Doctrine and Covenants is a sacred book of scripture that provides literally thousands of answers—answers to questions that have plagued the religious world for centuries. It is a treasure-house of doctrinal understanding.

WHAT IS THE SECOND COMING?

Jesus came to earth as a mortal being in the meridian of time. He taught the gospel, bestowed divine authority, organized the Church, and suffered and died as an infinite atoning sacrifice for the sins of the world. He stated that he would come again, would return not as the meek and lowly Nazarene but as the Lord of Sabaoth, the Lord of Hosts, the Lord of Armies. His second coming is thus spoken of as his coming "in glory," meaning, in his true identity as the God of all creation, the Redeemer and Judge. His Second coming is described as both *great* and *dreadful*—great for those who have been true and faithful and therefore look forward to his coming, and dreadful to those who have done despite to the spirit of grace and who therefore hope against hope that he will never return. The Second Coming in glory is in fact "the end of the world," meaning the end

---

Robert L. Millet is dean of Religious Education at Brigham Young University.

of worldliness, the destruction of the wicked (Joseph Smith–Matthew 1:4, 31).[1] At this coming the wicked will be destroyed, the righteous quickened and caught up to meet him, and the earth transformed from a fallen telestial orb to a terrestrial, paradisiacal sphere. We will live and move about among new heavens and new earth. The Second Coming will initiate the millennial reign.

DOES CHRIST HIMSELF KNOW WHEN HE WILL COME?

This question comes up occasionally, perhaps because of what is stated in the Gospel of Mark: "Heaven and earth shall pass away: but my words shall not pass away. But of that day and that hour knoweth no man, no, not the angels which are in heaven, *neither the Son,* but the Father" (Mark 13:31–32; emphasis added). The phrase "neither the Son" is not found in Matthew or Luke. Christ knows all things; he possesses the fulness of the glory and power of the Father (D&C 93:16–17). Surely he knows when he will return. If he did not know the exact day or time of his return in glory when the Olivet Prophecy was uttered, then certainly after his resurrection and glorification he came to know. It is worth noting that the Joseph Smith Translation of this verse omits the disputed phrase.

WILL ALL BE SURPRISED AND CAUGHT UNAWARE?

The scriptures speak of the Master returning as "a thief in the night" (1 Thessalonians 5:2; 2 Peter 3:10). It is true that no mortal man has known, does now know, or will yet know the precise day of the Lord's second advent. That is true for prophets and apostles as well as the rank and file of society and the Church. The Lord did not reveal to Joseph Smith the precise day and time of his coming (D&C 130:14–17). Elder M. Russell Ballard, speaking to students at Brigham Young University, recently observed: "I am called as one of the Apostles to be a special witness of Christ in these exciting, trying times, and I do not know when He is going to come again. As far as I know, none of my brethren in the Council of the Twelve or even in the

First Presidency knows. And I would humbly suggest to you, my young brothers and sisters, that if we do not know, then *nobody* knows, no matter how compelling their arguments or how reasonable their calculations. . . . I believe when the Lord says 'no man' knows, it really means that no man knows. You should be extremely wary of anyone who claims to be an exception to divine decree."[2] On the other hand, the Saints are promised that if they are in tune with the Spirit, they can know the time and the season. The Apostle Paul chose the descriptive analogy of a pregnant woman about to deliver. She may not know the exact hour or day when the birth is to take place, but one thing she knows for sure: it will be soon. It *must* be soon! The impressions and feelings and signs within her own body so testify. In that day, surely the Saints of the Most High, the members of the body of Christ, will be pleading for the Lord to deliver the travailing earth, to bring an end to corruption and degradation, to introduce an era of peace and righteousness. And those who give heed to the words of scripture, and especially to the living oracles, will stand as the "children of light, and the children of the day," those who "are not of the night, nor of darkness" (1 Thessalonians 5:2–5). In a modern revelation the Savior declared: "And again, verily I say unto you, the coming of the Lord draweth nigh, and *it overtaketh the world as a thief in the night*—therefore, gird up your loins, that you may be the children of light, and that day shall not overtake you as a thief" (D&C 106:4–5; emphasis added).

To certain brethren who would soon be called to the first Quorum of the Twelve Apostles in this dispensation, the Lord said: "And unto you it shall be given to know the signs of the times, and the signs of the coming of the Son of Man" (D&C 68:11). As we move closer to the end of time, we would do well to live in such a manner that we can discern the signs of the times; we would be wise also to keep our eyes fixed and our ears riveted on those called to direct the destiny of this Church. The Prophet Joseph Smith pointed out that a particular man who claimed prophetic powers "has not seen the sign of the Son of Man as foretold by Jesus. Neither has any man, nor will any man, till after the sun shall have been darkened and the moon bathed in blood. For the Lord hath not shown me any such sign, and as the prophet saith, so it must be: 'Surely the Lord God will do nothing, but he revealeth his secret unto his servants the prophets.'"[3]

IS IT TRUE THAT NOT EVERYONE WILL KNOW WHEN THE SAVIOR HAS COME?

Once in a while we hear something in the classes of the Church to the effect that not all people will know when the Lord returns. Let us be clear on this matter. There may be some wisdom in speaking of the second *comings* of the Lord Jesus Christ, three of which are preliminary appearances, or comings, to select groups, and one of which is to the whole world. The Lord will make a preliminary appearance to his temple in Independence, Jackson County, Missouri. This seems to be a private appearance to those holding the keys of power in the earthly kingdom. Elder Orson Pratt, in speaking of this appearance, said: "All of them who are pure in heart will behold the face of the Lord and that too before he comes in his glory in the clouds of heaven, for he will suddenly come to his Temple, and he will purify the sons of Moses and of Aaron, until they shall be prepared to offer in that Temple an offering that shall be acceptable in the sight of the Lord. In doing this, he will purify not only the minds of the Priesthood in that Temple, but he will purify their bodies until they shall be quickened, renewed and strengthened, and they will be partially changed, not to immortality, but changed in part that they can be filled with the power of God, and they can stand in the presence of Jesus, and behold his face in the midst of that Temple."[4] Charles W. Penrose observed that the Saints "will come to the Temple prepared for him, and his faithful people will behold his face, hear his voice, and gaze upon his glory. From his own lips they will receive further instructions for the development and beautifying of Zion and for the extension and sure stability of his Kingdom."⁵

The Lord will make an appearance at Adam-ondi-Ahman, "the place where Adam shall come to visit his people, or the Ancient of Days shall sit" (D&C 116). This grand council will be a large sacrament meeting, a time when the Son of Man will partake of the fruit of the vine once more with his earthly friends. And who will be in attendance? The revelations specify Moroni, Elias, John the Baptist, Elijah, Abraham, Isaac, Jacob, Joseph, Adam, Peter, James, John, "and also," the Savior clarifies, "all those whom my Father hath given me out of the world" (D&C 27:5–14), multitudes of faithful Saints from the beginning of time to the end. This will be a private appearance in that it will be unknown to the world. It will be a leadership meeting, a time of accounting, an accounting for priesthood stewardships. The Prophet Joseph Smith explained that Adam, the Ancient of Days, "will call his children together and hold a council with them to prepare them for the coming of the Son of Man. He (Adam) is the father of the human family, and presides over the spirits of all men, and all that have had the keys must stand before him in this grand council. . . . The Son of Man stands before him, and there is given him [Christ] glory and dominion. Adam delivers up his stewardship to Christ, that which was delivered to him as holding the keys of the universe, but retains his standing as head of the human family."⁶

President Joseph Fielding Smith observed: "This gathering of the children of Adam, where the thousands, and the tens of thousands are assembled in the judgment, will be one of the greatest events this troubled earth has ever seen. At this conference, or council, all who have held keys of dispensations will render a report of their stewardship. . . . We do not know how long a time this gathering will be in session, or how many sessions will be held at this grand council. It is sufficient to know that it is a gathering of the Priesthood of God from the beginning of this earth down to the present, in which reports will be made and all who have been given dispensations (talents) will declare their keys and ministry and make report of their stewardship according to the parable [the parable of the talents; Matthew 25]. Judgment will be rendered unto them for this is a gathering of the righteous. . . . It is not to be the judgment of the wicked. . . . This will precede the great day of destruction of the wicked and will be the preparation for the Millennial Reign."[7] Elder Bruce R. McConkie has likewise written: "Every prophet, apostle, president, bishop, elder, or church officer of whatever degree—all who have held keys shall stand before him who holds all of the keys. They will then be called upon to give an account of their stewardships and to report how and in what manner they have used their priesthood and their keys for the salvation of men within the sphere of their appointments. . . . There will be a great hierarchy of judges in that great day, of whom Adam, under Christ, will be the chief of all. Those judges will judge the righteous ones under their jurisdiction, but Christ himself, he alone, will judge the wicked."[8]

The Savior will appear to the Jews on the Mount of Olives. It will be at the time of the battle of Armageddon, at a time when his people will find themselves with their backs against the wall. During this period, two prophets will stand before the wicked in the streets of Jerusalem and call the people to repentance. These men, presumably members of the Council of the Twelve Apostles or the First Presidency—holding the sealing powers—"are to be raised up to the Jewish nation in the last days, at the time of the restoration," and will "prophesy to the Jews after they are gathered and have built the city of Jerusalem in the land of their fathers" (D&C 77:15; see also Revelation 11:4–6).[9] They will be put to death by their enemies, their bodies will lie in the streets for three and a half days, and they will then be resurrected before the assembled multitude (Revelation 11:7–12).

At about this time, the Savior will come to the rescue of his covenant people: "Then shall the Lord go forth, and fight against those nations, as when he fought in the day of battle. And his feet shall stand in that day upon the mount of Olives, which is before Jerusalem on the east, and the mount of Olives shall cleave in the midst thereof toward the east and toward the west, and there shall be a very great valley; and half of the mountain shall remove toward the north, and half of it toward the south" (Zechariah 14:2–4). Then shall come to pass the conversion of a nation in a day, the acceptance of the Redeemer by the Jews. "And then shall the Jews look upon me and say: What are these wounds in thine hands and in thy feet? Then shall they know that I am the Lord; for I will say unto them: These wounds are the wounds with which I was wounded in the house of my friends. I am he who was lifted up. I am Jesus that was crucified. I am the Son of God. And then shall they weep because of their iniquities; then shall they lament because they persecuted their king" (D&C 45:51–53; see also Zechariah 12:10; 13:6).

Finally, and we would assume not far removed in time from his appearance on the Mount of Olives, is Christ's coming in glory. He comes in glory. All shall know. "Be not deceived," the Master warned in a modern revelation, "but continue in steadfastness, looking forth for the heavens to be shaken, and the earth to tremble and to reel to and fro as a drunken man, and for the valleys to be exalted, and for the mountains to be made low, and for the rough places to become smooth" (D&C 49:23). "Wherefore, prepare ye for the coming of the Bridegroom; go ye, go ye out to meet him. For behold, he shall stand upon the mount of Olivet, and upon the mighty ocean, even the great deep, and upon the islands of the sea, and upon the land of Zion. And he shall utter his voice out of Zion, and he shall speak from Jerusalem, and *his voice shall be heard among all people;* and it shall be a voice as the voice of many waters, and as the voice of a great thunder, which shall break down the mountains, and the valleys shall not be found" (D&C 133:19–22; emphasis added).

When the Lord Comes, Who Will Come with Him?

The righteous dead from ages past—those who qualify for the first resurrection, specifically those who died true in the faith since the time the first resurrection was initiated in the meridian of time—will come with the Savior when he returns in glory. The Prophet Joseph corrected a passage in Paul's first epistle to the Thessalonians as follows: "I would not have you to be ignorant, brethren, concerning them which are asleep, that ye sorrow not, even as others which have no hope. For if we believe that Jesus died and rose again, even so them also which sleep in Jesus will God bring with him. For this we say unto you by the word of the Lord, that they who are alive at the coming of the Lord, shall not prevent [precede] them who remain unto the coming of the Lord, who are asleep. For the Lord himself shall descend from heaven with a shout, with the voice of the archangel, and with the trump of God; and the dead in Christ shall rise first; then they who are alive, shall be caught up together into the clouds with them who remain, to meet the Lord in the air; and so shall we be ever with the Lord" (JST, 1 Thessalonians 4:13–17).

What Happens to Those Living on Earth When He Comes?

Those who are of at least a terrestrial level of righteousness shall continue to live as mortals after the Lord returns. The Saints shall live to "the age of man"—in the words of Isaiah, the age of one hundred (see Isaiah 65:20)—and will then pass through death and be changed instantly from mortality to resurrected immortality. "Yea, and blessed are the dead that die in the Lord, . . . when the Lord shall come, and old things shall pass away, and all things become new, they shall rise from the dead and shall not die after, and shall receive an inheritance before the Lord, in the holy city. And he that liveth when the Lord shall come, and hath kept the faith, blessed is he; nevertheless, it is appointed to him to die at the age of man. Wherefore, children shall grow up until they become old"—that is, no longer shall little ones die before the time of accountability; "old men shall die; but they shall not sleep in the dust, but they shall be changed in the twinkling of an eye" (D&C 63:49–51; see also JST, Isaiah 65:20). President Joseph Fielding Smith pointed out that "the inhabitants of the earth will have a sort of translation. They will be transferred to a condition of the terrestrial order, and so they will have power over disease and they will have power to live until they get a certain age and then they will die."[10]

IS THE BURNING SPOKEN OF IN SCRIPTURE LITERAL?

Malachi prophesied that "the day cometh, that shall burn as an oven; and all the proud, yea, and all that do wickedly, shall be stubble: and the day that cometh shall burn them up, saith the Lord of hosts, that it shall leave them neither root nor branch" (Malachi 4:1; cf. 2 Nephi 26:4; D&C 133:64). In 1823 Moroni quoted this passage differently to the seventeen-year-old Joseph Smith: "And all the proud, yea, and all that do wickedly shall burn as stubble; for *they that come* shall burn them, saith the Lord of Hosts" (Joseph Smith–History 1:37; emphasis added). In the Doctrine and Covenants the Lord of Armies declares: "For the hour is nigh and the day soon at hand when the earth is ripe; and all the proud and they that do wickedly shall be as stubble; and *I will burn them up,* saith the Lord of Hosts, that wickedness shall not be upon the earth" (D&C 29:9; emphasis added), "for after today cometh the burning," a day wherein "all the proud and they that do wickedly shall be as stubble; and *I will burn them up,* for I am the Lord of Hosts; and I will not spare any that remain in Babylon" (D&C 64:24; emphasis added).

The second coming of Christ in glory is a day in which "every corruptible thing, both of man, or of the beasts of the field, or of the fowls of the heavens, or of the fish of the sea, that dwells upon all the face of the earth, shall be consumed; and also that of element shall melt with fervent heat; and all things shall become new, that my knowledge and glory may dwell upon all the earth" (D&C 101:24–25;

cf. 133:41; 2 Peter 3:10). President Joseph Fielding Smith wrote: "Somebody said, 'Brother Smith, do you mean to say that it is going to be literal fire?' I said, 'Oh, no, it will not be literal fire any more than it was literal water that covered the earth in the flood.'"[11]

WHY WILL THE SAVIOR APPEAR IN RED APPAREL?

Red is symbolic of victory—victory over the devil, death, hell, and endless torment. It is the symbol of salvation, of being placed beyond the power of all one's enemies.[12] Christ's red apparel will also symbolize both aspects of his ministry to fallen humanity—his mercy and his justice. Because he has trodden the wine-press alone, "even the wine-press of the fierceness of the wrath of Almighty God" (D&C 76:107; 88:106), he has descended below all things and mercifully taken upon him our stains, our blood, or our sins (2 Nephi 9:44; Jacob 1:19; 2:2; Alma 5:22). In addition, he comes in "dyed garments" as the God of justice, even he who has trampled the wicked beneath his feet. "And the Lord shall be red in his apparel, and his garments like him that treadeth in the winevat. And so great shall be the glory of his presence that the sun shall hide his face in shame, and the moon shall withhold its light, and the stars shall be hurled from their places. And his voice shall be heard: I have trodden the wine-press alone, and have brought judgment upon all people; and none were with me; and I have trampled them in my fury, and I did tread upon them in mine anger, and their blood have I sprinkled upon my garments, and stained all my raiment; for this was the day of vengeance which was in my heart" (D&C 133:48–51).

WHEN DOES THE MILLENNIUM BEGIN?
WHY WILL IT BEGIN?

The second coming in glory of Jesus Christ ushers in the Millennium. The Millennium does not begin when Christ comes to his temple in Missouri, when he appears at Adam-ondi-Ahman, or when he stands on the Mount of Olives in

Jerusalem. The Millennium will not come because men and women on earth have become noble and good, because Christian charity will have spread across the globe and goodwill is the order of the day. The Millennium will not come because technological advances and medical miracles will have extended human life or because peace treaties among warring nations will have soothed injured feelings and eased political tensions for a time. The Millennium will be brought in by power, by the power of him who is the King of kings and Lord of lords. Satan will be bound by power, and the glory of the Millennium will be maintained by the righteousness of those who are permitted to live on earth (1 Nephi 22:15, 26).

WHAT ARE THE TIMES OF THE GENTILES?
THE FULNESS OF THE GENTILES?

In the meridian of time, by command of the Savior, the gospel of Jesus Christ was delivered first to the Jews and then later to the Gentiles. In our day, the gospel was delivered first to Joseph Smith and the Latter-day Saints, those of us who are "identified with the Gentiles" (D&C 109:60), those who are Israelite by descent (see D&C 52:2; 86:8–10) and Gentile by culture. The gospel is given to us, and we bear the responsibility to take the message of the Restoration to the descendants of Lehi and to the Jews (1 Nephi 22:7–11). We therefore live in "the times of the Gentiles." "And when the times of the Gentiles is come in, a light shall break forth among them that sit in darkness, and it shall be the fulness of my gospel" (D&C 45:28). It is a time, in the words of Elder Marion G. Romney, in which "in this last dispensation, the gospel is to be preached primarily to the non-Jewish people of the earth."[13]

In a day yet future, a time when the Gentiles—presumably those outside the Church as well as some from within the fold—sin against the fulness of the gospel and reject its supernal blessings, the Lord will take away these privileges from the Gentile nations and once again make them available primarily to his ancient covenant people (3 Nephi

16:10–11). This will be known as the fulfillment, or the "fulness of the times of the Gentiles," or simply the "fulness of the Gentiles." Because the people of earth no longer receive the light of gospel fulness and turn their hearts from the Lord because of the precepts of men, "in that generation shall the times of the Gentiles be fulfilled" (D&C 45:29–30). In the purest sense, this will not take place until Jesus sets his foot upon Olivet and the Jews acknowledge their long-awaited Messiah. Thus the fulness of the Gentiles is millennial.[14]

WHAT ARE WE TO EXPECT ABOUT THE RETURN OF THE TEN TRIBES?

As we all know, there have been numerous legends, traditions, vague reminiscences, and a myriad of folktales that deal with the location and eventual return of the ten lost tribes, those from the northern part of Israel who were taken captive by the Assyrians in 721 B.C. During my youth in the Church, I was brought up to believe a whole host of things: that the lost tribes were in the center of the earth, on a knob attached to the earth, on another planet, and so forth. Each of these traditions had its own source of authority. Since that time, and particularly since I discovered the Book of Mormon, I have concluded simply that the ten tribes are scattered among the nations, lost as much to their identity as to their whereabouts (1 Nephi 22:3–4). Thus it seems to me that the restoration, or gathering, of the ten tribes consists in scattered Israel—descendants of Jacob from such tribes as Reuben, Gad, Asher, Naphtali, Zebulun, and, of course, Joseph—coming to the knowledge of the restored gospel, accepting Christ's gospel (1 Nephi 15:14), coming into the true church and fold of God (2 Nephi 9:2), congregating with the faithful, and receiving the ordinances of the house of the Lord.[15] That is to say, the ten tribes will be gathered as all others are gathered—through conversion.

The risen Lord explained to the Nephites that after his second coming, once he has begun to dwell on earth with his faithful, "then shall the work of the Father"—the work of the gathering of Israel—"commence at that day, even when this gospel shall be preached among the remnant of this people. Verily I say unto you, at that day shall the work of the Father commence among all the dispersed of my people, yea, even the tribes which have been lost, which the Father hath led out of Jerusalem" (3 Nephi 21:25–26). It will commence in the sense that its magnitude will be of such a nature as to cause earlier efforts at gathering to pale into insignificance. The return of the ten tribes is spoken of in modern revelation in majestic symbolism: "And the Lord, even the Savior, shall stand in the midst of his people, and shall reign over all flesh" (D&C 133:25). Further, those who are descendants of the northern tribes shall respond to the gospel message, come under the direction of those prophets or priesthood leaders in their midst, traverse that highway we know as the "way of holiness" (Isaiah 35:8), and eventually participate in those temple ordinances that make of us kings and queens, priests and priestesses before God; they will "fall down and be crowned with glory, even in Zion, by the hands of the servants of the Lord, even the children of Ephraim," those who are entrusted with the keys of salvation (D&C 133:26–32).[16] In addition to that portion of the record of the ten tribes in our possession that we know as the Doctrine and Covenants—the record of God's dealings with modern Ephraim—we thrill in the assurance that other sacred volumes chronicling our Redeemer's ministry to the lost tribes shall come forth during the Millennium (2 Nephi 29:13).

MUST EVERY PERSON LIVING ON EARTH HEAR THE GOSPEL BEFORE THE LORD CAN COME?

In November 1831 the early elders of the Church were authorized to preach the gospel: "Go ye into all the world, preach the gospel to every creature, acting in the authority which I have given you, baptizing in the name of the Father, and of the Son, and of the Holy Ghost" (D&C 68:8). "For, verily, the sound must go forth from this place into all the world, and unto the uttermost parts of the earth—the gospel must be preached unto every creature, with signs following them that believe" (D&C 58:64). It is true that every person must have the opportunity to hear the gospel, either here or hereafter. Eventually "the truth of God will go forth boldly, nobly, and independent, till it has penetrated every continent, visited every clime, swept every country, and sounded in every ear, till the purposes of God shall be accomplished, and the Great Jehovah shall say the work is done."[17]

Not all, however, will have that privilege as mortals, and not all will have that privilege before the Second Coming. Jesus had spoken to the Twelve about the last days as follows: "And again, this Gospel of the Kingdom shall be preached in all the world, for a witness unto all nations, and then shall the end come, or the destruction of the wicked" (Joseph Smith–Matthew 1:31). As we have seen, the great day of gathering—the day when millions upon millions will come into the true fold of God—is millennial. But there is more. Elder Bruce R. McConkie explained that before the Lord Jesus can return in glory, two things must take place: "The first . . . is that the restored gospel is to be preached in every nation and among every people and to those speaking every tongue. Now there is one immediate reaction to this: Can't we go on the radio and preach the gospel to . . . the nations of the earth? We certainly can, but that would have very little bearing on the real meaning of the revelation that says we must preach it to every nation, kindred, and people. The reason is the second thing that must occur before the Second Coming: The revelations expressly, specifically, and pointedly say that when the Lord comes the second time to usher in the millennial era, he is going to find, in every nation, kindred, and tongue, and among every people, those who are kings and queens, who will live and reign a thousand years on earth (Revelation 5:9–10).

"That is a significant statement that puts in perspective the preaching of the gospel to the world. Yes, we can go on the radio; we can proclaim the gospel to all nations by television or other modern invention. And to the extent that we can do it, so be it, it's all to the good. But that's not what is involved. What is involved is that the elders of Israel, holding the priesthood, in person have to trod the soil, eat in the homes of the people, figuratively put their arms around the honest in heart, feed them the gospel, and baptize them and confer the Holy Ghost upon them. Then these people have to progress and advance, and grow in the things of the Spirit, until they can go to the house of the Lord, until they can enter a temple of God and receive the blessings of the priesthood, out of which come the rewards of being kings and priests.

"The way we become kings and priests is through the ordinances of the house of the Lord. It is through celestial marriage; it is through the guarantees of eternal life and eternal increase that are reserved for the Saints in the temples. The promise is that when the Lord comes he is going to find in every nation and kindred, among every people speaking every tongue, those who will, at that hour of his coming, have already become kings and priests. . . . All this is to precede the Second Coming of the Son of Man."[18]

The revelations declare: "Prepare ye the way of the Lord, and make his paths straight, for the hour of his coming is nigh—when the Lamb shall stand upon Mount Zion, and with him a hundred and forty-four thousand, having his father's name written on their foreheads" (D&C 133:17–18). This group of 144,000 are high priests after the holy order of God, men who have themselves received the promise of exaltation and godhood and whose mission it is to bring as many as will come into the Church of the Firstborn, into that inner circle of men and women who have passed the tests of mortality and have become the elect of God.[19] I have often thought that the 144,000 high priests called in the last days to bring men and women into the Church of the Firstborn (see D&C 77:11) is a symbolic reference: in that day of division, of unspeakable wickedness and consummate righteousness, temples will dot the earth, be accessible to the Lord's covenant people everywhere, and thus the fulness of those temple blessings will be sealed upon millions of the faithful Saints worldwide by those holding those transcendent powers.

IS THE TIME OF CHRIST'S COMING FIXED, OR MAY IT BE ALTERED BY US?

We hear once in a while the plea for us as Latter-day Saints to repent and improve, so that the Lord may come quickly to us. It is true that we are under obligation to be faithful to our covenants, to deny ourselves of every worldly lust and cross ourselves as to the pulls of a decaying society, and to live as becometh Saints. It is true that our labor is to build up the kingdom of God and establish Zion, all in preparation for the Second Coming. The full redemption of Zion depends on the urgency with which the Saints of the Most High pursue their sacred duty. Further, our righteous obsession to be a light to a darkened world assures our own readiness to receive the Savior. But the time of his coming is a constant, not a variable. It may not be postponed because of the Saints' tardiness or sloth, any more than it can be hastened through a burst of goodness. The Father and the Son know when the King of Zion (Moses 7:53) shall return to earth to assume the scepter and to preside over the kingdom of God. As was the case with his first coming to earth in the meridian of time, so it is in regard to his second coming. The Nephite prophets, for example, did not encourage the people to be faithful so that the Lord could come; rather, they stated forthrightly that in six hundred years he would come (see, for example, 1 Nephi 10:4; 19:8; 2 Nephi 25:19)—ready or not! It will be a time. It will be a specific day, a designated hour. That day and that hour are known. The time is set. It is fixed.[20]

HOW CAN WE KNOW WHO ARE FALSE CHRISTS AND FALSE PROPHETS?

We must keep our eyes fixed on those charged with the direction of this Church, the prophets, seers, and revelators of our day. What they stress in their instruction to us should be what we stress. Any who come before the Saints claiming some special insight, gift, training, or commission to elucidate detail concerning the signs of the times beyond that which the Brethren have set forth is suspect, is running before his or her leaders. Their teachings are not to be trusted or received. Truly, "it shall not be given to any one to go forth to preach my gospel, or to build up my church, except he be ordained by some one who has authority, and it is known to the church that he has authority and has been regularly ordained by the heads of the church" (D&C 42:11).

With the exception of those few deluded persons who claim to be Jesus, when we speak of false Christs we speak not so much of individuals as of false spirits, false doctrines, false systems of salvation. Latter-day Saints who "stick with the Brethren," who study and teach from the conference reports, the official pronouncements and proclamations, and the monthly First Presidency messages in the *Ensign*— these are they who treasure up the word of the Lord, who will not be deceived or led astray at the last day (Joseph Smith–Matthew 1:37). Elder Boyd K. Packer declared: "There are some among us now who have *not* been regularly ordained by the heads of the Church and who tell of impending political and economic chaos, the end of the world. . . . Those deceivers say that the Brethren do not know what is going on in the world or that the Brethren approve of their teaching but do not wish to speak of it over the pulpit. Neither is true. The Brethren, by virtue of traveling constantly everywhere on earth, certainly know what is going on, and by virtue of prophetic insight are able to read the signs of the times."[21]

WHAT ARE THE BEST SOURCES FOR UNDERSTANDING THE EVENTS INCIDENT TO THE SAVIOR'S COMING?

At the October 1972 and April 1973 conferences of the Church, President Harold B. Lee warned the Latter-day Saints about what he called "loose writings" by members of the Church in regard to the signs of the times. "Are you . . . aware of the fact," President Lee inquired, "that we need no such publications to be forewarned, if we were only conversant with what the scriptures have already spoken to us in plainness?" He then provided what he termed "the sure word of prophecy on which [we] should rely for [our] guide instead of these strange sources." He instructed the Saints to read the Joseph Smith Translation of Matthew 24 (what we have in the Pearl of Great Price as Joseph Smith–Matthew), and also sections 38, 45, 101, and 133 of the Doctrine and Covenants.[22] It is of interest to me that President Lee cited primarily the revelations of the Restoration. He did not refer the Church to Isaiah or Ezekiel or Daniel or Revelation. In 1981 President Marion G. Romney explained: "In each dispensation, . . . the Lord has revealed anew the principles of the gospel. So that while the records of past dispensations, insofar as they are uncorrupted, testify to the truths of the gospel, still each dispensation has had revealed in its day sufficient truth to guide the people of the new dispensation, independent of the records of the past.

"I do not wish to discredit in any manner the records we have of the truths revealed by the Lord in past dispensations. What I now desire is to impress upon our minds that the gospel, as revealed to the Prophet Joseph Smith, is complete and is the word direct from heaven to this dispensation. It alone is sufficient to teach us the principles of eternal life. It is the truth revealed, the commandments given in this dispensation through modern prophets by which we are to be governed."[23]

Even given the divine direction of living oracles and the words of sacred scripture brought forth in this final age, we really cannot plot or calculate the signs of the times or lay out a precise scheme of events. That is, as one apostle pointed out, "It is not possible for us . . . to specify the exact chronology of all the events that shall attend the Second Coming. Nearly all of the prophetic word relative to our Lord's return links various events together without reference to the order of their occurrence. Indeed, the same scriptural language is often used to describe similar events that will take place at different times."[24]

CONCLUSION

We obviously could go on and on. But these feeble efforts at providing answers point us to the glorious reality that modern revelation, especially the Doctrine and Covenants, represents, in the language of Parley P. Pratt, "the dawning of a brighter day."[25] The Doctrine and Covenants is indeed, as President Ezra Taft Benson explained, the "capstone" of our religion.[26] It is truly "the foundation of the Church in these last days, and a benefit to the world, showing that the keys of the mysteries of the kingdom of our Savior are again entrusted to man" (D&C 70, headnote).

The early elders of the Church were instructed: "Wherefore, be of good cheer, and do not fear, for I the Lord am with you, and will stand by you; and ye shall bear record of me, even Jesus Christ, that I am the Son of the living God, that I was, that I am, and that I am to come" (D&C 68:6). Answer after answer after divine answer concerning such matters as the divine Sonship of Christ, his infinite and eternal atoning sacrifice, the principles of his eternal gospel—these things are made known with great power and persuasion. In addition, the revelations testify—

that he will come again to reign among the Saints and to come down in judgment upon Idumea or the world (D&C 1:36);

that he will gather his faithful as a mother hen and enable them to partake of the waters of life (D&C 10:64–66; 29:2; 33:6);

that Satan and the works of Babylon will be destroyed (D&C 1:16; 19:3; 35:11; 133:14);

that this dispensation of the gospel represents his last pruning of the vineyard (D&C 24:19; 33:2–3; 39:17; 43:28);

that the elect in the last days will hear his voice; they will not be asleep because they will be purified (D&C 35:20–21);

224 Robert L. Millet

that we will have no laws but his laws when he comes; he will be our ruler (D&C 38:22; 41:4; 58:22);

that from the Lord's perspective, according to his reckoning, his coming is nigh (D&C 63:53); he comes tomorrow (D&C 64:24); he comes quickly, suddenly (D&C 33:18; 35:27; 36:8; 39:24; 41:4; 68:35).

Mine is a certain witness as to the divine calling of the Prophet Joseph Smith and of the keys of authority that have continued in rightful apostolic succession to our own day. I know, as I know that I live, that The Church of Jesus Christ of Latter-day Saints, is, in the language of the revelation, "the only true and living church upon the face of the whole earth" (D&C 1:30). Truly, "the keys of the kingdom of God are committed unto man on the earth, and from thence shall the gospel roll forth unto the ends of the earth, as the stone which is cut out of the mountain without hands shall roll forth, until it has filled the whole earth" (D&C 65:2).

That we will follow the Brethren, search the scriptures, pray mightily for discernment and for awareness and understanding of the signs of the times, is my hope. That we will be wise, receive the truth, take the Holy Spirit for our guide, and thereby have our lamps filled (D&C 45:56–57), is my prayer. "Wherefore, be faithful, praying always, having your lamps trimmed and burning, and oil with you, that you may be ready at the coming of the Bridegroom—for behold, verily, verily, I say unto you, that I come quickly" (D&C 33:17–18). In harmony with the soul-cry of John the Revelator, we exclaim: "Even so, come, Lord Jesus" (Revelation 22:20).

NOTES

1. Joseph Smith, *Teachings of the Prophet Joseph Smith,* sel. Joseph Fielding Smith (Salt Lake City: Deseret Book, 1976), 101.

2. M. Russell Ballard, *When Shall These Things Be?* Brigham Young University Devotional Address (Provo: 12 Mar. 1996), 2.

3. *Times and Seasons* (1 March 1843), 113, cited in *Joseph Smith's Commentary on the Bible,* comp. Kent P. Jackson (Salt Lake City: Deseret Book, 1994), 109.

4. Orson Pratt, in *Journal of Discourses,* 26 vols. (London: Latter-day Saints' Book Depot, 1854–86), 15:365–66.

5. *Millennial Star* 21, 582–83.

6. Smith, *Teachings of the Prophet Joseph Smith,* 157.

7. Joseph Fielding Smith, *The Progress of Man* (Salt Lake City: Deseret Book, 1964), 481–82; see also Joseph Fielding Smith, *The Way to Perfection* (Salt Lake City: Deseret Book, 1970), 288–91.

8. Bruce R. McConkie, *The Millennial Messiah* (Salt Lake City: Deseret Book, 1982), 582, 584.

9. Bruce R. McConkie, *Doctrinal New Testament Commentary,* 3 vols. (Salt Lake City: Deseret Book, 1974), 3:509.

10. Joseph Fielding Smith, *The Signs of the Times* (Salt Lake City: Deseret Book, 1942), 42.

11. Ibid., 41.

12. Smith, *Teachings of the Prophet Joseph Smith,* 297, 301, 305.

13. Marion G. Romney in Conference Report, October 1971, 69.

14. McConkie, *Millennial Messiah,* 241.

15. Smith, *Teachings of the Prophet Joseph Smith,* 307.

16. McConkie, *Millennial Messiah,* 214–17, 325–26.

17. Joseph Smith, *History of The Church of Jesus Christ of Latter-day Saints,* 2d ed. rev., ed. B. H. Roberts (Salt Lake City: Deseret Book, 1972), 4:540.

18. Spencer J. Palmer, *The Expanding Church* (Salt Lake City: Deseret Book, 1978), 141–42.

19. Orson Pratt, in *Journal of Discourses,* 14:242–43; 16:325; 18:25.

20. McConkie, *Millennial Messiah,* 26–27, 405.

21. Boyd K. Packer, in Conference Report, October 1992, 102.

22. Harold B. Lee, in Conference Report, October 1972, 128.

23. Marion G. Romney, "A Glorious Promise," *Ensign,* January 1981, 2.

24. McConkie, *Millennial Messiah,* 635.

25. *Hymns of The Church of Jesus Christ of Latter-day Saints* (Salt Lake City: The Church of Jesus Christ of Latter-day Saints, 1985), no. 1.

26. Ezra Taft Benson, *A Witness and a Warning* (Salt Lake City: Deseret Book, 1988), 30–31.

INDEX